"What a clever, useful book, this *Fast, Cheap and Written That Way*. Cheap may be in the title, but this is one of the richest screenwriting books going. Rich with talent, wisdom, humor and the stuff that made all of these writers GET PAID!! Write on, John Gaspard, a Part Two is needed."
— Dr. Lew Hunter, producer/writer, UCLA Screenwriting Professor and Chair Emeritus, and author of *Lew Hunter's Screenwriting 434*

"A perfect read for anyone who wants to write a film script or for anyone who just enjoys watching movies."
— Fred Willard, actor (*A Mighty Wind, Best in Show, Waiting for Guffman*)

"Packed with war stories and savvy advice for beginning screenwriters, the 23 interviews in John Gaspard's *Fast, Cheap and Written That Way* also constitute a highly worthwhile history of the last quarter-century phenomenon called 'Indie Film'."
— Larry Gross, screenwriter (*48 Hrs., Streets of Fire, True Crime*)

"Just finished reading *Fast, Cheap and Written That Way* and thoroughly ENJOYED IT! Coming from a low-budget filmmaking background myself, I don't think ANYONE writing or making a low-budget film can afford NOT to read it."
— The Unknown Screenwriter (*www.unknownscreenwriter.com*)

"An invaluable handbook for anyone with the passion and resources (no matter how little) to bring their dream to the independent screen where the heart of the American cinema survives."
— George Hickenlooper, director (*Factory Girl, Hearts of Darkness, Mayor of the Sunset Strip, Man from Elysian Fields*)

"This volume is full of useful little nuggets of information and, as you might expect from a book of interviews with writers, many of the views expressed are completely contradictory. Pick and choose what works for you."
— Jonathan Lynn, director (*My Cousin Vinny, Nuns on the Run, Clue*)

"John Gaspard has gathered the perfect mix of filmmakers, each of whom brings something vital to the party. This is one of those books you wish you'd read before you made your last film. Fortunately, you can read it before your next."
— Jeffrey Hatcher, screenwriter (*Casanova*, *Stage Beauty*) and author of *The Art & Craft of Playwriting*

"Gaspard's terrific new book is an essential guide for writers who want to produce good, low-budget scripts. This collection of interviews with screenwriters who've done just that reveals plenty of critical lessons learned through the rigors of the ritual itself. Experience counts, and this book is the best way to gain some short of going into production."
— Derek Pell, editor, *www.dingbat.com*

"A very realistic read and one that captures with honesty what each writer went through: the scars and bruises of writing a script."
— Mark Andrushko, President, Scriptapalooza Screenplay Competition

"The next best thing to learning by doing is finding out how others did it. *Fast, Cheap and Written That Way* is a well-researched must-read for new screenwriters and filmmakers."
— D. B. Gilles, author of *The Screenwriter Within*

"In a low-budget film, the script is the one department you can't afford to cheap out on. This book introduces us to some fascinating people whose craft and vision overcame tiny budgets to bring us rich movies."
— Alex Epstein, co-writer of *Bon Cop/Bad Cop*, co-creator of the TV series *Naked Josh*, and author of the books *Crafty Screenwriting* and *Crafty TV Writing*

"If you are interested in screenwriting or you just enjoy a good read, this book is a must. Fast, fun, and informative."
— Eric Colley, President, *IndieClub.com*

"There is nothing fast or cheap about this book. Gaspard has put together an informative, insightful collection of interviews on writing screenplays for low-budget films, which include revealing looks at the development process and the hurdles the writers faced."
— *www.donedealpro.com*

"Gaspard's book is not just a 'must read' for screenwriters new and seasoned, but inspiring as well because the writers included share the varied carnivals of creativity that have no set rules or guidelines other than to, yes, write on with hope, passion, endurance, and a little luck and humor too!"
— Andrew Horton, Jeanne H. Smith Professor of Film and Video Studies at the University of Oklahoma, award-winning screenwriter, and the author of 18 books on film, screenwriting and cultural studies

"It is not very often that we are treated to the art and craft of writing for low-budget movies, which is what most students will be doing when they leave the university to seek their fortune. This book provides them (and others) with valuable insight and information, culled from the voices of the people who have done it, are doing it and will continue to do it and who are making their mark in the industry."
— Myrl Schreibman, producer, director, author, and professor, UCLA School of Theater Film and Television

"Emerging screenwriters will always have the option of writing spec scripts with big imaginary budgets, but the collected wisdom of this book revolves around alternative approaches to screenwriting that almost seem tailored for the screenwriter looking toward the burgeoning international market for ultra-low-budget, digital cinema. Writers who defer to this advice are far more likely to find their way not just into production, but also into film festivals and beyond. *Fast, Cheap and Written That Way* is an indispensable guide to the new era of indie authorship."
— Dan Nearing, program coordinator, The Master of Fine Arts in Independent Film & Digital Imaging, College of Arts and Sciences, Governors State University

"Great book exploring the idea of the low-budget film world through the writers that created it! Everyone started somewhere; that somewhere is described here."
— Matthew Terry, www.hollywoodlitsales.com

"*Fast, Cheap and Written That Way* by John Gaspard is the go-to source for aspiring filmmakers big on vision but light on cash. The book is informative and it's also a page-turner. Learn and be entertained at the same time. Gaspard has truly opened a revealing door into independent cinema."
— Kristofer "Grand Guignol" Upjohn, *www.b-scared.com*

"Thanks to John Gaspard, the mysterious task of screenwriting seems less so after reading *Fast, Cheap and Written That Way*, his helpful book of intriguing interviews with a variety of screenwriters who have written successful screenplays for low-budget films. What a treat to read stories like the one from Tom DiCillo about why and how he wrote *Living in Oblivion* — or from Ali Selim concerning his process in adapting a short story into the feature film *Sweet Land*! *Fast, Cheap and Written That Way* may be aimed primarily at wannabe screenwriters, but it's also a great read for anyone who loves the cinema."

> — Betty Jo Tucker, lead film critic for *ReelTalkReviews.com* and author of *Confessions of a Movie Addict* and *Susan Sarandon: A True Maverick*

"The basic fact of independent filmmaking is that the lower your budget, the higher your chances of getting the movie made. Gaspard has assembled the creative minds behind many of the pivotal films that laid the foundation for the current independent film movement, thereby giving these screenwriters a forum where they can share their wisdom and insight. It's like a road map to Sundance that can help you avoid the deer crossings, slippery shoulders and falling rocks along the way."

> — Catherine Clinch, Associate Publisher, *Creative Screenwriting Magazine*

"There are plenty of screenwriting textbooks that will teach you what a plot point is or how to write the next big Hollywood movie, but if you want in-the-trenches advice on how to write a script that anyone can produce, *Fast, Cheap and Written that Way* is the book to buy."

> — Randy Steinberg, Visiting Assistant Professor of Screenwriting, Boston University

"This is a one-of-a-kind book that is a must-read for any filmmaker or screenwriter who aspires to break into the world of low-budget film. Plenty of anecdotes and great advice make it a fun, valuable read."

> — Howard Meibach, President, *HollywoodLitSales.com*

"A must read for any aspiring filmmaker. I'll be telling all of my students and clients to think 'fast and cheap'."

— Pilar Alessandra, instructor/consultant: *On the Page*

Fast, Cheap and Written That Way

Top Screenwriters on Writing for Low-Budget Movies

John Gaspard

MICHAEL WIESE PRODUCTIONS

Published by Michael Wiese Productions
3940 Laurel Canyon Blvd, #1111
Studio City, CA 91604
mw@mwp.com
www.mwp.com

Front cover by
Interior design by MWP
Copyedited by Paul Norlen
Printed by McNaughton & Gunn

Manufactured in the United States of America

Library of Congress Cataloging-in-Publication Data
Gaspard, John, 1958-
  Fast, cheap, and written that way : top screenwriters on writing for
low-budget movies / John Gaspard.
      p. cm.
  ISBN-13: 978-1-932907-30-8
  ISBN-10: 1-932907-30-0
  1. Motion picture authorship. 2. Low budget motion pictures. 3.
Screenwriters--Interviews. I. Title.
  PN1996.G36 2007
  808.2'3--dc22
                          2007013944

For Frantisek (Frank) Daniel, John Fenn,
Sara Sexton and Jim White.

In this life, you're lucky to encounter one great teacher.
I had the incredible good fortune of encountering four.

Table of Contents

Acknowledgments

A book of interviews with screenwriters would not be possible without the aid and assistance of the people who support those screenwriters — their agents, managers, publicists and friends. Without their help, contact could not have been established and you'd be holding a book of blank pages in your hands right now. I am grateful to all of them for their help. The ones who went above and beyond include: Richard Arlook, Monica De Armond, Toby Ascher, Lyne DuFort-Leavy, Scott Greenberg, Marcus Hu, Nicole Jefferson, Jennifer Levine, Tom Lieberman, Chris Romero, Bethany Schwartz, Ali Selim and Helen Springut.

The advice and counsel of friends was invaluable in selecting the films for this book and for ongoing and unending support: Matthew G. Anderson, Dale Newton, David Garfield, John Jansen and the original grown men: Patrick Coyle, Peter Moore and Michael Paul Levin.

Daniel Berks deserves particular thanks for his careful editing and poofreading of the manuscript.

And finally thanks to my lovely wife, Amy, who patiently endured my absences during the long hours that it takes to cobble together a book like this.

Introduction

Screenwriting is easy.

At least that's the impression you'd come away with after reading many books and articles on low-budget filmmaking. In most you'll find numerous instances of filmmakers talking about the arduous process of making the movie — but precious little on how the script was actually written.

I realized this sad fact when I was proofing the companion book to this one, *Fast, Cheap and Under Control: Lessons Learned From the Greatest Low-Budget Movies of All Time*. Among all the wonderful gems gathered in that book, I realized that there was really very little on the actual screenwriting process. The closest we got to any meat were phrases like, "The script just poured out of me" or "So I sat down with my writing partner and we drafted a script." There was very little real information about the actual experience of writing.

Now, I don't want to come off as some sort of writing bigot, but the problem with screenplays is that they all look alike. Spread the pages of an Academy Award–winning script on a table next to a properly formatted first draft by an ambitious neophyte and you'd be hard pressed to tell the difference. At least at a glance. And therein lies the problem.

To many people, if it looks like a screenplay and it's formatted like a screenplay ... well, it must be ready to be shot. Such is the downfall of many an independent (and Hollywood) film.

The screenplay is arguably the most important element in the filmmaking process and yet it remains the most mysterious. Someone goes off into a small, dark room and then a few days (weeks, months) later emerges with a finished, polished script, ready to be shot.

Which begs this question: What the heck happened in that room?

That, in a nutshell, is the goal of this book: To blow the doors off that room, peer over the writers' shoulders and crawl into their brains as they conceive, develop and refine the blueprint for their movies.

To that end, I spoke with twenty-three different screenwriters and got (not so surprisingly) twenty-three very different responses on how to go about writing a successful, low-budget screenplay.

A quick glance at the Table of Contents will demonstrate that I was able, with a modicum of blood, sweat and e-mailing, to assemble interviews that cover the last forty years of filmmaking and touch on just about every style and genre of low-budget filmmaking. I hand-picked movies that I think made a difference at the time they came out and that still have a lot to teach us.

Each writer very kindly detailed the steps they went through in the process of writing their low-budget script. In each instance, we talked about where they were in their career before that script; how they conceived and developed the idea; how they did or didn't adapt their work to their intended budget; and the impact that process has had on their subsequent work.

Interspersed with that chronology came their philosophy of screenwriting, and that's where it really gets interesting. These folks have opinions about what works, what doesn't, and what's wrong with movies today. You won't necessarily find agreement, or even consensus, on many points. But you will undoubtedly find a point of view that matches your own, along with some contrary ideas that are worth considering.

I've organized the interviews into like-minded genres, for easier reference, although to be fair, many of them span multiple topic headings. Henry Jaglom's *Venice/Venice* could easily move out of its current location (Chapter One: This Is Your Life) and slide cleanly into Chapter Two: Keeping It Real or Chapter Six: Love Stories. The same is true of Roger Nygard's *Suckers*, which would be just as at home in Chapter One as in its current location, Chapter Five: Playing with Genres. And any of the screenplays deserve a place in Chapter Six: Original Visions. But since everything has to be somewhere, for better or worse this is where I've positioned these interviews.

Then, in the final chapter, I recap some of the key ideas that I took away from the interviews, providing my own (highly subjective) two cents on what I heard.

While I hope that you find much that inspires and motivates you in these conversations, never think for a moment that this project wasn't born out of anything more than my own selfish desire to chat with these writers and somehow, via osmosis or proximity, become a better screenwriter in the process.

The simple truth is, these folks are great storytellers. It was terrific fun to sit back and listen to accounts of their low-budget high jinks.

[In the interest of full disclosure, I must confess that a few of the interviews (Eric Bogosian, Alex Cox and portions of the Whit Stillman and Ali Selim interviews) were conducted by e-mail. However, their story-telling prowess came through the digital ether loud and clear. And while I'm disclosing things, the interview with Richard Glatzer about *Grief* was done long before these other interviews — way back in 1995 — and portions of that interview appeared in my first book, *Persistence of Vision*. There. Got that off my chest. I feel much better now.]

I've always been a sucker for film books, and interview books in particular, so it's been a special kick to put an interview book of my own together. As a youngster I devoured such classics of the genre as Joe Gelmis' *The Film Director as Superstar* and John Brady's *The Craft of the Screenwriter*.

And while we're on the subject of books worn out from constant re-reading, we can't forget William Bayer's *Breaking Through, Selling Out, Dropping Dead (and Other Notes on Filmmaking)*, which every filmmaker should look through before starting a film, regardless of the film's length or budget.

It's my fervent hope that some film geek not unlike my early self wears out this book like I wore out those books, and carries some of the ideas found within throughout his/her filmmaking career.

Happy reading. And, if this book serves its purpose, happier writing.

CHAPTER ONE

This Is Your Life

Finding inspiration from within your own life is a time-honored approach in low-budget filmmaking. While anyone can scribble down funny, sad and sexy moments from their life, the real trick is finding those events in your day-to-day existence that are truly universal.

None of the four films highlighted in the chapter would be correctly labeled "biographies." But each was taken from the writer's life experience and then filtered through their dramatic sensibilities to create classic stories that connected with audiences around the world.

Living in Oblivion
Tom DiCillo

TITO

Why does my character have to be a
dwarf?

NICK

He doesn't have to be.

TITO

Then why is he? Is that the only way you
can make this a dream, to put a dwarf in
it?

NICK

No, Tito, I...

TITO

Have you ever had a dream with a dwarf
in it? Do you know anyone who's had a
dream with a dwarf in it? No! I don't
even have dreams with dwarves in them.
The only place I've seen dwarves in
dreams is in stupid movies like this!
"Oh make it weird, put a dwarf in it!"
Everyone will go "Whoa, this must be a
fuckin' dream, there's a fuckin' dwarf
in it!" Well I'm sick of it! You can
take this dream sequence and stick it up
your ass!

You're crossing a potentially deadly minefield when you attempt to take a short film and expand it into a feature. What was once sharp and clever can quickly turn repetitive and dull if you take a wrong step or make the wrong choices. Tom DiCillo successfully navigated that minefield when he turned his short, Living in Oblivion, *into what is unquestionably one of the classic low-budget movies of all time.*

More importantly, he also took what at first appears to be a very narrow and "inside" story — about a director nearly losing his mind while shooting his movie — and turned it into a universal story about the creative process.

(Be aware that this interview contains spoilers about key plot points.)

What was going on in your career before you made *Living in Oblivion*?

My first feature was a film called *Johnny Suede*, starring Brad Pitt. I busted my ass on that one for at least four years to get it made. The film never quite found an audience and the distribution of it was, frankly, really disappointing. It made making my second film really, really difficult.

I had written a screenplay called *Box of Moonlight* and could not get the money for it. Years and years went by, two, three, four, five, and I just reached a point of such maniacal desperation that I said, "I have to do something, no matter what." It was out of that intense frustration that *Living in Oblivion* was born.

It wasn't born out of, "Hey, I want to make a funny movie." It really came out of one of the most intense periods of anger and frustration in my career. And, ironically, it turned out to be the funniest movie I've ever made. I think in some way that is part of what makes my humor my humor: It's humor based upon real, human intensity, desperation, and foolishness.

To use a screenwriting term, what was the inciting incident that kicked off the creation of *Living in Oblivion*?

I was invited to the wedding of my wife's cousin. It was a three-day event and on the first night — you have to understand, I was carrying with me four and a half years of frustration — I had a martini.

I had never had a martini before in my life. And I said, "Wow, if that's how you feel after one martini, let's have another one." So I had two. And I said, "This is just unbelievable." And I had three. Later I realized that I should never, ever, ever do that again.

But it was after the third martini that this guy came up to me, who I vaguely recognized from an acting class I had taken maybe four or five years earlier. And he says, "Oh, Tom, it's great to see you, man. You're so lucky, you made *Johnny Suede*, you made a movie. Lights, camera, action."

And I just erupted at him. I said, "Shut the fuck up. Making a movie is one of the most tedious, frustrating, intense experiences I've ever had in my life. And not even just getting the money. What about when you're getting ready to do a shot and suddenly something screws up and the actor's moment that they've been working on for hours just disappears and you never get it back again?"

Well, that's where I had the first idea. I swear, right there at that moment, I thought, "You know, that could make a little fifteen-minute film. Just confront an actor with an endless number of disruptions and see what happens." And that's where the idea was born.

That first half-hour just kind of jumped out of me. I went home and wrote the first half-hour as it exists, word for word, frame for frame in the final version.

So *Living in Oblivion* was essentially based on a single idea that later, completely by accident, turned into a feature film. You never quite know how something is going to turn out, and that one for some reason just all came together. I'm very proud of that movie.

What happened after you wrote the short script?

Catherine Keener was visiting us at that time and I gave her the script — it was about twenty-five pages — and I just heard her laughing in this back room that we have. She was just howling.

She came out and said, "We have to do this." And I said, "Okay, let's do it. Even if we have to shoot it on Super 8, let's make this movie."

The next thing I know, her husband, Dermot, said he would like to put in some money if he could be in it. He originally wanted to play Nick Reve, the director, but I said I had someone a little older in mind, and he immediately said, "What about Steve Buscemi?" I said, "That's a fantastic idea. You can play Wolf, the cameraman." He said, "That's great."

It was like a bunch of kids putting on a show in the garage. Anybody who wanted to be in the movie, who had a little money, got a part. That is how I cast it, I am not kidding you. Sometimes you agonize about casting, over and over for months trying to figure out which actor to choose. In this case, I never thought about it for a second. Never. And look how amazing those actors were.

So we started shooting. We had a five-day shoot in New York City and we had about $37,000 that my wife helped raise and that everybody put in. The cast and crew were amazed at how well it was turning out. On the fourth day we realized that it was going to end and there was a kind of depression that settled in on the set. People said, "Tom, you should make a feature out of this." And I went, "How? How? How would I ever do that?"

But it turned out so well that I thought, I have to somehow find a way to take this magical accident and develop it.

What steps did you take to do that?

After it was finished, I submitted it to the Cannes short-film festival, I tried a number of things, and I realized that as a short it wasn't going to go anywhere. First of all, it was too long. It was just under half an hour.

So I began to think about what was developed in the first section, the first third of the film? What ideas were kind of lurking in the background? And one of the ideas was that there was a relationship developing between the director and his leading actress. Another thing that seemed to be developing was a relationship between the cameraman and the First AD.

And I began thinking about, "What's the one fantasy that I've always thought about?" And that is having the lead actor and the director get into a fist-fight on the set. And so that's how I came up with the idea of Chad Palomino and how he disrupts the shoot — this Hollywood guy entering this little, dusty world of Nick Reve's independent film and totally screwing it up. So I had Part Two.

So then I said, "Where the hell is it going to go from here?"

And my wife, very astutely, said, "Listen, Part One is a dream. Part Two is a dream. Why don't you have Part Three be them making a dream sequence?" And I went, "Oh my God, that is so fantastic." Instantly, in an instant, I thought of Tito, the dwarf, erupting on set, "You stupid morons! Is that the only way you can make a dream sequence, by putting a dwarf in it?"

The two new segments evolve perfectly out of Part One. The movie never feels like a short with stuff added to turn it into a feature.

I put so much work into that screenplay. I wanted no one to think that it was just a short with two other segments tacked on to it. I wanted it to feel like it was seamless. And it took a lot of work to make that progression, to make that movement happen in the screenplay.

It sounds like you really drew from personal experience to write the script.

I've had a lot of experience of being on a number of sets. Even when I was going to film school, when you're on the set of a student film, it's just the most insane chaos that you can imagine. Even

6

then I noticed that the drama that was happening just off the side of the camera was a million times more interesting than the stale scene that everybody was so intensely focused on. I noticed that even then.

And I swear to God, the very first time that I experienced room tone, everybody standing there like these living statues in this forced silence, I said, "I'm going to put that in a movie one day. It's just so bizarre, I'm going to put that in a movie."

I've always been fascinated with the stuff that happens on the set. Not that I'm trying to say that just because it's a film set it's interesting. I don't feel that. But I do feel like there's a real crazy drama that happens when you get a group of people trying to do a task together.

I'm in love with filmmaking, but at the same time I also have moments where I absolutely despise it. The medium itself seems designed to thwart you whenever you really want to try to do something. Just when you're about to get a shot, a light goes off or a train goes by, a car alarm goes off, something. Everything is so fragile in the business. So I wanted to take my rage out on that, because it can be so frustrating at times. It was so liberating and freeing to do that.

It must have been bizarre, making a good movie about a movie where everything is going wrong.

I swear the first time I had the actor intentionally drop the microphone into the shot, they didn't want to do it. They didn't want to do it because everything that we've been taught is to keep the microphone out of the frame. Don't put it in.

I wanted to try to really peel back that curtain about what it's like to be on the set and the real struggle, because I think that struggle is what is interesting to me — the struggle to somehow capture something on film.

I also wanted to show the director in a way that I had never seen portrayed. I was really concerned about that. Most of the time the independent director, and directors in general, are shown wearing leather jackets and smoking cigarettes, brooding in a corner with sunglasses. Most directors that I've ever seen on a set of any movie look so desperate, so frustrated, so neurotic. So I wanted to address that and still let the director have some sort of dignity.

I think Nick Reve is not a total fool, but the struggles that he faces are really, I think, rather archetypical: How do you get what you want in a business that is all about pretension and ego? The way he has to deal with Chad Palomino is a monumental struggle. Here's a guy where all you really want to do is beat the shit out of him, but you can't. You have to say, "Oh, yeah, man, you did a great take. Great take."

Part One ended up being the idea of the technical desperation and screw-ups. Then I wanted to see what would happen if you drop emotional complications in and that served to be the core of the movement for Part Two. It's all about how emotional entanglements happening off the set can affect what's being captured on film.

For Part Three, I really wanted to bring the director to the point where he gave up. After all this frustration, I realized he would really get to that point. To me it was interesting to drive him to that point where he could not proceed — he really felt like he was failing and that he was not a director — and to see what would happen to him, to see how he would respond.

One of the things that makes the script so strong is that all the obstacles that you put in Nick's way are real obstacles that you've experienced in that position.

Whatever you write, you have to tap into something personal for yourself. I used to have an acting teacher who said to me, "If it ain't personal, it ain't no good." There's something to be said for that.

But at the same time, I don't want to ever make it seem like when I write that it's just about me. I'm not interested in that. Even with my first film, *Johnny Suede* — sure, I put a lot of myself into that character — but I also was very clearly trying to find a way to make it more objective, more universal, something that other people could relate to.

I absolutely believe that if you can find a way to tap into something that's very personal and then make a creative leap from there, that's the best way to do it. Anger by itself is not enough. You have to have the creative imagination coming into play as well.

How helpful was it to have Part One all shot when trying to get the money for Part Two and Part Three?

I took Part One all the way to the point of a finished print, with a mix, with titles, music, everything. I began screening that for people after I had written Part Two and Part Three, thinking that people wouldn't get a sense of what I was trying to do if they only read the screenplay. So therefore, having Part One all finished, I thought it would be perfect, because they can see exactly the characters, the actors, the humor, everything.

Well, it didn't happen. I had several conversations with all of the independent companies, and they all passed on the movie at the script stage. Completely. I offered it to Miramax for nothing and they said no.

Did they give reasons why they were passing?

They didn't get it. I'm not complaining, because I'm probably guilty of the same thing, but until something literally comes up and kicks you in the head and tells you what it is, no one knows anything.

They looked at this movie and said, "Why? Why should we put money into this movie?" And it's just bizarre to me, because most of the most impressive films — the ones that really have stuck in the minds and consciousness of audiences — are the ones that are absolutely original and have never been made before. Even *Star Wars*, for God's sake. He couldn't make that movie for years.

So, what happened was, I had put my wife's cousin and her husband, Hillary and Michael, in Part One — Hillary played the script supervisor and her husband Michael played Speedo, the sound man

— and at the last minute Hillary called me and said, "We'd like to put up the rest of the money and make the film as a feature."

And so they put up almost $500,000 of their own money and we were able to go off on our own, once again, and make the film.

This may be an apocryphal story, but I have heard that at the same time they offered you the money, you were on the phone with someone who had the money but with whom you didn't want to work.

Yes, exactly. He was being a real prick. He was this completely ego-driven guy. He was going to own everybody, he was going to tell everybody who to cast, all that stuff. Completely antithetical to the way the film had been created.

I was just about to make my travel arrangements to go out to L.A. to sign the deal with him, when my Call Waiting clicked in and it was Hillary and Michael. They were so apologetic — "Would you mind if we suggested putting up the money?" I said, "You've got to be kidding?!"

It was one of the most magical experiences, from beginning to end, really.

In Part One, how did you work with Catherine on the different levels of her performance? How did you map out the range she had to go through, from being just okay to being really good?

I was concerned about that. I actually numbered the takes; I think there's twelve takes. Number one, on the scale of one to ten, should be a seven. Number two should be a five. We did something like that, but eventually what it came down to the two of us deciding what the degree of distraction she was feeling at that time. That's basically how it came about.

How much rehearsal did you have?

None. Absolutely none.

I don't like to rehearse, anyway. My style of working is to just talk to people, get the costumes correct, talk a little bit about the character, and then just find it as the camera is rolling.

What was so fascinating to me was that none of these actors auditioned and they were almost instantaneously their parts.

Many people think *Living in Oblivion* is completely improvised, but there's only one scene that was improvised. That's the scene where Steve erupts at the crew at the end of Part One. Everything else was completely scripted.

What's your favorite memory of working on *Living in Oblivion*?

Oh, man, there are millions. I think I would have to say that it was the look on people's faces the first time Peter Dinklage, who plays Tito, erupted into his tirade against the director.

Most of the crew that we hired had not read the script, because we weren't paying anybody. And so we were getting people working for free and they might work one or two days a week. And so this crew was just standing by the lights, doing whatever they were doing, and all of a sudden Peter Dinklage, during a take, says, "I'm sick of this crap." He just erupted and everybody just turned and looked with their jaws open. They thought he was really saying it.

Then the laughter that erupted when they realized that it was just part of the movie, it was a fantastic feeling. It made me really feel that I had stumbled upon something and it was working.

Were there any things you learned writing that script that you still use today?

Yeah. I have a tendency, if I'm going to write a joke, I set it up with a one, two, three punch. But I realized that most of the time, when I get in the editing room, I usually only end up using the one or the two, never the one, two, three. That's kind of an interesting lesson to learn: if you're going to tell a joke, just tell the joke. Don't do three jokes.

I also learned the idea of setting in motion something that, once it's in motion it has a life of its own and people are really instantaneously eager to find out what's going to happen. That's a crucial thing.

Many screenwriting teachers will say a screenplay is all about tension and conflict. And, in some ways, that is absolutely true. But if that tension and conflict doesn't arouse enough interest to have people really want to know what's going to happen next, then you're screwed. I think *Johnny Suede* suffered from that a bit. It was my first screenplay and there's very little real dramatic tension in it.

I like the idea of setting something in motion — like a cart rolling down a hill — that once it's going, you can't stop it.

How do you make that happen while you're writing the script?

If it keeps me excited, if I kind of surprise myself and go, "Okay, what would be the conventional, expected way to do something?" I stop and think, "What if you just took a detour and went here? How the hell would you get out of that situation?" I find that really exciting. It prompts me to think of unexpected things.

What's your writing process?

Usually when I sit down to write a script, the first three days is the hardest. Literally, going into the room, turning on the computer and starting.

Usually what I do is I compile a notebook of notes for months, sometimes years, in advance. I did notes for *Living in Oblivion* years in advance; same thing with *Box of Moonlight*.

Once I actually sit down and get through the first day, then I just can't wait to get into the room. What I do is I get up early in the morning, turn everything off, make sure nobody's here, and work solidly from about 9:30 until about three in the afternoon. I just love it. The concentration is fantastic. I love the discipline. Even sometimes, when it's not working, you just take a ten-minute break and come back.

I love writing. To me it's a magical part of this business. It's the one time when you can be free to go wherever you want to go. The actors do whatever you want them to do. You get whatever location you want.

Do you have any self-imposed rules, like a certain number of pages per day?

I try to give myself goals, definitely. Writing is a very tricky thing. You have to have discipline, but at the same time you have to keep yourself excited. That's the thing that I find for myself: If I'm not excited, I can feel it, so what I do is I stop. And I say, "You have to get to a place, Tom, where you are re-excited about what you're doing." And when I am, the day goes by in about twenty seconds.

Sometimes you struggle with things and you have to literally take a day or two off, and when you do that, then sometimes, wow, the idea hits you and you can't wait to get back in there and get to work.

Do you ever put something in a drawer and come back to it months later?

Not when I actually sit down and start the writing process. If I'm still in the conception stages, then yes.

For example, my new script that I just finished shooting and am editing now, I had the idea years ago. And maybe once every two months I'd sit down and sketch out some ideas. And I started a whole folder just of ideas, putting some pressure on myself, saying, "Sooner or later, Tom, you're going to have to sit down and write this, man." But I just got to the point where the ideas were just building and building, until finally this thing started to write itself. But sometimes three months would go by and I wouldn't put a single note in.

What's the best piece of advice about writing that you've ever received?

The very first thing that comes to my mind is less about writing than it is about the creative process itself.

It was an experience I had when I went to Sundance, to the Director's Lab with my first screenplay for *Johnny Suede*. I had worked very hard on it and had just come from a rather negative experience at NYU, when I was there getting my Master's degree in directing. It was a very destructive process at NYU in terms of how they would critique you. Even though I did very well there, I still was quite aware of just how destructive it was and I was gun shy of that stuff.

So when I went out to Sundance for the Director's Lab, some of the more traditional guys out there were Hollywood, conventional guys, and they started giving me notes about the script that really bothered me and which were, again, destructive.

And then I had a meeting with Buck Henry, who was one of the advisors. He'd read my script and he sat down and just looked at me — this was the first time I'd met him — and all he said was, "Hey man, you're on to something. Go for it."

Now that wasn't specific, but what it completely did was just open me up to the fact that whatever you're doing, if you're trying something, just try it. Just try it. Things don't have to be instantaneously perfect or whatever, but if you really are trying something, then trust it and just try it.

And I would say that to any aspiring writer: It's a combination of confidence and innocence at the same time. You have to have both; you have to have absolute determination, but you have to be an innocent in the utmost sense of that word, where you are completely free and open to anything happening and that everything around you supports you and loves you, like the world of an infant.

Because if you don't have that, this world is so brutal to any sort of creative failure — Arthur Miller wrote a beautiful essay about how American culture deals with failure — and that's a struggle that we all face. Everybody faces it: giving yourself the creative and imaginative playground just to go ahead and try your idea for God's sake. Try it.

How do you make yourself do that every day?

It's a discipline. It's hard.

There are some days you just go, "Fuck. I can't do this anymore." Or you start getting angry, you start getting bitter, because you feel like you've done good work and nobody recognizes it or whatever. But it's not about that; you can buy into that crap so quickly.

Our whole entertainment industry is really about celebrity, for everybody, the directors included. It's the most destructive aspect of our entertainment culture; it's less about the work than it is about the celebrity.

So what I constantly do is say, "Listen, am I proud of this movie?" That's what it's about. Ten years from now, am I watching this movie and going, "Jesus Christ, man, you put your soul into that and that's all that matters."

Metropolitan
Whit Stillman

                    NICK

    The titled aristocracy are the scum of
    the earth.

                    SALLY FOWLER

    You always say "titled" aristocrats.
    What about "untitled" aristocrats?

                    NICK

    Well, I could hardly despise them, could
    I? That would be self-hatred.

Whit Stillman's Metropolitan *exists in a timeless New York past brimming with debutante balls and ultra-classy cocktail parties. His clever examination of this universe is set primarily at after-parties, allowing him to comment on the upper class without going to the expense of recreating their soirées.*

This true comedy of manners, based on Stillman's own experience of skirting the upper crust, put him on the map as a filmmaker to watch and resulted in a well-deserved Academy Award nomination for his literate and witty screenplay.

**What was going on in your life and your career before
Metropolitan?**

I was in transition. I had a journalism job; it was for a publication
where they overpaid us a bit and they went out of business. So I
was left in 1980 with some savings and I wanted to get into the
film business.

On a trip to Spain, I read a *Variety* special issue on the Spanish
film industry, which showed that there were opportunities to sell
Spanish films in the United States. I met a few Spanish filmmakers on my trip, talked to them about the opportunities to sell their
films in the United States, and I ended up within a year being a
sales agent for a lot of really good Spanish films.

So I did that from 1980 until 1983 and that was when it really
started paying off, in the sense that one of the filmmakers, Fernando
Colomo, came to New York to make his own film, *Skyline*, and I
helped him on it. It was made for nothing, with a four-person crew
and one comic actor brought over from Spain.

We re-enacted Fernando Colomo's real experiences in New York, so
I was in the film in an analogous role to my real role with Fernando.
The film turned out really well; it was in the New Directors series
at the Museum of Modern Art and got a release and good reviews
and did really well in Spain.

That same summer, another filmmaker I was representing, Fernando
Trueba, who did the film *Belle Epoque* that later won the Oscar,
made his second film, and I was hired to play the Stupid American,
an annoying character. I was in Madrid quite a bit that summer
— since I was an unimportant guy they could schedule around me
— so I had long weeks of waiting. With the per diems, I made more
money than I think I ever did as a foreign sales agent for Spanish
films. It was right before that shoot that I started to write the script
for *Barcelona*. And I realized, as time went on, it was too big and
ambitious a project to do first.

In the summer of 1984 I had an idea of a film I could do cheaply,
which was *Metropolitan*. So I put aside the work I'd done on

17

Barcelona and started working on that. Also, I had to take over a family business — an uncle's illustration agency, representing artists and illustrators in New York — and that became my day job. That anchored me to Manhattan and I started thinking of this Manhattan idea for a cheap film that would look good.

From childhood I remembered a production of Shaw's *Don Juan in Hell*, which all took place in one room and I thought that this was, theoretically, a film that could be shot in a room. You'd just have people all dressed up in some fancy room and there it is.

Of course, in writing the script it went different places, but that was the premise.

Were you drawing on your own experience to create those characters and those situations?

I was, but it was long enough ago that it was shrouded in the mists of time. But the idea of the group was sort of based on a group, the rat pack was based on the rat pack, there was a funny, snobbish character who was like the Chris Eigeman character, Nick Smith. But really it was fictional, it was all made up. There were some people who were sort of like someone or other, but it had to be created anew and that's what always takes me a long time.

You've used the phrase "social pornography" to describe the movie. Can you define what you mean by that?

What I mean by that is that it's a taboo to talk about this kind of society in the United States; it's not supposed to exist. And there's a feeling of disgust and excitement in talking about the idea of Americans who camouflage themselves as upper middle class but really think of themselves as upper class.

On the surface, the idea doesn't really lend itself to a low-budget treatment: a lot of characters, a lot of short scenes, a lot of locations — some of them high-end — and plus it's

a quasi-period piece. Did you consider any of those issues while you were writing?

Well, I remembered how cheap it was for me to go to those parties. It didn't cost me a dime, it was the least expensive part of my life. And so I thought, in a way, the film could be done the same way. If people donated tuxedos and a location, it would look rich but it's not.

I knew that for a very minimal amount of money you could get permits to shoot on the streets of New York, so you had a beautiful set for free. And moving around doesn't really cost that much. In a way, it's more expensive to stay in one place, because you really need to lock down the location and not have a chance of losing it.

One of our rules was that we wouldn't shoot in any apartment where we couldn't finish the scene in that day, because we assumed we'd be kicked out of the place. The lengthier apartment sequences were actually done in townhouses faked to look like apartment buildings.

One of the eureka moments for deciding to do the project, if I can use that term, was the director of one of the Spanish films I sold was talking about the actual cash budget for the film he had done was $50,000. And at that time I knew that — if we bought our rental apartment at an insider price, held it for a year and later resold it — theoretically we could make $50,000 on our apartment. That number encouraged me, because I knew I could shoot a film for that money. To finish it, I'd need other people's money, but I could start it with my own.

What was your writing process like on *Metropolitan*?

I actually dreaded the thought of writing alone. I had written short stories and gotten some good reaction; I'd been commissioned by *Harper's* to write a story and people liked them. Tom Wolfe was quoted as liking one of the stories. But I hated the solitary writing process.

So I actually started writing *Metropolitan* with a college friend — not exactly a college friend, a fellow who hung around college without actually going there. We sat around, talking about ideas, for about three hours and I realized that wasn't going to work. And so I went and wrote the script.

It was good because I had this interesting job that was sort of challenging, representing artists, and I liked the vicarious work of being an agent for people whose work I liked. It was a social job, where you had lunch with people and saw a lot of people and it was a good day job while I was writing the script. It meant that I could take two weeks without writing anything and then I'd get in an intense mode, then I'd have vacation where I'd expect to write all the time but instead I'd get excited about another topic and write a stupid article for a newspaper. It allowed time to pass and let me reconsider what I was doing.

At a certain point I decided that the Tom Townsend character really wasn't sympathetic, because he was in love with the girl he shouldn't have been in love with and he ignored the girl he should have liked, and that really the sympathetic character was the Audrey Rouget character and the film should be about her. I tried to make the film about her, but I realized that too much is involved in the Tom Townsend character, I'd done too much of that and was too attached to it. So I gave up making it explicitly Audrey's film, but a lot of what remains having tried to make it Audrey's film is still in the movie.

And then I thought the important thing in film is how you end it. So the challenging thing was where was all of this going to go? And so I started writing the end of the movie. I had a process where I had the first three-fifths of the movie and the last fifth of the movie and I had to attach them at some point. For me, it was like the transcontinental railway and finding where would the golden spike be to attach these two ends of the narrative.

How did you do that?

I can't remember exactly, but there was a year where the tracks would never quite sync up. It ended up working.

How was that process different from how you work now on studio projects?

I think it was good writing a film that wasn't in the development process, because I'm not sure it's very helpful having a lot of voices in on the creation of a script. I think they try to smooth things and homogenize things and explain things. It's better making it a kind of goofy voyage and ride, when you have to just be honest with yourself about what you're doing and where your mistakes are and what isn't working.

On *Metropolitan*, I found the least helpful comments were from people who thought they were in the film business. Unsuccessful screenwriter friends, who were very, very critical of certain things, while my sociology professor/godfather was very, very supportive and loved the things that the screenwriter friends said were breaking the rules.

Do you remember what their criticisms were?

I remember I had this long monologue that the Chris Eigeman character recites about this girl, Polly Perkins. It went on for pages and pages. My screenwriter friend was indignant about how terrible that was and my sociology professor/godfather thought it was a wonderful story.

What I found when we shot the film was that there were long speeches that didn't work, but they were the sociological speeches by the Charlie character, played by Taylor Nichols. If it was a very long sociological speech, we really had to fight hard to whittle those down and make them pertinent, while the long narrative about Polly Perkins, although it's just one guy talking, actually works perfectly fine. It's a story. People are interested in hearing a story. And film is so wonderful in the sense that you can have people's reaction.

How long was the whole writing process and how long were the gaps where you just let it gestate?

I would say the gaps would be a month or two. It was slightly more than a four-year process. I started in the middle of the summer of 1984. I finished four years later in August of 1988 and went out to try to find people to produce or invest in the film. I think I did another draft where I cut things, to try to make it more production friendly. But the actors had already seen the older script, so often we'd restore stuff.

How long was the script?

It was very, very long.

Also, I didn't really get into film formatting too much; I didn't really see the point of centering the dialogue, because my computer skills in those days weren't so good as to have to re-tab all that. I remember a woman at the Tisch School refusing to help us with casting because it wasn't in proper screenplay format, therefore we weren't serious.

That's why I don't take people very seriously when they criticize a script for being too long. I don't think we cut any scenes but one — it's a very brief phone conversation between Tom Townsend and his father, and it came off as mawkish. The line producer, Brian Breenbaum, made a very funny, cutting remark about it: He said, "Put it in an envelope and mail it to your father."

The other cutting we did was cutting within scenes, to try to whittle things down and pick up the pace. And of course we cut out all the improv stuff. We came up with some jokes that we thought were funny on set and we ended up cutting them out.

Did the actors have any problems with the long speeches and the heightened language?

Nope. It's good for them, I think. I think it's good for actors to have a lot of words to say, they seem to like it.

THIS IS YOUR LIFE

Did you do any readings of the script before you finished it?

There was a casting reading of it — after we had done most of the casting we had a read-through.

It was odd, because I had had the Charlie character have something of a stutter in the script. And then I thought, "This is too hard. We've got so many hard things to do, let's not have another hard thing with a guy stuttering through all this dialogue." And I thought it might sound fake, someone acting a stutter.

And then, in the read through, Taylor stuttered a couple of times, and there was one moment when it was a little bit too much. And I stopped the reading and said, "Actually, the idea of this character is he should stutter, so if you can do that, it's great." Taylor completely dominates his stammer, he can do a flawless performance. But he did have a stammer in childhood, and he brought it out for that part. I found it fantastic; somehow a stammer is like when an actor eats. Eating and food and business of that kind in a film is usually wonderful, people are relaxed. And the stammer was kind of the same, it made things really real and unrehearsed.

One of the great things about the script was that these characters are very likeable, even at those times when they may not be behaving in a likeable manner. Was that planned?

That was the intention. I think we give them their problems. They do have that reality in their sad-sack qualities and a lot of it is the success of the performance by the actor. It's a thing I've noticed: Some actors can do a technically perfect performance of scripted lines, but there can be a warmth that's lacking, a human quality, that takes away from what's intended. In this case, our cast delivered the warmth.

Did you write with any actors in mind?

Yeah. I wrote with Audrey Hepburn in mind. The Audrey character is Audrey Hepburn. I did not write with known actors in mind.

I knew that known actors wouldn't do it. It didn't occur to me which known actors would do it; only actors from the past — like Audrey Hepburn — who is the aunt of the actual Sally Fowler.

Although it's a talky film, you also made good use of just showing us things, without commenting on them. For example, when Tom Townsend finds his childhood toys have been thrown out by his father. We never see him come back for the toys, but they simply show up in his room in later scenes. Those scenes could have been painful to watch ...

It was painful to watch; we actually cut some stuff out there. We had a mawkish scene, going back to the box. We shot it and cut it out.

Why did you choose to set the movie in a sort of timeless past?

Well, in my head it was in the past and I couldn't afford to set it in a specific past. So I had to just try to do the best we could for a past identity to the film by trying to exclude what we could exclude and include what we could include, without stating anything too explicitly.

Did that choice help during production?

It didn't hurt us. It was helpful for production because we weren't specifically doing period, so that freed people up not to go crazy with things. It was the guiding principle to make it seem past.

How would you define the theme of *Metropolitan*?

I can't nail down themes. It gets me in trouble now when people ask me about my new script. Unfortunately, I answer when I should say, "Well, I don't know. Draw your own conclusions."

How did you know when you were done with the script?

That's odd. It happened faster than I thought — that sounds funny for a four-year project! I thought it was interminable, I thought it would never end. And suddenly it seemed like, whoa, we're ending. This is it. This is the film. And so it was a bit of a surprise.

I find that generally happens in an interminable scriptwriting process — suddenly you're close to the end or at the end before you even thought it was possible.

What's your writing schedule?

Well, it changed completely from the *Metropolitan* period to subsequently, because at the time of *Metropolitan* I had a day job, and so I would have dinner and I'd go back to writing after dinner. So I was drinking coffee late at night and often I would be at the computer at 1:00 a.m., really dreamy and half-awake and my mind wandering into dreams and I'd usually keep at it until 2:00. So it was a very strange process writing from 11:00 p.m. until 2:00.

Was there anything you learned writing *Metropolitan* that you still use today?

Pretty much everything. I changed the time of day, but everything else is pretty much the same as that process. I still don't use the screenwriting programs and cheat a little bit on the formatting, so it doesn't look as long.

What was it like to get an Academy Award nomination for *Metropolitan*?

I have to confess that I was always terribly, terribly anti-Academy Awards — until I got nominated for one. But as a want-to-be or not-yet-successful filmmaker, there's something terribly disheartening about that spectacle. But then you're nominated and — it's great, even losing.

Virtually the entire cast came and, with Line Producer Brian Greenbaum as ring-leader, we had a blast. But after I quickly reverted to anti-Oscars mode (the exception being 1995, when Mira Sorvino won hers and a lot of films I loved were nominated).

So many interesting, likable and sometimes great films are getting no — or next to no — coverage on their theatrical release, while madly expensive campaigns and over-the-top coverage is devoted to a handful of films (and not normally the ones I'd most like). It just seems to get more and more extreme and disconnected from the honest pleasure of going to the movies and discovering ones you like.

I now get a sort of early winter depression from the screeners Academy members are sent. You feel obliged to watch a lot of them, but very often they are not the films you'd ever go to see on your own and you end up seeing so many images you wish you never knew about. I can't believe that so many intelligent film journalists get caught up in covering this horse race — which must lead to an abdication of coverage for many untrumpeted releases.

The modern age's motto in the arts seems to be: "More recognition, less achievement." So many of the great cinema milestones date from the thirty years before there were film festivals or highly touted awards (such as the Oscars at their start). It'd be fascinating to see what a three-year awards and festivals hiatus might be like. Or at least to stop, or sharply tone down, the campaigning for awards.

Did you use any tools to get yourself up to speed as a screenwriter?

It was terribly helpful that I found a version of *The Big Chill* screenplay, in screenplay format. One publisher had the wise idea of issuing a screenplay-size edition of various screenplays, including *The Big Chill*. I used that to crib format from, to try to get close to film format. And it was actually a good script to have around, because it's an ensemble piece. And the *She's Gotta Have It* production book that Spike Lee did was very helpful.

And there's a book called *The Craft of the Screenwriter* by John Brady which has interviews with people like Ernest Lehman and Paul Shrader. I found that a very helpful book. I thought it was terrific.

Grief
Richard Glatzer

PAULA

Isn't it a year this Thursday since he died?

MARK

I should have known you'd remember. When Kenny went into ICU, Jeremy came down to the hospital and we went to get something to eat. I was sort of crazy, you know, over this idea that we'd had so many great times, Kenny and I, and I was like the custodian of everything. I mean, I have such bad memory and I felt like it would be this major crime if I forgot even one minute. But I was forgetting; I was forgetting all the time. Jeremy said to me, "What's the matter, don't you remember your Proust?" All those memories, just because you can't call them up, doesn't mean that they won't come back, that they aren't there.

There's a well-worn adage that says you should "write what you know." That's what Richard Glatzer did when he decided to make his first feature film. He took his experiences as a writer/producer of the TV show Divorce Court, *and combined it with the loss he had recently suffered after the death of his partner.*

The subsequent film — filled with such indie stalwarts as Craig Chester, Illeana Douglas, Alexis Arquette, Paul Bartel and Mary Woronov — is really a quintessential independent film: funny, sad, personal and in its own way, universal.

What was going on in your career before you wrote *Grief*?

I had sold some scripts to Disney and had written afternoon specials for ABC — one of which actually got produced — but mostly I found that I was making some money as a writer and getting very frustrated at never seeing any of my words come to life. I basically had given up on the idea of doing anything in Hollywood; I was doing a nightclub one night a week and just goofing off, after having produced *Divorce Court* for a couple years.

Producer Ruth Charney suggested that we work on a movie together. I said I had no interest in doing anything unless it was a movie that we could make on as little money as anyone could make a movie. Otherwise it wasn't going to get done. I had enough experience trying to get things done through more conventional channels. So I thought if I conceive of a movie that's basically one location, and think of it as an independent, independent, independent film, then maybe we can actually do it.

She suggested that I do something inspired by my experiences working on *Divorce Court*. I thought about it and thought I didn't want to do some *Soap Dish*-y thing; that I wanted it to have other stuff going on. A lot of the film is autobiographical, and I had been dealing with my lover dying at the time I was working on that show. And I thought that would make it more interesting then if it were just some sort of satire of *Divorce Court*.

So then the idea of it began to take shape. To me, that became more interesting, if you limited it to one location. To conceive of a film from the outset as ultra-low budget is the way to do it. You don't start with a bigger idea and then whittle it down.

Let's back up. How did you get into producing *Divorce Court*?

I sold these two scripts to Disney, when there was a different group of people in charge there. And then one of them ended up as the producer-story editor for *Divorce Court*. I was still living in New York at the time and thinking about going to L.A. I spoke to the guy who had been the head of the studio and he said I should talk to this woman who's over at *Divorce Court* and see if she can get me some work there. And I thought, "Oh my god — *Divorce Court*." But it ended up being more regular employment and more fun than anything else I ever worked on. I thought I'd be there for a week and it ended up being five years. I ended up producing the thing.

Once you had the idea, how long did it take to write *Grief*?

I wrote it quickly; it was the easiest script I've written. I usually don't keep journals, but I happened to write down in a little notebook the day that Ruth suggested thinking about this. It was the end of October in '91, and I had a draft of the script by early January '92; and I hadn't even started thinking about it at the end of October '91. So it was pretty fast.

How did you go about funding the movie?

I had about $20,000 saved and we raised another $20,000 from people who were willing to put up $5,000 investments — none of which was easy.

I think the gay content helped a little bit, that people felt that it was some sort of community function or something. But it also, obviously, limited the film in terms of people thinking they were ever going to see a lot of money coming back. Ruth put up $5,000. It was mostly little bits and pieces, mostly from friends.

We raised $40,000, and at the same time we were doing that, I put together my cast just by going to Sundance and seeing Craig Chester in *Swoon* and meeting people at parties or wherever.

That's where I met Illeana Douglas. Just as I was leaving — I hadn't even spoken to her, really — and I got my coat and was on the way out the door, it suddenly clicked that she was perfect for Leslie. I just went up to her and said, "Hey, you wouldn't by any chance do some low-budget, independent fag film, would you?"

And she said, "I bet you're the kind of guy who loves Edgar Ulmer movies." And I was a big Edgar Ulmer fan, so within a day or two she said, "I'll do your movie," as soon as I got her the script.

So I assembled the cast and felt like I had this really great group of people. We'd all been hoping to get more money than $40,000, but there was nothing coming.

Did you write the script with particular actors in mind?

No. I knew Alexis Arquette and Jackie Beat from this club I was doing; they both performed there. I was thinking of them as I was writing the script; not from the outset, but as I was writing it, I started to realize that I was hearing Jackie Beat saying these lines. So by the time I finished the script I definitely had them in mind for those two roles. But it wasn't like from the beginning I was going to write a role for Jackie Beat or write a role for Alexis.

How long did you shoot?

We shot for ten days. It was ten days for the bulk of the shooting and then we did an extra half day in the courtroom. That was our big production value, which of course we made look like shit by deteriorating it. We shot it on film and it looked really good and then we went and shot it off a monitor.

At the time we didn't know how it was going to work. I thought if I shoot it on film, I have the option to use it on film and if I shoot it on video, then I'm stuck with video. It was basically a half day; we were out of there at three, three thirty.

Did the script change much during shooting?

It was an ongoing process; I was always scrutinizing it and always fiddling with it. Then working with the actors was really helpful.

We did have a week of rehearsal and that was really great and crucial, especially for doing a movie that fast — and one like this, which was so character and performance oriented. I felt that was the highest value of the film, the quality group of people I put together and I wanted to make sure that the parts really came alive.

Did you change the script after the week of rehearsal?

There was a lot of re-writing in rehearsal and throughout the whole process — in the editing room as well. The finished movie is maybe 75% of what was in the original script, but there are little things tweaked here and there.

This was especially true of emotional stuff; you'd see it and think, "Wait a minute, there's not enough here, it's not sounding right." So I would scribble things down on slips of paper and hand them to them. Later I had to get a continuity script together for TV stations and I was like, "Oh my God, where did I put that scene?"

It's not really like I threw the script out, it's not that. It's basically about three-fourths of what was in the script. It's trying to make all of it right. It was just constantly fiddling with it.

And I felt really good about that, because I think everyone's hesitation about a writer-director is that you're going to think that every word is sacrosanct. I felt like I was very able to put the writing behind me and just listen to it and watch it and see if it was working or not.

My actors were a really smart group of people, so I could trust them, if they said "Wait a minute" about their character. Most of the time they were right and that was really good, because it was a great sounding board. Actors are always like that, but I think some actors are better able to see what's missing, or know when something's not sounding right, than other actors are. I credit them with a lot of that.

Then also, in the editing room, I thought, "Oh, everything's fine," and then you'd put it together and realize, "Wait a minute, there's a beat missing here," or you've got to move this thing before that thing or it doesn't pay off. Just all that kind of stuff.

So you were re-writing even while you were editing?

I shot the bulk of the movie in ten-and-a-half days, but six months down the line — after I had a rough cut of the movie — I realized that there were some important emotional beats that were missing. So we went back and shot an extra day's worth of stuff.

These were pretty crucial scenes. There are other scenes they replaced. All the stuff that was taking place near the stage — because we couldn't have access to our original location again.

The big scene where Jackie Beat talks about being fat and the scene where Illeana asks Craig to marry her, that was done somewhere else and we just made it look like it was part of the sound stage in that same building.

There were things that were replaced by those scenes, but those new scenes were really crucial.

The Love Judge scenes were very funny. Did you ever intend to include more of them?

I wish I'd had money to really do the whole shooting of _The Love Judge_, rather than just do scenes from the episodes — to actually see the judge carrying on, to see the actors have the scripts re-written under their noses, and all that kind of stuff. I thought that could have really been fun.

But it just seemed like then we'd have to rent real video cameras and real lights and all that stuff that we didn't have a budget for. That was the closest we could get to it.

Since you lost your original set for the re-shoots, how did you come up with the idea to set the scenes backstage at the show?

It was just a way for us to make up for not being able to re-shoot in the original location. I don't know if I would have even tried that if we'd had access to the original location. So it turned out to be a blessing that we didn't have access to it, because it let us fake it. And all that set was, was a stage at this place called Lace, which is a performance art theater/gallery downtown. There was nothing there, it was this black, empty space. So we made it work.

Do you think there were any advantages to not having a larger budget?

I set out to make a movie in one location for financial reasons. I think the whole idea of grieving and the fact that Mark's dealing with the death of his boyfriend, to me is so much more interesting indirectly and seen only in the office.

I think if we'd had money to go shoot Mark crying at home, or something — just because we maybe had the money, and you'd think, "Oh, we have to cover that" — to me the movie gained its identity and meaning from giving him that sense of privacy and from being limited to the office. That was a budgetary limitation that ended up working in the movie's favor.

Of course, it probably would have been distributed wider and seen as a more mainstream movie if we'd had more locations — a lot of running around and all that stuff.

Did you write the scenes from *The Love Judge* for an existing set?

No. My producer, Yoram Mandel, made phone calls to see what he could get cheap. The people liked him over the phone; he explained how there was no money in this film, and they said, "We'll let you have the set for $500," which by L.A. standards for a day is great. The only thing they said was that we had to go with their schedule and I never knew from one day to the next when it would be available.

So we only had two days' notice to get up there. I had Tim Roth and a couple other people who were going to do cameos in those scenes and they couldn't because of the last-minute scheduling. But I was thrilled that Paul Bartel and Mary Woronov were willing to do it.

How long did it take to finish the movie?

It took forever to post it. We didn't have enough money; the $40,000 was to shoot it, but we didn't have anything left to do any of the post. We were trying to raise money and trying to find free-bie stuff. There was this UCLA student who had this KEM deck at home and she was synching dailies for us. She let us in there to cut some stuff.

It's so frustrating when you've got this in the can and you want to work on it and you can't. It took us about a year to edit the thing, getting a few bucks here, a few bucks there and begging favors everywhere. There was a post house near me, an editing facility that would let us go in there for free. They were sympathetic and trying to help us out.

And really the only reason it ever got finished was because Mark Finch, who was the head of the Gay & Lesbian Film Festival in San Francisco, saw a rough cut of the film and loved it and said he would give us the closing night if we could finish. So then it was this panic to finish it.

I put up more money — fool that I was — in order to finish it. No one was coming up with any money. I made him a personal guarantee that I was going to get the film done and we had two or three months and there was no money and so I finally just put the money up.

Did that festival help?

It was a partial success story. It was a huge hit there and it was like a dream come true to be there. It's a 1,500 seat theater and that town's just insane. These people go there and they have these wild opinions — they either love it or they hate it — and luckily with me they loved it. They just decided very early on that they loved this movie and they were screaming and carrying on throughout the whole movie.

Then we got a great review in *Variety* and all of a sudden all these festivals wanted the film and there was this big Hollywood pro-ducer who had to meet with me and who loved the film. It just felt like, oh, now everything's happening.

Festival-wise, the film did really, really well. It played everywhere.

St. Petersburg, New Zealand, Jerusalem, just every corner of the globe I could think of, it's been.

Most of the time I went with it; a lot of these people can't afford to fly you all around. But I went to Australia with it and I went to Berlin with it and I went to Italy and London a whole bunch of times. I could have gone to Hong Kong if I wanted to pay half my airfare, but I said no. I also could have gone to Jerusalem and I stupidly didn't. It was right when it was with all these Italian festivals and I would have had a day here and a day there and it just seemed like, what's the point?

I traveled with the film for about a year and a half, which was fun.

How was your Sundance experience?

Not very good. The film had been to Toronto and to Vancouver and to the Gay & Lesbian Festival in San Francisco and in Los Angeles. Most Sundance films are pretty new to the public, so by the time the film got there, it was sort of considered old news. I heard that in the first show audiences were pretty good, but by the time the second show happened, it was all these Hollywoody people. And they'd literally walk out during the opening credits.

I've talked to a lot of people who have had similar experiences. And then we didn't win any prizes and however stupid that is, you still want it. And you have to keep reminding yourself that Sundance prizes don't really mean a hell of a lot. It's usually the audience award that seems to indicate something about any commercial success. But nothing else seems to indicate anything.

I guess for my film, Sundance wasn't that important. I've seen my film with audiences, like in Germany where the film was not subtitled, where they loved the film. Or in Toronto, where the film went over really, really well.

And then I was there at Sundance and it felt like a total bomb. The audience, those Hollywood people, were completely inattentive and didn't get it and didn't give a shit and it just felt really bad.

That's not the festival's fault, but that's who's going there these days. And they go there wanting the new Tarantino or something. My film is very quiet and you have to pay attention and stick with it. And I definitely don't think Sundance is the place for a film where you have to stick with it. Because they just don't; they get up and they leave after five minutes. So that wasn't fun.

What have been the positive effects of writing and shooting *Grief*?

Creatively, it's the most gratifying thing I've ever done. No question. And financially, not. If I had it to over again, I would absolutely do it.

It's been an amazing thing to me, just really amazing to think how many thousands of people have seen this thing around the world and that it's really moved some people and really gotten to some people and that I've gotten to meet so many people, filmmakers, through this.

I really feel that there's this great community of independent filmmakers, which is so unlike the Hollywood community and which has a real integrity to it. I'm just amazed how open filmmakers are. I've met so many people — and I hope I'm this way, too — who really are encouraging with other independent filmmakers. There's no sense of competition, there's only support. That's been fantastic.

You meet so many different people from different aspects, from the people at Channel 4 in London, to the people who run the festivals, to the filmmakers themselves. On that level, I haven't been disappointed at all.

There really is a great deal in common; I've formed really strong friendships with people. That whole thing felt great. Especially living in L.A., you feel like, "Who are these fuckers who are making movies? God, get me out of here." And then, to do the festival circuit is such another perspective on film and so different from the Hollywood perspective on film and so much more valid.

What were the downsides?

The financial, really. Because of the financial thing, at times I'll get down. I'll see a film like *Go Fish*, which I really enjoyed, but which to me was like, that film, there was such a hoopla over it, such a huge amount of money given to them and such huge distribution for it. And I would think, "Is my movie not as good as *Go Fish* and why can't my movie get that kind of release?"

And I get resentful — not toward Rose, who's great, and not because of the film, because I really enjoyed the film — but because of that sense that the marketing thing, that this is the first hip lesbian movie and so it's going to get this big send-off and my movie's just not.

I've always fought with myself not to be resentful — especially over films I like — but still there is such a freaky quality to what's hot and what's not. It doesn't have anything to do with the reviews, because my film was really well reviewed. It doesn't have anything to do with anything but how we can market this film and we can't market that film or somebody at one of the distribution companies suddenly gets really worked up over something or whatever.

It's hard to be satisfied. At one point I would have been satisfied just to finish the film, because I thought we'd never get the money to finish the film and I thought, "Oh, if I can only finish it — it doesn't matter if it's distributed, if only I can finish it."

Then you get it finished and then you see it received well, and then you're like, "Oh, well now I want more and I want more and I want more." And then you think of all the films, independent films, that never get finished or never get out there or get to two festivals and then they disappear. I was so much luckier than that.

Mostly, I'm really grateful for the whole thing and feel like — absolutely — if I had it to do over again, I would do it over again, because it was a really great experience.

Would you do things differently?

Yeah. Not so much creatively. There's a million things wrong with that movie, but give me some money and I'll fix them.

I think the big thing that I would do differently was the way we tried to sell the film. That's what I really think about. We were so desperate for $5,000 investments or whatever, that we took the film in various stages to all the big distributors and showed them rough cuts. I had no perspective on it. I didn't realize that it was going to look really stodgy and static and that they weren't going to get it. And they didn't.

We should never have shown them a rough cut. We should never have let any of them see the film except with an audience, because it was working with an audience. When you say what mistakes did you make, that's the big thing.

You get so desperate and you think your film's so good and it's like, "I've got to show it to them and they're going to love it and they're going to give us money," but I think it's really important to realize as a filmmaker you are able to see the finished product more than what's in front of your eyes and other people won't necessarily respond to it.

I would say be damn sure that you're getting the same kind of enthusiasm from other people. If not, hold out and don't show it to them.

Especially if it's a comedy. You need that kind of audience response to convince them that it's working and if you're showing it to them with just a few people in a screening room, they're never going to get it. Or, worse yet, a rough cut on a video tape — forget it. It would have to be really an unusual film to work as a rough cut on a video tape.

One last question: Am I nuts, or is the actor who plays *The Love Judge* doing an impression of Lionel Barrymore?

Yes, the Love Judge is doing Lionel Barrymore. You're the only person who's ever figured that out.

The actor, Mickey Cottrell (the clean freak in *My Own Private Idaho*) loves to do shtick. That morning, when we were at the location of the courtroom scene and he's getting dressed, he said, "You know, I do a really mean Lionel Barrymore." I said, "Let me hear it." And he did his Lionel Barrymore. And I said, "That's perfect, just do that."

It was perfect, it was just what I wanted — a curmudgeonly character. But no one else has picked up on it. That's so funny.

Venice/Venice
Henry Jaglom

                    JEANNE

What are you thinking?

                    DEAN

I was thinking, what if this is all a
movie that I'm making? What if you're
all actors in a movie that I'm making?
Then what? What if the camera's there?
There. Does that make this less real?

Henry Jaglom's style of filmmaking was probably best described by his dear friend, Orson Welles, who said of Henry's films, "You have a different way of making movies than almost anybody else." Not to question Mr. Welles' judgment, but that's actually a bit of an understatement.

Jaglom's films are at once deeply personal and completely universal. He looks at big themes, but only as they affect people individually.

In his film Venice/Venice, *he examines how movies influence our perceptions of reality and romance. To bring that examination to life, he uses improvisation, bits of reality, semi-structured scenes, and on-camera interviews with a wide array of real people, providing a larger framework for his small story. And in the process, he also delivers one of the most surprising and enlightening "twist" endings in the history of movies.*

(Be aware that this interview contains spoilers about key plot points.)

When did you start using improvisation in your movies?

To make my first movie, *A Safe Place*, I had to write a script to get the money from Columbia Pictures. I had written a play called *A Safe Place*, so I adapted it into a very funny screenplay. It was a more hip version of a Neil Simon thing. The studio loved it, everybody loved it.

It starred my two friends, Jack Nicolson and Tuesday Weld. I knew them extremely well and I'd written this wonderful scene and I'd done it on the stage and it worked beautifully. So I had them do the scene, and they're tremendous actors, but there was something missing and I didn't know what.

So I said, "Okay, let's do it again." And I did about five takes, and I said, "This is really strange. This isn't as interesting to me as Tuesday actually is or as Jack actually is in life."

So I said to them, "Look, just forget what I wrote. You know what has to be accomplished in this scene. Just get through that, but don't worry about my words."

And it was magical. And I didn't look at the script for the entire rest of that movie, to the horror of Columbia Pictures.

What did that experience teach you?

The biggest lesson that I got was that actors are to be encouraged to delve into their own lives and into their own expression and their own language and their own memory, because they will come up with fresh and extraordinary things that you could never in a million years create.

And all you have to do is get that to happen once on film and then figure out how to put it together with the next moment. For me, that was it. I never looked at my script again. I drove the crew crazy, but I made the movie I wanted to make.

Your process is a little less conventional than most film-makers.

It's a lot less conventional.

But it works for you.

I think it works great. I never thought that "conventional" was connected with something that worked and "unconventional" not. I don't think there's any relationship there.

At what point did you start using on-camera interviews as part of your process?

That was on *Someone to Love*.

And why did you continue to use that technique on later films?

A really simple reason: I found that every movie by definition tells a story of one, two, three people. In some of them you might learn about four people's stories. But it's very unusual that it's more than three people.

When I'm doing a film like *Someone to Love*, it's a thematic film rather than about a particular individual. The point of the film was to cover the whole range of the theme. I wanted to enlarge the canvas. I wanted to be able to make a film that doesn't just tell you the story of two or three people.

If it's about two or three people, you're always able to say to yourself, "Well, that's these particular two or three people." When you have a large tapestry of individuals, relating their specific experiences connected to that theme, it's much harder to dismiss it as just an aberrant story about one or two particular people who have this issue.

So each time I've used on-camera interviews, there's been a very central reason for it, in terms of expanding the canvas and creating a tapestry which would reverberate around the theme and give it more heft. Give it more variety and make it harder for people to just say, "Well, this is one particular story about one or two people who are going through something."

What inspired the theme of *Venice/Venice*?

My movies are always in direct relationship to what's going on in my life.

I was invited to be, strangely enough, the American representative at the film festival in Venice with my film *New Year's Day*. It was the only film from America that was in the official competition.

Certainly from the conventional point of view, my films are not the traditional fare that comes out. And festivals, no matter how creative and art-oriented they are, seem to like to support themselves with big, commercial, mainstream films.

In any case, I was stunned that I was invited to be the American representative. *New Year's Day* had gotten very good reviews in America and had a nice little run, but there was no reason to expect that anybody would take it on that kind of a level. But the Europeans really liked it and they invited it to the festival with all the hoopla that goes along with being an official invitee, representing of all things the United States.

I'm such a counter-cultural figure here, I thought it would be a really interesting opportunity to make a film about a counter-cultural figure like myself, someone who's far from the mainstream, being invited to represent his country at this oldest and most prestigious of film festivals.

So I made it a condition of accepting their nice honor that anyone who interviewed me, I could interview them at the same time. I would have a crew with me. The festival people were all too happy to do it, they thought it was fascinating.

I brought no crew from America. My cinematographer, who's Israeli, I brought from Israel. He put together a five or six-person crew of Italians in Venice.

I had three actors come: My star, Nelly Alard, came from France. My friend Suzanne Bertish, came from London. And against my wishes and without my economic support, Daphna Kastner, an actress who I'd used in *Eating*. I had told her, "I'm sorry, I can't afford to bring anyone over for this, it's all going to be shot there," so she got on a plane and came by herself anyway. So I cast her as my assistant that I could annoy and drive crazy.

And that was it. David Duchovny was there, because David was in *New Year's Day*. So I said to David, "Okay, I want you play a little part in this as well," and he said, "Sure."

I decided I would make it up as I went along, based upon what was happening to me, because that would give a sense of what happens to somebody who comes to the film festival.

Then I thought that the second half will take place in California. I structured that half to reflect my feelings about Venice, America, movies, real life and all of that.

And that's the part where I did the interviews in my office, and for that part I wrote a much more structured script and brought several of the characters into it who had been in the European half.

The movie has an amazing twist, where at the end we find out that the first half of the movie — in Venice, Italy — is not actually reality, but is the movie that you're talking about making in the second half of the film. At what point did you decide to make that switch?

As I was doing this, I realized that one of my main themes was the effect of movies on our sense of reality and on our romantic dreams, and that this whole movie was kind of a romantic dream. I'm meeting this extraordinary creature, this journalist who falls in love with me and who I fail to attract because I'm being such an asshole and she's expecting the person I am in the movies and all of that. So I thought, that really sounds like a movie.

I didn't think about it while I was shooting the movie in Italy. I just shot it the way I would have shot it anyway. I shot it for its own reality. But when I came back I realized that the Italy segment should be the film that I'm making.

That film does reflect more profoundly, for me, my sense of what my life is like. It really captures in some way, deeply for me, my own interior sense of life. So that's why I'm very attached to it.

Did you go to Italy with any structure in mind?

Absolutely none. Absolutely none. I didn't have a script. I decided that I would just see what happens to a person who goes to a festival. I'd been to several — Cannes and Rotterdam and Berlin and other film festivals — but I'd never gone to Venice. So I just decided I would go and see what it was like, with a film crew. And that's exactly how I did it.

How much backstory did you provide to the actors?

I gave Nelly her backstory — she's a journalist, from Paris — but not much, because she had been in America and she had done a documentary on me for French television. So I said, "Okay, you're a journalist who's here because of an obsession with me and with what you think is this sensitive male that you've gotten from my performances in the movies you've seen." That's all I told her.

I said to Suzanne Bertish, my friend from England, a really wonderful actress, "You play an ex-girlfriend of mine who I run into there." She said, "Fine."

I said to the guy who was my escort from Germany who was arranging for distribution of foreign sales, I said, "You're going to play my foreign sales rep."

I said to Daphna Kastner who showed up without my permission, "Okay, you're my assistant and I'm really going to treat you like shit." She said, "That's nothing new."

You made good use of Nelly's background in physics, particularly when she compares moviemaking and movie watching to the principles that Heisenberg developed.

I always do this with my actors, if they have a particularly interesting bio. So I said to her, "Listen, the most important scene in this movie is going to be a scene — and you're not going to know when it's going to take place — but it's going to be a scene where I'm pointing out that this feels like a movie I'm making."

I said, "What I would like to do then is for you to bring in Heisenberg, because it becomes this whole metaphor for films and how we see them and seeing them affects our perception of reality and all of that." She said, "Great."

It's like in *Can She Bake a Cherry Pie?* and the guy with the pigeon. He throws the pigeon and the pigeon keeps coming back to him. That guy happened to have a trick pigeon. It was his pet. So I turned it into a metaphor for a guy who mistreats women and they keep coming back to him.

To me it's just a question of finding out what the actor's equipment is, what special aspects they might have handy, that might further help explicate a point in the thematic intention. That's why we used the Heisenberg Principle. It worked very nicely.

How much time was there between shooting in Venice, Italy and Venice, California?

I think we had six or seven months.

How structured was the California segment?

Very. The story was very structured; within the story I always encourage the actors to come up with their own dialogue.

We happened to shoot at this guy's house in Venice; he happened to be a songwriter. I didn't plan that. So I had him play the part of somebody who's trying to convince me to use his song in the movie.

The relationship with my local girlfriend, played by Melissa Leo, and her reaction to Nelly coming there, all of that was very planned.

I show them the structure, scene by scene: "In this scene, you're sitting with her, talking about this guy you're both involved with, my character. Nelly, you know me, you've come from Venice to see why I haven't followed up on the relationship. Melissa, you've learned enough from our relationship that you're ready to move on and hand me over, and you're also responding in whatever real way you respond to her."

Do they know the full arc of the story or just on a scene-by-scene basis?

The main characters know the arc of the story and they know where they are in that arc; they have to know that as good actors, I feel. But not the smaller characters, people standing around at the party. They don't know anything that they don't need to know.

The last time we spoke, we talked about how you hate rehearsals —

I don't hate rehearsal; I'm *terrified* of rehearsal.

Why?

Because the worst thing that can happen to me is a great moment that's not on film, because I know it's not going to happen again.

It might be that wonderful actors after a lot of work and takes might be able to recreate it fairly well. But I'm a great, great believer in inspiration and moment-to-moment reality. I come out of the Actors Studio, that's my background. I think that the more open and available a person is to the moment, and the less restricted he or she is, the more they're going to come up with completely fresh, surprising behavior, some of which is going to be wonderfully useable.

I just like the surprise. I also know that the surprise means that the other actor in the scene will be surprised and you will get really true behavior. And when I'm surprised by my actors I know the audience is going to be surprised.

That's why so many people say of my films — sometimes positively, sometimes negatively — that they don't feel like they're watching a movie, they feel like they're almost eavesdropping on something very personal and private. For me, that's the goal, to take down that fourth wall to such a degree that they're not completely sure what's real and what isn't.

Life is not rehearsed and I don't think movies should be rehearsed.

Do you shoot the scenes more than once?

Oh, of course! But I shoot them differently and I don't say "Use the same words," unless I need a close-up or something. I just say, "Okay, that was good. Let's do that again." If I'm not in the scene I stand behind the cameraman and whisper to him, "Go to her. Pull back. Do a two-shot." Because I'm also thinking about how I can cut the scene while it's happening.

Some scenes just happen once, but many scenes are created in the editing. I might do ten, twelve takes sometimes, but they're not the same dialogue. They're the same intentions and they have to get to the same place, but they're completely different.

Do you show rough cuts to people for feedback while you're editing?

Oh my God, yes. I'm sort of famous for my rough cut screenings. They start when the movie's about three-quarters finished. I have twenty or thirty people come to the screening room on Sunset, and I do it at least fifty or sixty times as I'm finishing the movie.

What I do is I ask people afterwards, "What worked, what didn't work, what bothered you …?" I really listen to audiences. I like to do that, that's a big part of the process.

What advice would you give to a filmmaker who wanted to make a movie like yours?

It's really simple: Don't do my kind of movie, do your kind of movie. Figure out what your kind of movie is, not my kind of movie. That would be my advice.

And once you've figured out what your kind of movie is, don't let anybody tell you that anything about it is wrong. Don't let anybody diminish your enthusiasm or excitement about it. And insist that you know what you're doing, even if you don't know what you're doing, because you will find out what you're doing as you go along.

Try as much as you can to tell your own particular truth on film. Insist on not letting anybody change your mind about what your truth is, what your goal is, how you should convey it. You can learn all kinds of technical things and become very proficient, but most people lose the impetus that made them want to be filmmakers to begin with, because they learn all kinds of things that people tell them you shouldn't do or you can't do.

When I was shooting my first film, I had a crew and a cameraman that came from *Love Story*. *Love Story* was a huge hit. Columbia Pictures assigned them to me because they didn't know exactly what to do with me and they were a little scared, so they assigned this very conventional crew. It was during the Vietnam War, I had long hair and white capezio shoes and I was totally weird to them, so they showed up wearing American Flag pins in their lapels the next day. They were rather hostile toward me.

I was trying to invent my own style. And seeing Tuesday and Jack be so good at being themselves made me throw away my script. And the crew kept getting more and more irritated. But mainly they said, "It won't cut. It won't cut. It won't cut. You can't shoot that, it won't cut."

And it was driving me crazy. So at lunch I said to Orson Welles, "What am I going to do? They're driving me crazy. Everything I try that's different, they tell me it won't cut."

And he said, "Tell them it's a dream sequence." I said, "What?" He said, "Just tell them it's a dream." I said, "Why?" He said, "Never mind, just tell them that."

So after lunch, sure enough on the first shot I said, "I'd like the camera to go from here down to here." The DP said, "The camera go from here to here? How are you going to cut that? That can't possibly cut."

I said, "It's a dream sequence."

"Oh, a dream sequence! How about this?" And he got down on his back on the floor and said, "Look, I could shoot it up against the sky ..." And I said, "Great, great." And I had no problem for the rest of the movie with anything I said, because I kept saying it was a dream sequence.

I went to Orson that night and said, "What the fuck is this? I don't understand, why did this change everything?"

He said, "Most people — a crew is very much like average people, not artists, but good technicians — they think life has rules. And life has order. And life has structure. The only place in their life where they know there are no rules, no order, no structure, is in their dreams. When they dream, they know things jump around, things aren't logical, and they accept that, because that's a dream.

"So if you tell them this is a dream sequence, they are freed from all the conventional requirements or the logical, structured, tech-nologically-adept way of doing things. And the artist in them is suddenly freed."

There's not a single movie since then that I haven't used that on somebody. Even on actors, who say, "I don't understand why this person would do that," and I say, "It's a dream sequence." "Oh! Oh, okay!"

You mentioned how people either love your films or hate them. There seems to be no middle ground. And the critics

are the same way. Do you remember the headline for the review of *Venice/Venice* in *The Rocky Mountain News*?

Yes. "Jaglom on Jaglom. Again. Who Cares?"

And the first paragraph is something like "Henry Jaglom has made the single worst movie in the history of cinema." Not just in the 1990s or in recent memory, but in the history of cinema.

I collect those. I love them.

People who don't like your films seem to be particularly vocal about it. People (and critics) seem to take your movies personally.

That's because my films are so personal.

People magazine said of *Sitting Ducks*, "If this film were a horse, you'd shoot it." On *Can She Bake A Cherry Pie?*, *People* magazine said, "Some people look forward each year to their root canal. That's how I feel about my yearly Henry Jaglom film."

To a lot of people, the airing of your emotional dirty laundry is so terrifying that they hate you. I run into men like that a lot. Women very rarely; women are very responsive to the films, and men who are artists and creative men. But there are a lot of men who just think I'm just the devil, the absolute devil.

You seem to have no problem with getting bad reviews.

I love them. From the beginning, when I got a bad review — a fun one, like a real attack — I just copied them and sent them to all my friends. I thought it was just hysterical that people would get so upset about somebody else's playing with paint brushes. I've always enjoyed it.

I found, on *A Safe Place*, because I violated all of those rules on my first movie, the anger started right there. I remember *Time* magazine saying "this movie looks like he threw the pieces of the film up in the air and it landed totally at random in a mixmaster."

People really expose themselves in my movies. And a lot of people don't want to see that. It's understandable. I'm never surprised by the negative reactions. I'm always surprised and delighted by the degree of openness with which so many people are willing to receive and accept the films.

And those people who do like them, they really do become a part of their lives. I get these incredible letters with very touching things about terribly sad and painful moments in these people's lives when the films were really helpful. They feel less alone, they feel less isolated, which is really the goal for me of making films like this.

CHAPTER TWO

Keeping It Real

There are many different ways to use reality to your advantage when creating a screenplay, as the following three screenwriters ably demonstrate.

You can use real people to tell a fictional story (*Bubble*); fictional characters to tell a real story (*Henry: Portrait of a Serial Killer*); or use actors to bring real people to life on screen (*Capote*).

Each format has its benefits and pitfalls, but all three approaches share the same goal: an attempt to bring a reality to the screen that you won't normally find in traditional "fiction" films.

Capote
Dan Futterman

TRUMAN

On the night of November 14th, two men
broke into a quiet farmhouse in Kansas
and murdered an entire family. Why did
they do that? Two worlds exist in this
country: the quiet conservative life,
and the life of those two men -- the
underbelly, the criminally violent.
Those two worlds converged that bloody
night.

Although it ended up becoming an Oscar-winning film, Capote *started out the way many independent films do: Someone gets an idea, writes a script, and then gathers his/her friends together to make a movie.*

First-time screenwriter Dan Futterman started that traditional process with a couple of distinct advantages: He chose a compelling subject matter (Truman Capote's relationship with murderer Perry Smith while writing his classic In Cold Blood*) and the friends he gathered to make the movie included his talented long-time pals director Bennett Miller and actor Philip Seymour Hoffman.*

Where did the idea to write *Capote* come from?

I got interested in Truman Capote in sort of an oblique way, and it was almost incidental that it ended up being specifically about Truman Capote.

There was a book that my Mom, who's a shrink, gave me called *The Journalist and the Murderer*, by Janet Malcolm. It's about a case in California where a doctor named Jeffrey MacDonald was eventually convicted of killing his wife and children. Joe McGinniss was writing a book about him and eventually, when the book came out — it was called *Fatal Vision* — Jeffrey MacDonald sued Joe McGinniss for fraud and breach of contract.

Malcolm's book is sort of a meditation on how could this happen. How could a convicted triple murderer sue the writer who's writing about his life? How could he convince himself that the writer was going to write something good about him? It dealt with the fact that the journalist is posing as a friend to get the subject to talk, and that the subject has hopes that he's going to be portrayed in a good light, and that the journalist is always playing off of that desire. The relationship is premised on a basic lie that it's a natural relationship. It's not. It's a transactional relationship.

That seemed interesting to me, and had there not been a TV movie made about that incident, I might have written about that.

Some years later I picked it up again and read it — it's a pretty short book and I recommend it — and just on the heels of reading that I read Gerald Clarke's biography of Capote, called *Capote*, and there are two or three chapters that deal with the period in his life where he was writing *In Cold Blood* and his relationship with Perry Smith.

I wanted to write about that kind of relationship and deal with those kinds of questions. The fact that it was Truman Capote was an extremely lucky accident, because he's fascinating in so many ways and he's so verbal and also was a man who was struggling with some real demons, I think. That made the work I was doing that much more interesting and deeper.

Up until that point, you'd made your living as an actor. Where did the impulse to tackle a screenplay come from?

I'd written, as you do, bad poetry in high school and college. And I had written a short story or two. I'd always admired playwrights and screenwriters; it seemed to me like a real trick to get a story told primarily through dialogue.

I thought about writing this as a play, initially, and then for some reason a screenplay felt more liberating. The play, I think, would have felt a little bit closed down and would really center too much on the discussions in the jail cell.

I always thought I wanted to write a screenplay, but I never wanted to do it just theoretically. I wanted to do it with a specific idea in mind that would really become something of an obsession, which is what this became. I almost felt like I would have been terribly disappointed with myself had I not done it. And feeling like I had to write this, or had to try to write this, was not a feeling I'd had before.

Did you like that feeling?

It was great, because there were no expectations that it would be any good, either on my part or anybody else's part. I knew that if it sucked, I would read it, my wife would read it, and she'd love me anyway. So it didn't feel like there was any pressure.

You had the distinct advantage, as a beginning writer, of being married to a working writer. How did she help you in this process?

Although it doesn't seem like there's a lot of plot in the movie — it's about a guy writing a book about an event that already happened — but it is quite plotty when you get down to it. And she was clear and strict with me, saying "If there are any scenes where people are just talking about something that you think is going to be interesting, cut it, because if it's not moving the plot forward it doesn't belong in the script." That was important to learn. And it was something that I had never considered.

I did an outline, somewhere between twenty and twenty-five pages with a paragraph for each scene, with dialogue suggestions. The script came out probably 80% tied to that outline.

Did you change the script after showing it to people?

Not right at the beginning. It kind of was what it was. It was long, almost 130 pages, a lot of dialogue, but you got a very strong sense of what the movie might be from it.

We let it sit for a while. I know Bennett did a lot of thinking about it, as did Phil. And when we finally were getting to the point where it looked like we were actually going to get some financing for this, we got to work. The basic work that happened on the script was altering the first act.

What sort of work did the first act need?

I think I had written a tonally different first act from the second and third acts of the movie. By that I mean that it was as if Capote was off on a lark — he saw this thing in the paper, it grabbed hold of him, he asked his buddy Harper Lee to come with him. In life, he asked her to take a gun with her to protect him. The tone was of high jinks and fun and an adventure and there was a slightly campy road trip quality to it. Not that any of the scenes were that different, but there was a tonal quality to it that changed abruptly when Perry Smith was caught and brought to town and Truman saw him for the first time. And then everything changed.

That was my conception of it, and what Bennett suggested to me — and I think it was very smart — was that was probably how Capote told the story to himself, that he sort of fell into this situation and then Perry was caught and then everything changed. But the story Bennett was more interested in telling was built around the structure of a Greek tragedy, where the hero is meant to confront something in himself by going on this journey. The way I went back and re-wrote the first act telegraphed that much more, that this was going to be a movie where the main character was going to go to a place he'd never been before and see himself in a way he'd never seen himself before.

Did you take any classes or read any books on screenwriting before you sat down and wrote the outline?

No, I didn't take any classes. I read the Robert McKee book (*Story: Substance, Structure, Style and the Principles of Screenwriting*) that I guess everybody reads, and I found that pretty helpful — his clarity about story. I think that was an important lesson for me to learn over and over again, that story is primary. Clever dialogue is not what it's about. It's got to ride on the story, and then you can hang stuff off of that.

Then it was just a matter of trial and error. And the lucky fact of having a subject who has been quoted as having said a lot of funny things, of which I put as many as possible into the screenplay.

What were the upside and the downside of writing about a real person?

I always hated that moment in school when the teacher, I think inevitably a somewhat lazy teacher, would give the assignment, "Write a story about whatever you want," and I would just panic. My mind would just be a complete blank. But if I got a very specific assignment to write "Why does this character have to confront this thing in this story in Chapter Three," then I was off and running.

Rules are good for me. In that way, I think writing about a real person, knowing basically what the rules are — you can take a little bit of license, but try to stick to the facts as much as humanly possible — that felt liberating to me. It has a way of focusing my imagination, I guess, instead of feeling like anything goes and then I'm screwed.

I recently have had correspondence with Wallace Shawn, who is William Shawn's son. He and his brother are not terribly happy about the way William Shawn is portrayed in the film.

I knew that Capote had three different editors involved in the book. One was William Shawn of *The New Yorker*, one was Bennett Cerf at Random House, and then when Cerf retired, a guy named Joe Fox took over. That just seemed too confusing to present in a movie. We needed one editor and I choose that to be William Shawn, and he would do everything that all the other guys did as well. That upset Wallace and I feel badly about it. If I were able to go back, I would try to solve it.

What you encounter is that, even if the people have died, there is a moral debt owed to them in terms of trying to adhere as strictly as possible to the truth. It's something I tried to be very conscious of, but in this particular case, I think I came up short.

Did you ever consider just fictionalizing the character's name, since he was already a composite of three people?

It didn't occur to me at the time that any of the things I had him doing could possibly be upsetting to anybody, but that was my own take and I see now why his sons are upset. Looking back now, I would try to find a way to fix it.

How did your background as an actor influence your screenwriting? Did it help?

I guess I'd like to think that it helps. I've worked on a lot of great scripts as an actor and I've also worked on some that have stuff that's difficult to play or difficult to say. I think that the basic questions that one asks as an actor (and this will sound completely elemental to anyone who's taken a second to think about it) — what do I want, how do I go about getting that, what's my action on this particular line — I think that those things were very much in my mind as I was writing and I really wanted to write stuff that was eminently playable.

I think the way that it gets in the way is that different actors have a different barometer for what feels playable to them, or a different take on the scene that's equally valid, and so there were certain times during rehearsals where lines would come up and I'd hear "Let's try to change this, this part of the scene's not working," and I'd think, "I played that scene up in my room just last night and it was great. So I don't get it, what's the problem?"

But I'd like to think that I was sensitized to the difficult work that actors go through to try to make things feel real.

At what point were you in the writing process when you approached Bennett Miller?

I think I told him about the idea; I've known him since we were thirteen or so, and I'd only ever made money as an actor, and so he basically gave me a friendly pat on the head, "Sounds great. Good luck."

And then I sent him an outline after I'd written it, and I think to this day he has yet to read the outline. But his response was equally blandly encouraging. Then I sent him the script when it was done.

My feeling about his reaction to the script was that he was a little upset that he had responded so well to it. He'd been reading a lot of scripts since a documentary of his, called *The Cruise*, came out, and I think the last thing he wanted to do was a period piece and a piece that was clearly going to be hard to get made. So he read the script and he thought, "Oh, fuck. I like this. It's one of the few things I've really liked in the last number of years. And it's going to take a really long time to actually make this movie."

We then decided to give it to Phil. Bennett physically handed it to him and Phil's enthusiasm for it — and fear of it — I think really convinced Bennett that we should try to do this.

Did you do any readings or workshop the script?

We did a table reading in New York with Phil and some actor friends of ours, just a few weeks before rehearsals started. The reading highlighted the problems that we had been kind of skating over, scenes where we thought, "Oh, I'll fix it later." It focused our minds on actually fixing the problems.

Did you have much rehearsal?

We had a decent amount of rehearsal and I loved it. It was a terrific experience.

Bennett and I had an important talk about how, mechanically, we were going to run rehearsals. The decision was that he, because he was directing the movie, he needed to develop rapport, relationship, trust with the actors without me around.

We were all up in Winnipeg and in the morning I would go sit with whomever was going to rehearse that day with Bennett and they would read through the scenes. We'd talk about any questions, and then I'd take off and go up to this little room I had and do re-writing from the day before that needed to be done, tweaks, whatever. Then I'd come back at the end of the day and we'd read it again. I think it worked enormously well. I think the actors came to really trust Bennett and it was just a better use of my time instead of just sitting and poking my nose into rehearsals, which would only have been disruptive.

Did the script change much in rehearsal?

It did. What I remember was that there was a lot of re-arranging in one particular section, not in enormous ways, but there was a lot of re-arranging of Perry and Truman scenes and topics. I remember in the second act of the movie, where Truman is visiting him repeatedly in the penitentiary, there was a lot of adjusting: "We'll take this half of the scene and put it on the back of the scene a little earlier." It was all about trying to figure out what the natural development of that relationship should be.

And then there was an ongoing discussion about what the opening of the movie was going to be. The third act of the movie now opens with a shot in Capote's brownstone. It's a shot through these glass doors and he's talking on the phone. He's kind of drunk and he's talking to William Shawn about how the killers have gotten another appeal at the Supreme Court. In the way I'd written the script originally, that scene opened the movie, and then it flashed back to the beginning of the movie and you worked your way back to that scene starting the third act.

I think it was necessary for me to identify, in my writing process, what felt like the crisis point that Capote had come to. But Bennett was right, and I came to realize, that it was not a dynamic way to start the movie.

I then wrote about six versions of what an opening scene could be. We finally thought, "You know what? We're going to save a little money for re-shoots and, upon watching the movie, we will hopefully then have figured out what needs to be the opening scene." And that's eventually what we did.

The first introduction to Capote, in the party where he's telling the story about Jimmy Baldwin, that was written and shot months later. It feels perfect, Phil was perfect. What I wrote was largely taken from the Clarke biography, but then Phil was off and running with it. Phil is a gifted improviser, even though I don't think he would say he is. The party scenes in particular are places where he made some great additions to my script.

Did any other significant changes take place in editing?

There was a lot of streamlining of the movie.

The first version that I saw was probably twenty minutes longer than the finished version. I'd never been through the process of seeing a movie that was so fat in that way. Bennett was feeling quite good about it and I think he could see where the target was. At that point I couldn't and it felt fat, it felt not terribly funny, sluggish, and I got kind of terrified at that point.

It was just through months of carving it and carving it and carving it that it got to the place where it didn't have anything extra in it — and it only got to that place after a laborious process. Bennett and Chris Tellefsen, the editor, knew where they were headed, but it was a little bit difficult for me to see, so to my mind that transformation was enormous, although I don't think it was a tremendous surprise to them.

I saw, finally, a version that I felt really happy with. There was no sound work done on it, there were a couple of little things that needed to be fixed, and I thought, "I'm going to stop watching it now and I'm going to wait to see it all the way through with everything set, color-corrected and all the sound work done." I did that at the Telluride Film Festival, where it was properly projected and there was an audience, and that was a pretty thrilling moment.

What's the best advice you're ever received about writing?

I think it's got to be what I learned from my wife, that it's all about plot. It has got to move. You have to move through the scenes from one to the other. It's got to feel inexorable that this scene follows upon that scene.

There's no point to moving around capriciously. You're only going to get lost and you're going to lose the audience. As many screenplays as I may write, I don't think I'll change my point of view about that.

Did you have to do any re-writing to fit the budget?

Yes. There's a section of the film that takes place in Spain, and that was shot right at the end. There was a big question about if we were going to have the money to shoot it in California, in Malibu, or if we were going to have to do it in Winnipeg in an interior that was supposed to be a ski chalet. It was a matter of "do we have the money or do we not have the money?"

We were pretty despairing, we just knew — having seen the dailies and talking about what the film looked like — there was an awareness that it needed a breath of fresh air at the point, it needed some sunlight, it needed some different vibrant bright colors of the ocean and the sky. It had been oppressively Kansas in the late fall and winter. So I did do some re-writing, to be able to set it all indoors in some ski chalet.

There was some transferring of scenes from outdoors to indoors and cutting down the scope of them. Thankfully, we got to shoot those scenes on the California coast as they'd originally been written.

By and large I would say that for a relatively low-budget movie, a good 90 to 95% of what I wrote ended up getting shot as it was. It was kind of remarkable and I think it was due in large part to the fact that Bennett and I had some time — some months leading up to shooting — to make sure we were on the same page and were wanting to make the same movie.

What was it like to be nominated for an Academy Award?

I hope this doesn't come out the wrong way, but because the season is so long — we'd been to Telluride, Toronto and the New York Film Festivals, and then we opened — and the movie had gotten a great deal of good response, even before it opened, so we knew we had something that people were responding to.

And then sometime in January they announce what's going to be nominated, and by that point you've been through so many different awards announcements — the critics' awards that have been handed out or nominees have been announced, Independent Spirit awards nominees were announced by then — there starts to be a little list that people are saying, "These are the contenders."

Unfortunately, it kind of ruins the experience, because I think that you start to develop expectations, because people are saying, "Oh, look, it's a real possibility," while all along you've been thinking, "Oh, come on, don't be ridiculous." It can't help but eat at you and so you think, "Well, that would be great, wouldn't it?" The fear of being disappointed almost replaces what should be simply shock and elation. And that's unfortunate.

However, having said that, the biggest reaction I had was looking at the list of people I'd been nominated with. I'd never understood before when people said that something like that could be humbling, but, at that point, I got it. And it was largely because Tony Kushner's name was on it, someone whose play I had been in — *Angels in America* — and someone whom I've admired for as long as I've been aware of his writing. To be included in a list with him was simply incredible.

So I had all those emotions at the same time.

It's a heady time, it's fun. There was no expectation on my part that I would win, because *Brokeback Mountain* was such a big event. Larry McMurtry and Diana Ossana wrote a great script and I think people felt that he was due and the script was great. So it was kind of a fun way to go into the Oscar season, which was that I had no expectations of winning but I was just going to enjoy it.

Any advice to someone starting a low-budget script?

I know that the premise of this book is about writing stuff that will fit into a certain budget, but I don't know that I would give that advice off the bat. I mean, look, obviously if you're writing scenes where spaceships get blown up, you know where you are. If you're even slightly aware that big things cost money, then you're not going to write things like that.

But to be thinking in that way, I feel, can also get you thinking like, "Well, how will critics respond to this? How will producers respond to this? How will ...?" And you cannot have that in your head while you're writing. You simply have to be thinking, "Do I like this? Do I believe it? Is it interesting to me? When I go back and read it, if I can be as objective as possible, is it exciting to me to read?"

If you're honest with yourself and have some sort of decent barometer for how things are playing, then you can't help but have the right reaction to it. That's the most important thing, to write something that is successful on the page. That sort of second-guessing, I think, is going to be defeatist.

You already have enough voices in your head – and the superego perched on your shoulder, saying, "That's terrible, that's not good enough" — so the fewer voices you can add to that chorus, the better.

Henry: Portrait of a Serial Killer
John McNaughton

                    HENRY

You kill that high school boy, they're
gonna slap your ass back in jail, Otis.
That's a promise. I mean, people have
seen you together.

                    OTIS

I'd still like to kill him, though.

                    HENRY

I bet you would.

                    OTIS

I'd like to kill somebody.

                    HENRY

Say that again.

                    OTIS

I'd like to kill somebody.

                    HENRY

Let's you and me go for a ride, Otis.

*The phrase "not for the squeamish" may well have been invented
for John McNaughton's* Henry: Portrait of a Serial Killer. *Although
you'll find it in the "horror" film section of the video store, it's*

far more than a simple horror film. The film is a starkly realistic, almost documentary-style fictionalized look at a few days in the life of confessed serial killer Henry Lee Lucas.

McNaughton, who went on to direct in a number of different genres including the comic-drama Mad Dog and Glory *starring Robert De Niro, Bill Murray and Uma Thurman, drew on his roots producing documentaries to construct the film. But as he admits, it was co-writer Richard Fire's keen understanding and use of the basics of dramatic construction that helped to make* Henry: Portrait of a Serial Killer *the milestone it has become.*

What was going on in your life and career before *Henry: Portrait of a Serial Killer* came along?

I had a long-standing dream of wanting to make a feature film. But I'd had to put that on hold because — being that I lived in Chicago and was not connected in any way to the mainstream industry — I really didn't know how I was ever going to achieve that dream.

I was working on these small documentary projects that were being distributed by a company in the south suburbs of Chicago called MPI. I had worked in the commercial field in Chicago, but the first time I was ever on a feature film set I was the director.

Where did the idea for the story come from?

I had done this series of documentaries for MPI called *Dealers in Death*, which were about American gangsters, primarily from the Prohibition era. We had scoured the archives for a lot of public domain photographs and footage, got Broderick Crawford to narrate it for us and made a little money on that project.

I was going to produce and direct another documentary piece, based on professional wrestling, because I'd found someone who had a collection of wrestling footage from the 1950s and 1960s with Bobo Brazil and Killer Kowalski and Dick the Bruiser and Andre the Giant, from the period of wrestling before the WWF or the WWE.

MPI was owned by two brothers, Waleed and Malik Ali. I went out to meet Waleed to talk about doing these wrestling documentaries. When I got to their offices Waleed informed me that he had contacted the person who had the footage for sale. The person with the footage had quoted a price and when the Ali brothers approached him, saying, "Okay, we'll negotiate on that price," the guy realized that the brothers had money so he increased his price. The Ali brothers were not to be dealt with in that manner, so Waleed informed me, "Listen, we're not going to do business with this guy. He's a crook."

Early on in the video business — and the brothers got in at the beginning — the major studios weren't interested in video rights, because there just wasn't enough money involved. So they were selling off the rights to their films. A couple of companies, like Vestron and Pyramid, became wealthy for a short period of time, until the studios saw the potential in the video market and started creating their own video divisions. And then those companies went out of business.

But in the early days of video you could buy the video rights quite cheaply for low-budget horror films, and since a lot of "B" horror titles hadn't been seen widely, they were very successful on video. A "B" schlock horror film that people may not have been interested in going to the theater to see, they were more than happy to rent because they're a lot of fun.

So what was happening at this time was that those titles were becoming so popular that the rights acquisitions were becoming more and more expensive. And so Waleed had determined that it would make sense for them to fund a horror film and thereby own all rights in perpetuity, rather than just buying the video rights for a limited period of time. So he proposed to me that we should join forces and make a horror film.

I went in thinking I was going to be doing these documentaries and instead, it was the day that my dream came true, completely unexpectedly. I was kind of in shock.

Down the hall was the office of an old friend of mine who I had grown up with, Gus Kavooras. Gus was always a collector of the strange and the arcane and the weird. I stopped in to see him and I was kind of in shock. I said, "Gus, Waleed just offered me $100,000 to make a horror movie. I have no idea what my subject will be." And he said, "Here, look at this."

He took a videocassette off the shelf and popped it in the machine. It was a segment from the news magazine show, *20/20*, and the segment was on Henry Lee Lucas and Ottis Elwood Toole, who were serial killers. The term "serial killer" was coined in 1983 by the FBI. In 1986 I had never heard the term before and this was something new to me, the idea that there were these random murderers going around.

Most murders are committed by people previously acquainted with the victim. Husband kill wives, wives kill husbands, husbands kill wives' lovers, wives kill husbands' lovers. Most murderers are committed by people who are known by the victim. But this was a new trend in murder where there were these individuals who were just randomly murdering strangers. It was, indeed, very horrifying. There were some interviews with Henry and a lot of photographs. He was really a creepy character. And so that became the germ for the story.

Was the budget an issue while you developed the story?

The budget was written in stone. That was the mandate from Waleed, "Make me a horror film for $100,000." So the budget was always a consideration.

How did you and co-writer Richard Fire work together?

I put together a set of 3x5 index cards delineating a scene structure, but I was not an experienced dramatist, screenwriter or otherwise. But I had the money, I had the mandate to make the picture, and we had our subject: the true story of Henry Lee Lucas.

I had a friend, Steve Jones, and he was working as a director of animated commercials in Chicago, primarily doing Captain Crunch commercials. He was very well connected into the production community in Chicago and I was not. So I arranged with Steve to be the producer and I said to him, "I need a co-writer."

There was a theater company in Chicago called The Organic Theater Company. The Organic was a really wild bunch of characters who had quite a bit of success in Chicago and were a really interesting theater company. One of the company members was Richard Fire, another was Tom Towles, who would play Otis. Other members of the company were Dennis Franz, Dennis Farina and Joe Mantegna. They had worked with David Mamet, they had produced *Sexual Perversity in Chicago*.

They did a play called *Warp* that was kind of an outer space fantasy and Steve Jones had done a bunch of video projection for them and knew the group. Steve recommended Richard Fire. Richard and I met and talked about the project and I hired Richard.

What was your working process with Richard?

I would go every day to Richard's apartment and we would sit and he would type. We would knock ideas back and forth and then when we came to what we thought was something worthwhile, he would type it out.

What's so interesting about the script is that — if you take out the violence — it's a very traditional, well-structured story. We meet Henry, he meets his friend's sister and a romance starts. Then there's a fight and he and the sister leave together. It's almost like a classic 1950s Paddy Chayefsky television play.

I brought the exploitation elements to it and Richard brought traditional dramatic skills to it. We made a very good team, because had it been left to me it probably would have been tilted more toward pure exploitation. Whereas Richard humanized it. Paddy Chayefsky is a good example. On the DVD, Richard talks about the Aristotelian unity of time, place and action from classic dramatic writing. I think his presence certainly elevated the script.

Did you set out to make such a controversial movie?

I intended to make something very shocking. I remember, in my youth, pictures that sort of crossed the line. Back in those days there would be these incredibly lurid radio advertisements that if you listened to rock music on the radio a lot — like most kids in my generation did — they had these incredibly lurid campaigns for pictures like *Last House on the Left* and *Night of the Living Dead* and *Texas Chainsaw Massacre.* Those pictures were sort of watersheds, alongside pictures like *The Wild Bunch. The Wild Bunch* was incredibly shocking; up until then in a Western, if somebody got shot they fell down. There was no squib work, there was no spouting blood.

So our thought was, "Okay, we've got $100,000 and a chance to do a film and it's going to have to be a horror film, so let's make a horror film that is going to horrify." Richard Fire and I set ourselves a goal, and it was if we're charged with making a horror film, then a) Let's redefine the genre, and b) Let's totally horrify the audience.

Like many things, the words "horror film" are like "liberal" and "conservative." The original meanings of the words have gotten lost. One would think that conservatives would be interested in conserving the environment, because the word comes from conservation. When you think of "horror film" now, it's a set of conventions and we meant to defy those conventions. The genre often includes monsters, creatures from outer space, ghosts, the supernatural or something beyond reality. But we didn't have a budget for any of that, so we set ourselves the goal of, "How can we most completely horrify an audience without using the traditional conventions?"

Was there any downside to ignoring the traditional conventions of the genre?

Well, when we did the home invasion scene, it was a pretty creepy feeling after finishing that scene. A lot of the stuff — fake blood and all that stuff — there's a certain fun factor to doing it on the set. It's kind of silly, it's fake blood and rubber heads and all that kind of thing. But when we did that scene of the slaughter of the family it left a really strange atmosphere in the room. We did two takes. It was pretty horrific stuff and we didn't know how an audience was going to react to this.

Was the use of videotape in the home invasion scene an aesthetic choice or an economic choice?

Absolutely an aesthetic choice. The video image had an immediacy that the film image did not have, so when we had them tape that home invasion we very specifically chose to use video because it does have that immediacy and that reality. It lacks that distancing and softening that film gives. Also, having grown up watching the Vietnam war on television, even though those were 16mm film cameras, there was a quality to that handheld footage that made it more real and more shocking.

Also I had read the book *Red Dragon*. In Henry Lee Lucas' case, they did not photograph or videotape their crimes. But in *Red Dragon*, Francis Dolarhyde worked in a film processing facility and he would go out and kill these people, photograph them, then come back and process the film. That book was a couple years old and by that time you could buy a decent home video camera, you didn't need to go through a lab.

The use and intensity of violence, from the static images that open the movie to the crimes we ultimately see Henry and Otis commit, seems very planned and measured. Was that the case?

With violence and action, you have to keep topping yourself. If you go backwards, the audience is going to be disengaged. So the violence was doled out and increased as the story went along.

How did you come up with the idea of opening the film on a series of tableaux of Henry's recent crimes?

Richard and I were sitting in his apartment and we had various materials — this was before the Internet — and we were quite limited as to what we could come up with compared to today. But we did have that *20/20* documentary and it did have images. One of the famous images was of a young woman who was allegedly murdered by Henry. She was a Jane Doe who was never identified. She was left in a culvert somewhere and she was nude but for a pair of orange socks. And she was always referred to as Orange Socks because there was no other way to identify her.

We were thinking, "What's our opening?" And we happened to be watching the *20/20* show and there was that photograph of Orange Socks, and Richard just went, "That's our opening."

That was indeed our opening, although we didn't have orange socks, we used pink socks. Once we established that, we decided to do a series of them.

The audience can only take so much. You'll notice that one of the bloodless ways we had them kill people was to snap their necks, which is how he kills the woman and the young boy in the home invasion. There's no overt gore.

We were borrowing from the exploitation genre but to me the movie is a character study about people who did extremely horrific things. And there's the horror. Again, not from monsters from outer space.

In the case of stabbing Otis, he's such a heinous character that he deserves it. When we stabbed him in the eye with that rat-tail comb, you can't believe how much laughter there was on the set with that silly looking head and the blood. It was kind of fun.

Each individual can create in their imagination something more horrific than the graphic expression you may be able to come up with, especially on that kind of budget. A great way to put across scenes of great mayhem is to lead the audience up, step by step, so they can see what's about to happen. It's very clear that somebody's about to get killed. If you lead the audience, shot by shot and step by step up to the deed and make it very clear what's about to happen and then give them a couple frames and then cut away to some other thing, but continue it with the graphic sound, I think it can be much more horrific. Each individual will be left to complete the horror in their own mind, from their own library of personal horror.

Again I have to credit Richard Fire for insisting that we make a serious drama rather than just a piece of pure exploitation.

The visuals are very clever, like the use of the guitar case to signal that Henry has killed the hitchhiker. Or Otis' sister's suitcase, which is used for comic effect when we first see it and then has a far grimmer use at the end of the film.

We had a fair amount of time to work on that script, which you don't often get. In Hollywood they say, "Okay, the money's here, you've got this actor, let's go!" I just shot a segment for *Masters of Horror* and normally they give you a seven-day prep, but since one of my days was Canadian Thanksgiving, I got a six-day prep. It's hard to iron out the details in that amount of time.

Once you lay out your story and your script, then you start to see these connections that can be made to really strengthen that through-line, so everything connects in some way or another. If you have time, you can work on those details. If you don't, you just shoot the script and hope for the best.

Did you write with any specific actors in mind?

No. We had the Chicago theater community to draw from, which is pretty rich. A lot of young actors come to Chicago to learn their chops because there's a lot of Equity theater where you can actually make a living working in theater. Unlike Los Angeles, where most of it is non-Equity so you don't really get paid.

Chicago's a cheaper place to live, so a young actor can make their way with perhaps a bartending job or waitress job, and when they're working in theater they actually make enough money to pay their rent in the Bohemian neighborhoods of Chicago.

What was the refinement process on the script before you shot it?

The refinement process was mostly with the actors. There weren't that many people in my circle who had wide knowledge of production. Most of the experience in actual film production in Chicago was in commercials. Occasionally a movie came to town, but that was not the bread and butter of Chicago, it was commercial production. At the time Chicago was the number two market, after New York, for commercial production.

Our actors came out of theater, so the script refinement was done with the actors in rehearsal. Tom Towles came from the Organic Theater, where Richard Fire was a member and they'd known each other forever. And Tracy Arnold also came from the Organic, although Tracy was more of a new arrival, she had only been with the company for a year or two. Michael Rooker was just a lucky find.

How did you use the rehearsal process?

I've worked this way almost ever since, when I'm fortunate enough to get rehearsals. If I can get two weeks or at least ten days with them, I'll work with the actors myself for the first half of the rehearsal period. And then once we get the shape of the thing I've almost always brought the writer in, because the actors will want to make changes, like, "My character wouldn't use this word," "My character wouldn't say it this way," "I can't get my mouth around this phrase, it doesn't feel right to me."

Once the actors take on those characters, they know them in a deeper way often than the creators do. But if you just open the door and say, "Sure, go ahead, change it," you're going to have a disaster on your hands because then everything will start to change. But if you bring the writer in and if the actor tells the writer the line they'd like to change and their reasoning, then if you allow the writer to tailor the line, you still have the writer's voice but you also have the actor's notes. I think when you work that way you get roles that are like custom-tailored clothing. They're tailored to the particular actor and their personality and their needs and their interpretation.

On the first day of rehearsal, Richard told the actors, "Okay, I want you to go home and write a character bio, all the backstory, all the family history." Since Tracy and Tom were both part of the Organic Theater this was common to them, but to Michael it was sort of an affront. So Michael actually went home and, truth be told, while he was sitting on the toilet he dictated his backstory into a little portable tape recorder.

They each came back to rehearsals with these backstories and a certain amount of that information then got worked into the script for each character. It was a lesson to me that I carry because it was invaluable.

How have you used this technique since then?

Well, when you're working with Bob De Niro, Bill Murray and Uma Thurman you don't necessarily send them home to write character bios. But you work with them in readings and discussions for four or five days. Then once you've really gotten the shape and everybody's in the same movie, then you bring the writer in and you use the writer to explain to them why things are the way they are. If they want dialogue changes, then you let the writer do it for them so that a voice is maintained rather than just throwing the doors open and letting everybody re-write your dialogue. You'll regret it if you do that.

Did you make any choices in the writing that you knew would save you money in shooting?

Well, a major one was setting it in Chicago. So far as anyone really knew, Henry Lee Lucas had never been near the city of Chicago. But there was no way we were going to go out on the road with a crew and house them and feed them.

What's the best advice you've ever received about screen-writing?

Probably, strangely enough, it was in Syd Field's book. I had read other books on screenwriting and filmmaking that tended to take a more academic, ivory tower approach to the artistic principles involved. Syd Field's book was just the nuts and bolts.

"Know your ending" was one thing I got out of that book. I live back and forth between Chicago and Los Angeles and I love road trips. When I come out to do a project I'll drive out and when the project is over I'll drive home. It's a three-day drive and I think a lot and clear my head. It's like a chapter in my life is beginning and a chapter is ending. But I always know my destination. I know where I'm going, so I can plan my route. It's the same thing with a script. You need to know where the story's going.

One of the principles that he laid out in his second book was the midpoint. The dramatic arc goes up and it comes down. It starts at the beginning, goes up to a peak, comes down to the ending. And the midpoint is the peak.

But most movies get in trouble in the middle. Establishing a mid-point for me was like knowing that I was going to drive from Los Angeles to Chicago, but I'm going to stop in Omaha. That was really an incredibly helpful idea, because after you leave the first act you're driving to the midpoint. You're going up. Now when I'm working on a script, once I've read it, I'll go to the last page and take the page number — let's say it's 120 pages — and I'll go look at what happened on page 60. I want to see if there's a key event that sort of divides the story in half.

In good screenplays, it may not be exactly on page 60. It may be between 58 and 63. But almost always in a good story you'll go back and find a key event that takes place that divides the story in half.

Bubble
Coleman Hough

```
                    TACKLE SHOPKEEPER
The darker the water, the darker the
bait …
```

It will be interesting to see how film history treats Bubble. *At the time of its release, it was heralded as the bellwether of a new paradigm for film distribution, called day-and-date release, in which the film was released to theaters, pay TV and home video all on the same day. It was also an experiment in HD video production, as well as an experiment in improvisation and working with non-professional actors. That's a lot of baggage for this simple story to carry, but the film bears up well.*

Writer Coleman Hough had previously worked with director Steven Soderbergh on Full Frontal, *a fully-scripted feature that incorporated some improvisational interviews with its professional cast. For* Bubble, *she had to create a story without the aid of one of screenwriters strongest tools — dialogue — because it was Soderbergh's plan to let his non-actors make up their dialogue in the moment.*

(Be aware that this interview contains spoilers about key plot points.)

What was going on in your career before *Bubble* came about?

Before I started *Bubble*, I had written a movie for HBO about the life of Katherine Graham and I was developing a TV series with some producers in Los Angeles. The thing for HBO, I was hired to do it, I did it and it was completed, but it's never been produced. It's still in development. Apparently, one of the re-writers is Joan Didion, which is kind of cool. If you're going to be re-written by anyone, Joan Didion's the one.

I went to Los Angeles and was developing this TV series. I ran into Steven and he wanted to know what I was doing. I told him and we started talking about working together again. He said that Mark Cuban and Todd Wagner had commissioned him to do six films in this new format, day-and-date release. And he said, "Why don't you write the first one?"

I was thrilled. And then he said, "I don't want to use actors, I want to use just people in the town. And I want there to be no scripted dialogue; I want it to be all improvised." So then I thought, well, what am I going to write?

He had an idea; he wanted to do a tale of jealousy that took place in a factory, a love triangle. So I said, "Well, what kind of factory?" And he said, "I'm thinking about an animal testing facility." And then we started talking about the political implications of that and we decided we didn't want that overlay of political implications.

We started brainstorming about other factories. I was researching industries in the Midwest, because I knew he wanted to film in the Midwest because it was during the re-election and Ohio specifically was such a hot swing state. I found two doll factories in Ohio and Indiana, the only two remaining doll factories in the country.

I started making some calls. I didn't tell them what I was doing, I just said I was interested in making dolls and I wanted to know if they did tours of their plant. So I went with a location manager and it was this fun research trip for two weeks, with a week in each town. It was really great; it was like working as a site-specific playwright. I fell in love with the Ohio town, because it was right on the Ohio River.

From the people I met in the town and the feeling I got from the town, just by observing the life that I had landed in the middle of, I fashioned this story. And then I presented it to Steven and he liked it. We made some adjustments and that gave us our shooting outline.

The fun thing, the great discovery, was that he wanted me on the set every day, because he wanted to be constantly incorporating the stories of the actors into the story.

So I found my job to be the best job of all, because I was there to put the non-professional actors at ease. Steven called me The Human Green Room, because they would hang out with me. I would listen to their stories and we'd share stories and we'd talk about things we'd done and I'd ask them a million questions.

Their stories were so great and so rich. So, whenever I would see Steven, on a break or whatever, I'd say, "Okay, I've got a good one. You've got to get Debbie to talk about ..." whatever story they had told me that day.

So you really established give-and-take with them — you told them stories from your life as well?

Exactly. For example, the scene where Rose is taking a bath in the house she's cleaning is a story from my life. I've always wanted to put that scene in a movie because I used to take baths at parties. When I was in my thirties I went through this weird phase where I would just disappear and take a bath at a party, because my idol Zelda Fitzgerald used to do that.

I've always wanted to put that in a movie and I thought, what if she takes a bath in the house where she cleans? And so, that day Misty, the actress, was very apprehensive about wearing the nude suit and being in the bathtub. So I told her that story from my life and it put her at ease. She just thought it was so funny and it just made it more delicious for her to do it.

How did you create the characters once you had the story roughed in? And did it change once you cast the non-actors?

I had a clear idea of the characters before we cast the actors. We cast the actors based on the characters I'd imagined. When Steven and I were reviewing the audition tapes, the criterion was, are these the people that I imagined? So we didn't have to make any adjustments to the story, because they were the characters.

So, Debbie just jumped out, she was Martha, and Misty was Rose. They couldn't have been more perfect. We found them, they found us.

How difficult was it for you to not write the dialogue and let the actors make it up on-camera?

It was very hard for me at first, because that's what I write. I'm a playwright and dialogue is what I love to write.

I felt a shift — Steven always talks about a writing head and a making head, which is developing a film and then actually making it. And it's true. So I got to experience that in terms of listening to their cadences and pointing out to Steven the things that really spoke of their characters. Like Misty would say, "Oh, *yeah*," that was one thing she said that was so much a part of that character.

We filmed in the bait and tackle shop for a long time. I would listen on the monitor through all the shooting, and I was thrilled when that woman said, "The darker the water, the darker the bait." I said, "Steven, you have to start there. It's such a great line."

So it was kind of like writing it as I heard it. It was such an honor, because it was like not making it up in my head, but listening to it and catching it. Which is what you do when you immerse yourself in a world or a culture, you start to hear certain phrases or certain intonations. That was a challenging adjustment to make.

I always thought dialogue was so important to me in writing scripts and I couldn't imagine what that would be like to relinquish the control of that. But it was thrilling. On the first day of shooting, we did the lunchroom scene, where's there's an awkward silence and then Rose says, "Do any of you all smoke?"

I got chills when I was watching that, because of the silence. That's what I love to write; in fact, in a lot of my plays the stage direction says, "There's an uncomfortable silence between them." And the fact that they just trusted that silence, and the subtext in that line "Do any of you all smoke?" I just couldn't have written anything better than that! Just by putting them in that situation, it was amazing to see the organic response.

There was a deleted scene on the DVD, where the police detective talks to a doctor about Martha and we learn about her brain tumor.

I never signed on to that. That scene was an explanation about why Martha had headaches and why she committed the murder.

Was that scene in your outline?

No, not originally. The scene was not organic to the feeling of *Bubble*.

How aware were the actors of the story, and the murder, as you shot it?

They knew something was going to happen. We filmed in sequence, so that they would live the story. So they only knew as much of the story as they needed to know that day.

One time Debbie, who played Martha, came in and said, "I know I need to set this up, because this thing is going to happen later …" And I said, "Debbie, don't worry about that. You know as much as you need to know today. It's fine. It will all take care of itself."

And I think that was the beauty of working that way, because it allowed them to immerse themselves in the whole thing and be in the moment with it. Especially in the interrogation scene. We did that in one take. One take. We used two cameras and it was just this incredible dynamic between Debbie and Decker.

There's a lot going on in that scene for Debbie, because as her character she is denying a murder that she, as an actress, really didn't think her character did.

That's the thing about Debbie. As a person, she is so in the moment, so alive in her guilelessness. She's an incredibly guileless person, loving, good, and she wants to look for the good in everyone. So I think in that moment when she saw those photos of what she'd done to Rose's neck, she truly was shocked. It made her cry, which made all of us watching it on the monitor cry.

Did the story change at all while shooting?

Yes. It wasn't originally in the outline that Kyle's mom would be hired at the factory. That was an idea that came while we were shooting.

And I love that the manager of the factory introduces her as "Kyle's Mom."

I also wrote in the outline that the scene in Kyle's bedroom between Rose and Kyle was written as a make-out scene. Steven and I discussed the possible awkwardness between them, and I said, "Misty is so comfortable when she talks about tattoo parlors, she loves to hang out in tattoo shops. Since Dustin has tattoos, why don't you get her to touch Kyle's tattoo and maybe that will spark some sort of seduction?"

And what happened was even better. That was one of the scenes that I could never have written that way, it was amazing, the tension between them. That tender awkwardness. It was lovely.

And I understand that Kyle's Mom was also not supposed to talk in the scene where the police tell Kyle that Rose is dead.

That was another example of the power of filming in sequence, because at that point she was so in the scene that she just said, "What? Something happened to Rose?" She just piped in. Laurie

Lee, who played Kyle's Mom, definitely entered into that scene.

But then there's another scene, the scene that followed it, where she says to Martha, "She was killed; she was murdered; she was strangled last night," or whatever. And that's because I didn't hear anyone say that Rose was murdered. We kind of left that out. So I said to Steven, "I don't think anyone's said 'murder' or that Rose was murdered yet."

And that's why Laurie Lee emphasizes it in that take.

What was the benefit for you of having Soderbergh edit the movie while he was shooting it?

It was great, because he was open to suggestions from me. Every two or three days he'd show me what he'd done, and we'd go over the story and discuss where it was going.

It was really fun, it was such a collaboration. It filled me with total confidence about directing something of my own. I really learned about the whole process of trusting the story.

Were there any other lessons you took away from the experience?

Trust was the biggest one. It was also an experience about instinct: finding the doll factory, finding the story, trusting that not writing dialogue was going to be a rich experience.

But the thing I took away from *Bubble* was trust: trusting the process of filmmaking.

Why did you call it *Bubble*?

That was Steven. When he said, "Let's write a film," he also said, "Let's make a movie called *Bubble*." And that informed my search for the story. *Bubble* is open to interpretation; it means a different thing to each person. But to me *Bubble* represents our stories, the fragility of our stories.

How did you feel about the film being part of the grand experiment of releasing a movie to theaters, pay TV and DVD all on the same day?

I think the whole day-and-date release idea is an amazing idea. Why should we be forced into the business construct of a two-hour movie with movie stars? People aren't going to stop going out to movies just because they can see them at home. They'll see more movies.

I just think it's a window that opens up more opportunity for young filmmakers to experiment and not use movie stars and have a way of bringing their films to more people.

What the best advice you've ever received about writing?

It's funny. When I was sixteen, I took a course in my school called Global History. And my Global History teacher said that the art of letter writing was dead. I challenged him on that. He said that the art of letter writing was dead because people reported, they didn't tell stories anymore. So I took that as a challenge and that was the beginning of my writing.

What advice would you give someone who wanted to create their own outlined-but-improvised movie?

I'd say listen. And trust what you hear.

CHAPTER THREE

Based on a Short Story By ...

There's something about the structure of many short stories that make them perfect starting points for a feature film. Unlike novels, with their multiple characters and often long time frames, the compressed nature of the short story is ideal for creating a tight little movie.

The four screenwriters highlighted here took wildly different short stories and created (not so surprisingly) wildly different finished films.

What they share in common is that they used a short story (or, in the cases of *Personal Velocity* and *Re-Animator*, multiple short stories) as their starting point, and then successfully (and artfully) bridged the gap from literature to film.

Personal Velocity:
Three Portraits
Rebecca Miller

                    THAVI MATOLA

What's your story?

                       GRETA

Manhattan. I was born in Manhattan.
Went to the Flemming School uptown -
- a small, private, you know -- then to
boarding school, then to college, then
to law school. My father's a lawyer;
we're not talking. My mother is -- dead.
They're divorced -- I mean, they were.
I'm twenty-eight. My father has a three-
year-old.

                       GRETA
                   (voice over)

God almighty please let me shut up.

The movie Personal Velocity *is actually three movies — three individual stories about three very different women. Writer/director Rebecca Miller adapted the stories from her short story collection (also titled* Personal Velocity*), bringing the stories to life via a low-budget DV production.*

The result is a movie as varied in its tone and emotions as the three primary characters whose stories it brings to life.

(Be aware that this interview contains spoilers about key plot points.)

What was going on in your life before *Personal Velocity*?

I had basically given up the idea of making films, at least for the time being, because it was so hard for me to get my films made. I had made one film, *Angela*, which had won the Filmmaker's Prize at Sundance.

Angela did well with some critics, but it didn't make money. It was a very uncommercial film. And then I had written *The Ballad of Jack and Rose*, which was something I would make later, and I wrote another film that collapsed in preproduction. So I had gotten to the point where I just felt like I didn't want to just wait and wait to make films. All I did all day was write these screenplays that nobody seemed to want. So I decided to write short stories.

I had a child — I was living in Europe at that time — so it was a perfect moment for me to do that. So I started writing these short stories and had a book of them.

My friend Gary Winick called me. He was making this series of films for the Independent Film Channel. He had come to them with this idea that he would make ten films a year for a million dollars, but what they ended up giving everybody was a $250,000 budget.

He asked did I have anything, did I want to make a film on mini-DV for that much money? None of the films that I had already written were really right for that, because I figured (and I was right about this), that you'd have to tailor a script for that medium and for that budget. You shouldn't just take one of your scripts and try to turn it into that kind of shoot.

I was sick of writing screenplays that no one was going to make, so I said, "If you want to look at the stories that I'm writing, I could maybe do something out of one of them." I gave him a few stories from the collection and he read them and he really liked them. He gave them to Caroline Kaplan, who was running InDigEnt with him, and they ended up green-lighting the film. It was also Gary's idea to use three stories and make a trilogy. When he said that, my mind took off.

The thing that's great about Gary is that he really insisted that I feel completely free. At first I was sort of checking with him and saying, "I'm doing this, I'm doing that," and he was like, "Look, do whatever. The point is that we want to get filmmakers who have experience and who we believe in to feel free."

And so I wrote the script for *Personal Velocity* in about two months. It took me about two years to write the book. I knew what everybody in those stories was feeling and I knew the characters from top to bottom, so writing the screenplay was mostly about finding the form and the structure.

How did you decide which of the three stories to use?

I chose the ones that were the most dynamic in terms of action, where there was conflict that was externalized, because some of them were very interior. And also where I thought that there was a good clash. I thought there was a very good clash between *Delia*, which is a story about a working-class woman struggling with an abusive marriage, and *Greta*, which is about an upper-middle-class woman struggling with the clash between her own ambition and a marriage which is feeling increasingly stultifying; finally her ambition propels her out of her own marriage.

They both involve crisis, but of a different order. And then, class-wise, *Paula* is kind of a floater, because she's an artist, she's from that class. Although she doesn't really produce anything, she's in-between the two classes.

It was a little bit crazy. When Gary first read the screenplay, he said, "Well, this is great, but how in God's name are you going to do this?", because there were many, many, many locations in the film. *Greta* had so many flashbacks and so much going back and forth with the past that it was just insane. Ideally, when you make a film for $250,000 in sixteen days, you're going to be in one room. We were all over the place.

The good news was that it was a kind of mosaic, so that you didn't really need the coherence from scene to scene. The coherence was something that really came with the editing, and then the whole thing was sewn together with voice over and music. So although there were complete scenes that had a beginning, middle and end a lot of the time, there were also very tiny scenes that were very short and all pieces of a puzzle.

How did you come up with the idea of using still images throughout the movie?

There were scenes that I wrote that the producer, Lemore Syvan, would look at and say, "We can't afford to shoot certain things." And that's where the idea of the stills came in. The stills turned out to be one of the things that distinguished the film and I think worked really nicely emotionally in the film. But the idea was born out of poverty.

Shooting MOS, without sound, is so much faster that we could just rip through those scenes. At first I thought we might shoot them as stills in the camera, but then I just decided to shoot and then pick the stills later, because it would give me more choices.

At what point in the process did you decide to use narration?

I always knew I was going to. The narration was built into it.

Early on Gary had said that he loved the way the narrator spoke in the stories and that it would be a pity to lose that. I also thought that with the three stories it would be a good way to link them together. It also gives you a lot more freedom, because we're jumping back and forth through time constantly. And the narration also carries a lot of the humor — it's a sympathetic third voice.

In the end there was a whole debate about whether or not to make it a male or female voice. I always knew that it was meant to be a male voice, but then there were some people who saw it and said, "You can't make it a male voice; it's about women."

But I just ended up really liking the male voice, because I thought it differentiated itself from the other voices. Otherwise, it was just another woman's voice; it was like a soup of women's voices and I thought it was good to have the male voice. Also, I thought it was kind of optimistic to have a male voice. It seemed to be sympathetic and unjudgmental of these women while some of their struggles were against men. And it was my overriding view that it's very possible to have sympathetic males in your movies.

How did you come up with the idea of linking the three stories with the car accident and how did that decision help you?

That came fairly early on, because I realized that something had to unify these three stories and I liked the idea of them all happening at once. It also created a sense of mystery, so that by the time you get to Paula's story, you know that she's the person that everyone is looking for and wondering who she is. That was a device that I came up with fairly early on, because I didn't want to do an interweaving of the stories. I contemplated all sorts of things, including cutting back and forth, but I didn't really want to do that. I wanted to give each woman her complete story and to make them three portraits.

I called it *Three Portraits* because there was something kind of humble about calling them portraits, because mini-DV is a modest medium. We looked at a lot of other films that had been made on DV and we realized that the lens just doesn't work very well in wide shots, the shots kind of fall apart. Because of that, for the most part, there aren't that many wide shots in the film, because they tend to look really cheesy when you go wide. I ended up focusing on medium shots and close-ups and some really, really intense close-ups.

The stories are very different, tonally, and you found a good way to visualize those differences.

Each of the stories has its own look that's quite distinct from the other ones. All of this was in the interest of doing whatever I wanted, because I thought, "Well, let me try all these crazy things that no one would ever let me do." If I sent a script out with three different points of view, three different women, with narration all over, I would have been sitting there for five years trying to get the money. But in this case, I was offered the money up front and told to experiment, so I thought I would experiment as much as I possibly could. So I came up with the idea of these three different looks and that each of them would have their own color palette as well.

With *Delia*, it was more earth tones. There's something archetypal and eternal about that character, the endlessly suffering person who rises up out of the ashes. I liked the idea of the muted, almost sepia colors, but it's all still very modern.

With *Greta* I wanted it to reflect her hard-edged intelligence, so we used more primary colors, like Mondrian. And then with *Paula* I had this idea of micro epiphanies, because she's in shock and so she's having these micro epiphanies, because in her world the edge of a donut takes up the whole frame, her hand on the steering wheel, the kid's eye — especially in the beginning, where we used a lot of claustrophobic, intense close-ups.

So once you decided that the accident would link the stories, then *Paula* had to be the last of the three. What was your thought process on how to order the other two stories?

Actually, in the script *Greta* came first. And then, when we were cutting it, I realized that if you put *Paula* after *Delia*, *Paula* became unbearably sad. But if you start with *Delia*, and then go to *Greta*, where you're laughing within a few minutes, then *Paula* becomes lyrical instead of sad. So that's why I made that switch.

How did your background in acting help the writing process?

I think that acting was a very necessary step for me. I had a weird, long apprenticeship. I was a painter for quite a while and then at a certain point realized that I wanted to make films. I acted for about five years while I was writing my first screenplays and still painting for some of that time — it was like a bridge.

Without the acting I don't know that I would have been able to successfully make that leap. When I was a painter, I was so far away from the mindset of being a filmmaker and being more sociable and being on a set where there are so many people. I just learned all sorts of things, just how it works, what a film set's like.

One of the problems with being a director is that you never get to go on sets — even if you go to film school, you don't usually get to be on sets when you're coming up. You learn when you get on your own set, but it was nice to just understand certain things, to have been around directors. For writing it probably helps, too.

You're writing to shoot, and that's what's important to remember. And I really remembered it with *Personal Velocity*. That screenplay was really tailored, it was absolutely tailored to the medium. I don't think I even cut any scenes out; there was no waste in that thing.

You shot what you wrote.

I shot what I wrote and I kept what I shot. Which is really unusual. Usually you end up realizing that there are internal repetitions that you didn't notice. But this was all done in a spirit of such economy, so I was very conscious of not wanting to shoot anything extra.

We had no overtime, so we *had* to finish our days, and we had no extra days. There was no leeway at all. If you weren't making your day, you had to start cutting scenes. There was one occasion where I did have to cut a scene, which was completely unnecessary. I think in the end I would have cut it anyway afterwards.

Was there anything that you hated to lose while making the adaptation?

Not really. There was a long dream that Greta had that I ended up not including. I think that was not a mistake to take it out.

I would have lost a lot of scenes if I hadn't come up with the idea of using the stills. In a funny way this was one example of where the poverty of it and the necessity of it totally worked in my favor. I was terrified that this was going to be a complete disaster. I was really worried, because sixteen days is not very long to shoot a feature film. But it worked because of the stills and because of the fact that a lot of it could be reshaped in the editing room. You could re-tool things if they didn't quite work.

It wasn't just unspooling like a red carpet folding out, which was true of *The Ballad of Jack and Rose*, which was much more a single line; if things really didn't work it would be very hard to fix it later. *Personal Velocity* didn't have that problem. It was a very wise idea to do something where the form is more fluid when things could so easily go wrong.

Did you find that you needed to re-write the narration during editing?

Yes, I did. As it went on I re-wrote a lot of it. I can't even say exactly how much or what, but I would re-write the narration as the images changed. The way I thought the film should move was like thoughts move, in that meandering, back-and-forth way, with that kind of freedom, where one thought triggers another thought.

Delia was the one that was most re-structured in the screenplay. If you read the story version of *Delia*, the way that it meanders back and forth is completely different in the screenplay. In the screenplay, where she's about to get whacked in the head, the narration says, "Wait, let me explain," and then you go back into her past, then you come back and her husband slams her head into the table. That was an example of where you're cutting into the narrative, looking through the skin of it into the entrails and then coming back up — that was completely just for the movie. It was much more fluid in the story.

And likewise with *Greta*, the flashbacks in the story are all higgledy-piggledy — some are earlier, some are later, some are here and there — and they were that way in the screenplay, too. But when I came to cut it, I realized that it was too confusing, so I ended up putting the flashbacks in chronological order in the film. Otherwise it just got to the point where it was too confusing.

As much as there is a level of apparent chaos in the film, you need a certain level of order for people to follow what you're doing.

How did you come up with the title?

Well, it was really just a line that Greta's father says when everyone thought, "Oh, wow, she was such a loser and now look at her!" Everybody has their own personal velocity. He means that everybody succeeds at different rates or everybody comes into themselves at different rates.

I thought it was a good title for everything because in a sense the whole movie is about these women and the question of being hurled through space by their own past and the accidents of fate. Like Paula and that stupid accident where she switches places with somebody and he gets killed. To what degree are we choosing our lives and to what degree is it something else? I think it's probably a cocktail of all those things, but that's what personal velocity means to me.

And speaking of the car accident, I thought that — regardless of the budget — it was conceived and executed beautifully. It never felt like, "We can't afford to show it." Instead, you found a way to do it in a way that was different, and better, than expected.

Thank you. I really love that whole sequence. It's one of these little moments — these epiphanies — where everything is being revealed. But you couldn't have had less: we just had two people, a shoe, and a flashing light to reflect in a puddle, and that's all we had. And the sound of a car crash.

But the truth is, I think especially with sex and car crashes, we've all seen so much of it on the screen, so why even bother?

Did you tweak the script after it was cast?

I'm sure I did. I'm usually kind of tweaking things until they get said.

But I do really believe very, very strongly in having a very, very strong script. Then you can throw it out. The thing is to have a really strong script and if you are the director then to fool yourself into thinking that you didn't really write it, that it's somebody else's. Then you can be totally irreverent with it and throw it out. It's a blueprint, it's only a blueprint. At the same time, if you're really well prepared, then you can always change everything. It's when you're not prepared, I think, that things get really scary.

How do you know when a script is ready to be shot?

It's very hard to answer that question.

I just made a film called *The Ballad of Jack and Rose* and that was a script I thought was ready and then I couldn't get the money together. Then I lived a little bit more, looked at it in a different way, wrote it a little bit more.

Cut to nine years after I'd started writing it and by now it's really changed, because my point of view had changed so much. I'd become a parent and the script is partly about a parent, so now it was as much about the parent as about the child. Now I feel like I waited the right amount of time, that script was finally ready. But had I gotten the money back all those years earlier, it probably would have been ready then. It just would have been a different film.

I think that to a degree we just abandon things. I don't think anything is ever really finished, ever really perfect. I wonder what filmmaker looks back and thinks, "Oh, yeah, that's perfect." Probably something's wrong with them if they do.

Personally I think that you do need to feel that it has a solid flow and that there's a certain causality that's respected — one thing leading to another, even if it's totally surreal. There has to be an internal logic that's respected.

And then also you should comb through it for internal repetitions, which you might not be aware of, but will only cost you money that you don't need to spend, shooting scenes that you're going to cut later in the editing room.

In other words, if you say the same thing two different ways, usually you don't need to do that. In a movie, it's so powerful; if you show someone smoking once, they're a smoker. You show them smoking twice, they're a chain smoker. Same thing with drinking: They drink once, okay, they drink. They drink twice, they drink heavily. Three times, they're going to have to have a liver transplant. It's a very powerful medium. It's got a completely different impact than the written word.

And it's hard, because when you read a script, you're *reading* a script, you're not seeing a script.

I also think it's a good idea to have a strong sense of what the seminal images are. I did that with *Angela* and very much with *Personal Velocity*, because it was so visual in the way it was expressed.

What were the seminal images for *Personal Velocity*?

Each story has a seminal image.

Greta crying behind her husband's shoulder while he reads her a piece of news out of the *New York Times* and she knows that she's going to leave him and he doesn't.

Delia standing in front of the mirror, all battered up, in that still where she's looking at her child.

The image of the boy who's all cut up, when Paula finally realizes what's wrong with him and sees what has happened to him.

Those are the power images. It's good to have them, because you're writing in a visual medium, so you have to think about an image that people can remember that will tell much more than words will tell. The emotion comes out of the images. Your dialogue can be great and witty and the rest of it — and there are certain movies that are much more dialogue heavy, like Woody Allen movies — and then there are movies that are much more image driven, like a Scorsese film.

For me, the best films finally have some images which you're not going to forget. Or, at least, that you hope people are not going to forget.

Was there anything you learned while writing *Personal Velocity* that you still use today?

Yes: the idea of freedom.

The whole point is to fool yourself into feeling completely free every time. And that becomes more difficult as people expect things from you. It's easier to write a screenplay when no one expects anything of you, because there's nothing to lose. As people start to expect something of you, it becomes more about fooling yourself into feeling completely free.

That was what made that experience so wonderful. But I would like to always have that, to remember that, to guard it and to cherish it. You need to feel free.

What's the best advice that you're ever received about writing?

The best advice I ever received was from a screenwriter named Tom Cole. He read the first screenplay I ever wrote. It was never produced as a screenplay, but I did actually cannibalize it and use a lot of stuff for other things, which often happens to your first work.

He said, "This is a very personal screenplay, it has your own stamp on it. Don't ever let people, with their advice, sand it down and make it smooth and turn it into something that could have been written by a lot of different people."

I think that's especially good advice because screenplays have no value unless they're produced. People give you a lot of advice, and a lot of that advice is just turning things into something average. That's fine if that's what you're wanting to do. But if you're looking to create something that's really your own, then you have to keep what's unusual about it and what's even jarring about it.

One thing I would say, especially for people who are starting out — this is a big piece of advice that I definitely learned from my first screenplay that was never produced — which is to allow yourself to be humble enough to boil a screenplay down to what's most important. I think when you start out, you tend to try to write about a lot of different things and put a lot of themes into your script. A lot of themes can exist in a piece, in a subterranean way, but that doesn't mean that your story can't be simple.

For example, in *Personal Velocity*, as many things that are going on there, there are three very simple stories: A woman is escaping from an abusive marriage. A woman is propelled out of her own marriage by her ambition. A woman nearly gets killed in an accident and then tries to make sense of that accident by rescuing a hitchhiker. They're simple stories.

When I first started out, I wrote a screenplay that was so complicated — it had everything I had ever thought of in it. There were these two little girls in it and they were the most real people in the screenplay. And my friend Michael Rohatyn, who is the guy who composes all the music for my movies, said, "Why don't you just write a movie about those two little girls?"

And I ended up doing that and that was *Angela*. And I'm so glad that I did it. It was such good advice. Sometimes you just take the fingernail off the giant and the fingernail is your story.

Re-Animator
Stuart Gordon

                    DAN CAIN

    Herbert, you're insane. Now what
    happened here?

                    HERBERT WEST

    I had to kill him.

                    DAN CAIN

    What?! He's dead?

                    HERBERT WEST

    Not anymore.

Director/Writer Stuart Gordon came to an interesting realization a few years after the success of his first feature: He suddenly had a new middle name. Any time he was mentioned in print, his name now read "Stuart 'Re-Animator' Gordon." Be assured, there are worse fates in the film business.

His new moniker came about simply because he (and his stellar team of actors and writers and creative folks) had taken the standard horror film and given it a much-needed jolt. Re-Animator, based on short stories by horror master H. P. Lovecraft, used all the standard elements of the horror film — mad scientist, pretty girl in distress, able lab assistant, lumbering monster/creature — and then gave the whole genre a surprising (and surprisingly funny) twist.

What was going on in your career before *Re-Animator* came about?

I was doing theater. I was the Artistic Director at the Organic Theater Company in Chicago. When I started working on *Re-Animator*, the original guy that I collaborated with was William Norris, who was an actor in our company and had written several of the plays that we had done.

Originally, we were going to do it as a limited series for television. That sounds kind of insane, but that was the plan. H. P. Lovecraft had serialized the *Re-Animator* stories, so there were six little stories. So our plan was to do six half-hour shows. Lovecraft's original stories are set in the past — the first one takes place around the turn of the century, and then the episodes go through about a thirty-year period. So the first draft was set in period.

We tried to sell that idea, based on the first episode, and had no luck. Then someone told us that half-hour shows were not really the way to go and that we should do an hour. So we went back and combined the first and the second story.

Around this point, Bill Norris was kind of losing faith in the process, so he dropped out and Dennis Paoli came in. When we wrote the second script, the hour-long version, someone again told us that setting it in period was making it a harder sell. It really should be set in the present day. So we shifted it into the present day, but were still unable to sell it.

At that point a friend introduced me to Brian Yuzna, who wanted to finance a feature. We showed him the hour version that we had developed and talked a little bit about how it could be expanded into a feature. We thought we could use the third story, and he said, "Why don't we use all six of them?" I said, "Well, what if we want to do a sequel?" And he said, "Let's just worry about doing as good a movie as we possibly can."

And that was the script that ended up becoming the film *Re-Animator*.

Why did you decide to work with the Lovecraft stories in the first place?

It began with a conversation I had with a friend. This was in the early 1980s and there were all these vampire and *Dracula* movies being made. I said, "I wish someone would make a *Frankenstein* movie," because I always liked *Frankenstein* better. This friend said, "Have you ever read *Herbert West, Re-Animator* by Lovecraft?" I had read a considerable amount of Lovecraft and I had never heard of this story.

It piqued my curiosity so I started looking for it and found that it was out of print. I eventually ended up going to the Chicago Public Library and found that they had a copy of it in their special collection. I had to fill out a postcard requesting it. A few months later they sent me a note saying I could come to the library and read it there, but I would not be able to take it out of the library. When I got there, they handed me what was essentially a pulp magazine that contained the stories. The pages were literally crumbling as I was turning them, so I asked if I could photocopy it and they allowed me to do that. The stories had been out of print for many years.

Were the stories in the public domain?

They were. All of Lovecraft's work is now public domain. This was something we didn't know at the time. We believed that we had to get the rights through Arkham House, which was the publisher of the stories.

What you usually do when you're working on something based on existing material, you do a copyright search, just to make sure that the people you're dealing with do indeed have the rights to it. We discovered that the material was public domain and that Arkham House did not have the rights. When we confronted them with this, they just sort of said, "Oh, well." They didn't argue about it at all. They knew that they had been trying to pull something.

Was one of the attractions of the piece that it was in the public domain?

That made things a lot easier for us. We were prepared to pay something for the story. If they had asked for a lot of money, that would have been difficult, because our budget was small. Finding out that it was public domain was great, it was one less thing to worry about.

Once you decided to do it as a feature, what was the process for determining what elements you'd use from the six stories?

One of the things that emerged was that the whole story was being told by West's assistant, in the first person, describing what it was like working with West and so forth. We realized that this character was really key to telling the story, because all of the other people that you meet in the stories are these insane characters. This guy really is, in a sense, the audience who's witnessing all this stuff.

We really got into the idea that we had to make this character very sympathetic and very normal. He would be like the audience, asking the questions that the audience wants to know and be someone that they could relate to. It also added a lot of contrast between this guy and all the eccentric types that populate the story.

In addition to reading through the stories, did you do any other research before you started writing?

I did. I went and visited some morgues, which was very helpful. I talked to several pathologists and even got thrown out of some places. I went to the University of Illinois pathology department and as soon as I told them I was working on a horror film, the professor started screaming at me to leave. They threw me out.

After this happened, I talked to a friend of mine who's a doctor, because I was kind of nervous about going to go to talk to more pathologists. I said, "Will they talk to me?" And he said, "Oh, yeah. They're the loneliest people in the world. No one ever goes to the morgue." Not when they're conscious, anyway.

It turned out to be true — the pathologists that I talked to were great. It started with a meeting with a guy named Dr. Stein who ran the Cook County morgue. He took me on a tour of the morgue that I'll never forget. At that point I had never really seen a dead body, other than someone at a funeral who had already been embalmed and made-up. The stench was just unbelievable. The bodies were just piled on top of each other on gurneys in these walk-in refrigerators. They didn't have those drawers like you see in movies; I've never seen that in any morgue.

Stein had a very dark sense of humor, and I found out that this was pretty common with these pathologists. If you're going to do that job, you really have to maintain some kind of distance and keep a sense of humor about it all. That worked its way into the screenplay as well.

The attitude about the dead was really interesting. The idea is that a doctor, when you're alive, will do everything he can to keep you alive. But as soon as you're dead, you become toxic waste. You're garbage. You're not dealt with in a loving way at all. The corpses that we saw in the Cook County morgue were literally in garbage bags, black plastic garbage bags. The ones that had been in operations still had all the tubes and everything still in them. They didn't even bother to pull those things out. It was like, "Why bother?"

It was an eye-opener and that also worked its way into the story. There's a sequence in *Re-Animator* where he's trying to re-animate this corpse and it's not working. The assistant says, "We failed." And West says, "I didn't fail. He did." And then he smacks the corpse.

Why did you decide to do a horror film as your first film?

First of all, I like horror films. I've always liked them. But it was also because I was told by a friend that they were the easiest kinds of movies to find financing for. The wisdom, and I think it's still true, is that no matter how badly a horror film turns out, you can always sell it to somebody and the investors will get their money back.

Did you bring any tricks from your theater background to help keep costs down?

I would say that 99% of the effects in the movie were done as live stage effects, what they call practical effects. They were the sorts of things that we could have done on-stage, to a large degree. I think there are only a couple of opticals in the whole movie. And this was before CGI or any of that.

I also rehearsed with the actors the same way I would when doing a play and that was very, very useful.

What's the value of rehearsing?

The main reason you rehearse when you're doing a low-budget film is because you don't have a lot of time on the set to be talking about motivation while the whole crew is standing around waiting. So it's a way to work out a lot of stuff beforehand.

But it was also good to hear the script read aloud. It amazes me that that is almost never done. We could see which lines sounded kind of clunky or other lines that weren't needed. In a couple of places we found dialogue that we really did need that was not in the script and we had to fill in some things.

Can you think of any examples of dialogue you created in rehearsal to fill in a gap?

In the movie, West kills Dr. Hill who is trying to steal his secret of re-animation. He beheads him, and then he re-animates both the head and the headless body. They both come back to life and end up attacking West and stealing his serum.

We had his assistant coming back and — in the screenplay — West didn't tell him any of the stuff that had gone on. The audience already knew this stuff, but the actor playing the assistant was asking, "How do I already know all this? Wouldn't I be asking him what happened?"

We didn't want to have a long scene where West tells us what we already know. And so it was one of those things where we had to find a way to explain it very quickly. So West says something like, "He wanted my serum. I had to kill him." And Cain, the assistant says, "He's dead?" And West says, "Not anymore." And that was it. That basically filled it in.

That's my favorite exchange in the film; it really encapsulates the tone of the movie.

There's always some key piece of information you always leave out in a script, too, I've noticed. Something you always take for granted and assume that it's there, and then you realize that it isn't.

Did you screen other genre films before you started scripting?

I looked at a lot of films. Brian Yuzna sat me down and for weeks we screened every horror film that had been made in the 1980s, just to get an idea of what was out there and what had been done.

One of the things that you have to do when you're making a horror film is that you have to somehow set it apart from the others. You have to go further or do something differently that really makes it unique. So it was important to see what else had been done and to get an idea where we could go, some uncharted territory that we could mine for the film.

With *Re-Animator* it really had to do with the sexual content. There were a lot of horror films out there, but most of them had the monster trying to devour the victim. That's a very typical thing. So the idea that the monster wants to have sex with the victim was something that was very seldom done. And if it was done, it was something that was very non-explicit.

You found a way to make it explicit and at the same time different and amazing and something no one had ever seen before.

Yes, we set up that Dr. Hill was in lust with the Dean's daughter and he finally has her, but now he's a headless corpse. But he still wants to have his way with her, and the question was, how's he going to do this?

I remember having discussions with Dennis about that. One night he called me up and said, "I've just written the world's first visual pun." It was the scene that everybody talked about in that movie, which was referred to as the "head gives head" scene.

How did you share the labor in the writing process?

Bill had written the piece as a period piece, but some of that language survived even into the modern versions of the script. It was almost Victorian language. West says things like, "That infernal beast," and things like that. No one uses a word like "infernal" anymore, but West does and it seemed right for him. Dennis modernized things a bit more. And the experiences that I had in the morgue worked their way into what became the final version of the script.

How conscious were you of budget limitations as you were writing?

With low budget, it really has to be minimalist. You have to have as few sets and locations as possible and as few characters as possible. You really have to determine what's really essential and what do I really need to tell this story. If it isn't essential, it usually will get cut.

There are no night exteriors in the film, except for some establishing shots. Was that by design?

Shooting outside at night is a very expensive thing to do. If you're outside, you need to light it and that can become very pricey.

The establishing shots were done later, because after looking at the movie we realized that we needed to go outside some times. So we just added establishing shots of the buildings.

At what point in the process did you add the film's Prologue, at the University of Zurich?

That sequence was in the script, but we thought that it was something that could be left out. We felt you could tell the story without that scene, so when we shot the movie we did not shoot that opening scene.

After we cut the footage together, the producer, Brian Yuzna, felt that we really did need to have that scene. The way he put it was (and I've also heard this many times from people who teach writing), "The movie has to declare itself early. You have to let the audience know what kind of film this is."

Brian's feeling was that you had to have an opening scene that really knocked the audience on its ass. That opening sequence could accomplish that. So we got everybody back together — this was several months after the original shoot — and went back and did that scene.

I remember you saying once that you never worried about what the critics would say about *Re-Animator*, because you always knew they would hate it.

That's true. I assumed that the critics would hate it and that the people I was really thinking about were the fans. I had seen all these other films and in my mind I knew that I had to outdo them — somehow. But I just wrote off the critics. In a way, that was a very healthy thing, because if you're worrying about the critics it can paralyze you or you'll get too self-conscious about what you're doing. To just be able to ignore them completely was actually a very healthy thing.

Did you think about the special effects at all while you were writing?

One of the most difficult things was the idea that there's a character walking around carrying his head through half of the film. That was the major special effects problem. So I sat down pretty early on with the effects guys and we talked about different ways of creating that effect. I also ended up storyboarding those sequences, once I knew what the techniques would be and what approach we'd use for each shot.

We used a variety of different gags. We resisted the idea of just having a guy with his shoulders built up, because what that does is make his arms look like he's a gorilla. So that was one technique we did not use.

The simplest technique we used was when we would shoot from the back. We would just have the guy who was playing the headless body lean his head forward and we had a fake neck stump on the back of his neck, and that was what you saw when it was shot from the back. You just had to make sure you didn't see his head at all. That way, we didn't have to do anything to his arms.

The one that was the most complicated was where we built an entire fake torso. That allowed the actor, David Gale, to stick his head through the torso and then the other actor could reach his hands around. That was the most complicated thing.

Once you had a draft done, what was your review process?

I think we mainly showed it to Brian Yuzna. Brian was always trying to come up with more and more things, more gags. One of the ones that he added was after West has beheaded Dr. Hill and puts the head into a pan. The head keeps falling over. Brian's idea was that he uses a paper spike to give the head a base so that it could stand up.

Did the story change much in the editing?

A lot of material got cut. You find out that you don't need as much explanation for things as you think you do sometimes. There were several long scenes that were cut. One that I remember cutting was after Dan Cain is expelled from school. He and West and Meg talk about what they're going to do now. And it ends up with the idea that they have to re-animate a human being to prove that this stuff really works. That whole scene ended up getting cut.

When it came time to cast the film, you didn't really follow Lovecraft's description of Herbert West.

West in the story is a blonde; Lovecraft refers to him as a towhead. But when Jeffrey Combs came in, he had the right attitude: a brilliant guy who is completely focused on only one thing and everything else is really not important to him. He captured that kind of drive. It was pretty clear from the first audition that this was Herbert West.

You did a very free adaptation of the original source material, just taking bits and pieces of the six stories. What was one of the significant changes you felt you needed to make?

Lovecraft very seldom writes female characters, and there were no female characters in *Re-Animator*. So the creation of the Dean's daughter was something that we added to the story, because we really felt that there needed to be a love interest and there needed to be a certain sexual tension in the story.

One of the things that's interesting is that whenever I'm dealing with Lovecraft purists, they're always very upset about the sexuality in the films I've done based on Lovecraft. But I always feel that Lovecraft stories are very, very sexual, that there is a sexual undercurrent running through them. And I felt that was even true in *Re-Animator*.

Was there anything you learned while working on that script that you took to future writing projects?

One of the things was that when you're working on a horror film, every single scene should have some tension in it. That was one of the things we really worked on with *Re-Animator*. You really can't have any scenes with people just sort of sitting around and relaxed. You have to find the tension in each scene. There needs to be something scary about every single scene in the film, otherwise you're letting the audience off the hook. What you really want to do is to keep people on the edge of their seats all the way through.

Is that something you brought to the process from your work as a theater director?

It's funny, one of the things that I always did when I was staging a play was, I would very seldom have characters sit down. People sitting down and talking is, I think, one of the most boring things you can do. I would try to avoid that, because I felt that if you have the character sitting down, then the whole story sits down.

When I was doing theater, one of our patrons was an older woman and she would always bring her husband, who didn't really like theater very much. But she dragged him along to see our plays. He was notorious for falling asleep in the middle of the plays, and sometimes snoring. His name was Lester. So I was always, in the back of my mind, thinking "We've got to keep Lester awake. We have to have something going on every moment to keep Lester from falling asleep." And I think I'm still trying to keep Lester awake.

What's the best advice you've ever received about writing?

The best advice I ever got was don't censor yourself. That applies to horror films, but I think it applies to anything. If the idea seems like a strong idea, don't worry about what the ramifications are. Just go for it.

You should always use yourself as the test, the guinea pig, rather than thinking in terms of, "Well, marketing people say if I want to appeal to an audience of teenagers I should do this." That's a really good way to destroy anything that's interesting. If it's something that you would like to see on-screen, then that's enough of a reason to put it in.

Also, although it's a cliché, they say that scripts are not written — they're re-written. And scripts are not finished, they're abandoned. I think that's really true. You're going to end up doing many drafts of that script and really boiling it down to what's essential. Movies are really minimalist, I think. Every single line of dialogue, every single stage direction is going to be questioned at some point — "Do we really need this?" So it's really a question of getting a sense of what you absolutely have to have and getting rid of everything that you don't.

One of the great things that Lovecraft said was "Never explain anything." I always thought that was a really good note, especially in horror films. It's really interesting when you look at a movie like *The Ring*, and then you look at the Japanese version of it, *Ringu*. *Ringu* is really spare and simple and they never explain anything. Whereas in the American version there's this tendency to want to explain everything — to the point where you kind of take away all the magic. Lovecraft's precept is a pretty good one to follow.

Hester Street
Joan Micklin Silver

MRS. KAVARSKY

I was in this country when you was still
in Russia, hauling away on the bellows.
You can't pee up my back and make me
think it's rain!

Hester Street *breaks many of the rules of low-budget filmmaking.
It's a period piece. It's shot in black and white. And half the dialogue is in Yiddish.*

*However, as we know, rules are made to be broken. Joan Micklin
Silver's passion for the story, from Abrahma Cahan's novella* Yekl,
is evident in every frame of Hester Street, *and her genius at casting
(which would surface again in her next feature,* Between the Lines*),
brought Carol Kane to national attention – and garnered her an
Academy Award nomination for Best Actress.*

At what point were you in your career before *Hester Street* came along?

I had made some short films for an educational film company and had written a screenplay which was — although much changed — made in Hollywood. And I was looking for an opportunity to direct. I found that in that particular time — we're talking about the early 1970s — the opportunities for women to direct were just nil, and while I could get work writing, I really wanted to be able to direct the work that I did.

How did you find Abraham Cahan's novella and what attracted you to it?

One of the films that I made for the educational film company was on immigration. I read just about everything I could find on immigration and one of the things that I read was the novella by Abraham Cahan called *Yekl*.

I was really floundering around and wanting very much to make my own films. My husband, Ray, who was a real estate developer, told me that if I could do a film that would not cost very much, that he would try to raise money from some of the investors that he'd been going to for real estate deals. And that was how we did it.

Frankly I didn't think I'd ever get to make another film. I was pretty discouraged about it all. My family were immigrants and I wanted to make a movie that would count for them.

Was the story in the public domain at that point?

Yes. And that was one of its attractions.

What challenges did you face in the adaptation?

Well, the story itself is more the husband's story. I think what grabbed me about it was what happened to the wife. So it was really just telling the story from the point of view that interested me. The challenge of it, of course, was to try to make it authentic.

I felt that because my father had told me so many stories about his life as an immigrant boy from Russia, I knew that language was a huge factor in getting along or not getting along. He told me stories of not quite knowing English and once leaving some money on a bus; he was a paperboy and he had made some collections and left the money by accident on the bus. He thinks people were trying to tell him and he didn't understand what they were saying. He got off the bus and then realized it — things like that. Knowing the English language was extremely difficult.

And also both my parents were Yiddish speaking and I can remember dinners at our house with all sorts of relatives and wonderful stories being told and then punch lines coming out in Yiddish and my mother turning to us and saying, "You know, it doesn't quite translate." She would try to translate it, but never could quite do it. And I associated that language with something very rich and interesting and enjoyable.

Were you worried about breaking some of the cardinal rules of low-budget filmmaking: You don't do period pieces, you don't do something that's half in English and half in Yiddish?

I didn't know enough to know that I was breaking cardinal rules and that's the truth. I had to tell this story and I had to do what I could to tell it.

Was there anything in the adaptation that you really wished you could have included, but budget prevented it?

There were many, many things. For example, just after we had made the movie, *Godfather II* came out. And in *Godfather II* there's a very long scene in Ellis Island in which there's an overhead traveling shot. The boy who will grow up to be Robert De Niro is sitting on the bench and you see him in isolation, all by himself. It's just a stunning shot, and I remember that Ray and I saw it and were just pinching each other's arms in jealously.

When it came time to do Ellis Island, I had to do what I think just about all low-budget filmmakers do and that is that you make a part work for the whole. You have to ask yourself, "What's the most important thing about this?" And I decided that it was the separation between the ones who were already there and the ones who had just arrived. Therefore, I thought if I could do some sort of a fence or something that would keep the two groups apart, that would help to say what I wanted to say.

I remember that the fence cost about $800, which was a huge portion of our budget. I think it worked — it isn't re-creating Ellis Island, which if I'd had a chance, of course I would have done. Those were the sorts of things that we did all the time.

What was your process for making the adaptation?

I think I just read it more than a few times and then just thought about it. I like to do research and I was also looking though lots and lots of material. For instance, I went to the public library and there were a lot of files available about immigrant life in New York, with pictures. I went to the YIVO Institute for Jewish Research, which had a lot of oral histories of immigrants.

There also happened to be an exhibition of Roman Vishniac photographs around that time and although his photographs were not of the period — they were about Polish immigrants between the wars — still the *shtetl* life I'm sure was pretty similar.

Did you use any of your family's immigrant experiences in writing the script?

Immigrants fall into two groups: the kind that want to talk about it all the time and the kind that never talk about it because it was traumatic and they really want to make the adjustment and be Americans.

My family was definitely the kind that talked about it all the time. I had heard so many stories about it all. I'd heard stories about people who came and people who left and people who went back and people who went crazy. I had a head full of all these sorts of stories, so I'm sure they fit into writing this screenplay.

Did the fact that you knew you wouldn't have much money to shoot this movie have any impact on you while you were writing the script?

Constantly. I was constantly thinking, for example, about how I could do Ellis Island, things like that. It was one thing after another, just constantly trying to figure out how I could tell the story without having a budget that would have allowed me to tell the full story, where you could recreate the Lower East Side, like they did in *Godfather II*.

We used one street, Morton Street, and we could only shoot in one direction, because that direction faced Bleecker, where the streets formed a "T," so that you only had to create the look on Morton up toward Bleecker.

If we faced the other way, it was Seventh Avenue and obviously we couldn't close Seventh Avenue, we didn't have that ability. In *Godfather II*, they had street after street, traveling shots that were gorgeous. So we just did what we could and everything was written and organized with that in mind.

My own experience in writing low-budget films is that you often have to do a part of something; a part has to stand for something larger.

Did you always plan to shoot in black and white?

No, I don't think I thought about it at all. But when I started doing the research and saw these pictures, particularly the photos by Louis Hine and Jacob Riis and some of the anonymous pictures I found in the Jewish file at the public library, it just seemed to me that it might be a wonderful way to tell it. And I happen to like black and white.

Were you worried about the balance of English and Yiddish in the script?

I don't think I was thinking in those terms. I guess my own experience had been that actors have very good ears. I knew that even if the actors had to learn the Yiddish phonetically, they would do it.

I was writing this screenplay for me to direct and I didn't think that I would be hiring too many actors who already knew Yiddish. I thought I'd be lucky if I hired some, but I didn't think all of them would. In the end, I did have a few that did, but many didn't.

But that wasn't something that worried me, because my own experience with actors had been that they really have very good ears, they're terrific mimics. Actors can hear someone and mimic them the next moment.

What resources do you use to get feedback while you're writing?

The feedback that I got was primarily from my husband. Usually you have to send the script to whoever the financial group is, but this was a group of investors that didn't really need to see the screenplay. They were making small investments and it was not the sort of thing where they were going to be reading it.

I know I got lots of ideas when I started working with the actors. For instance, I think that two of my favorite lines in the script came from Doris Roberts, who plays the neighbor, Mrs. Kavarsky. These were expressions that her grandfather had said and she said to me, "Do you think these are good lines?" And I said, "Doris, they're fabulous. They're going right into the script."

One of them is, "You can't pee up my back and make me think it's rain," and the other one was, "With one tuchis you can't dance at two weddings." Old Yiddish expressions and they were wonderful and just perfect — and, of course, she delivered them wonderfully.

Besides the addition of those lines, did the script change much once you started working with the actors?

I was quite open to changing it, but it didn't change as much as I thought it would, mainly because, with the Yiddish and the English and the period, the actors didn't feel really comfortable doing improvisations.

It did change somewhat when I was cutting it — it followed the original story more closely. There was a longer section of the husband's life in New York before the wife came. When we did the rough cut, it was just clear that the real story started when the wife came and that the life of the husband could be established in fewer scenes.

Two scenes really stand out for me and I'm not sure how you would have described them when you wrote them. The first is when Jacob finds out that his father has died and he goes home and tries to pray. You really get a sense that this is a guy who hasn't done this in a while.

Well, he hadn't done it, so that part wasn't hard. The actor wasn't trying to unlearn something or trying to show that he didn't know how to do something that he really knew how to do. He didn't know how to do the prayers.

And then there's a scene with Gitl and the boarder, Bernstein. We're not sure where the relationship is headed and as they sit at the table he reaches over and touches her garment.

That came from the actor. She was talking about her husband and not knowing where to turn. She sat down at the table across from Bernstein and he tried to reassure her and cover for her husband, although you could tell that he felt very sorry for her.

We shot it a few times, and I just didn't feel like we had it; it needed something. It wasn't quite there. And I was sitting there, trying to think about what it was that would bring the scene more to life. At that moment the actor playing Bernstein reached over and touched her shawl. And I said, "That's it."

It needed something to show that he had feelings for her, and it came from him — it was not in the script but came from the actor.

It just proves that you don't always need dialogue to show the relationship between characters.

That's very true. If you can get it that way, you've really got it. You get so many clues of people's behavior by watching them; we all do that, all the time. We do it with our politicians; it isn't just what they say, it's how they are.

Did you have actors in mind while you were writing the screenplay?

No. As a matter of fact, I was expecting to find someone who is like the Gitl in the story. She was described as dark and a little plump. So I thought I would find someone like that and that will be fine.

After I finished the script and while Ray was raising the money for it, I saw a film with Carol Kane in it, a Canadian film called *Wedding in White*. I was just entranced by her, I just thought she had such a wonderful film presence. She had a certain Old World quality to her.

We had a casting director and I told him I'd seen this young woman, but she seemed to be Canadian, and obviously with our low budget we couldn't afford to bring anybody in and put them up. And he said that as a matter of fact she lived across Central Park and she was a New Yorker and there wouldn't be any problem. She was the first one that we hired.

Was it difficult to put aside, as a writer, your vision of Gitl when, as the director, you found someone completely different than you had imagined?

I think every writer/director does the same thing. You write to give yourself a blueprint for the film that you're going to make. Then you see what comes up and you try to leave yourself open to what the actors bring to it and what the weather brings and what the locations bring. You're happy because it isn't just you; everybody's taking this thing and adding to it, bringing more to it. And that was just fantastic.

In casting the Jacob character, I felt that I understood his problem and I understood what he was going through and I really liked this character. But a number of the people who came and tried out wanted him to be more heroic and a little less harsh with her and a little less confused about his life. I had to reject those actors, because they didn't want to do the character as written, they wanted to do something else.

For Bernstein, the actor who was cast dropped out at the very last minute and I was quite stuck. It was one of the most devastating moments in the making of the film.

Ken Van Sickle, our cinematographer, said to me, "Well, what about Mel Howard?" And I said, "Mel Howard? Mel Howard came here for a crew job, he's not an actor." And Ken said, "Yes, but when he came you told me you liked the way he looked and you liked his eyes for Mr. Bernstein."

I didn't even remember that I'd even said that. So I said, "Bring him in," and he came in, and of course he'd grown up in a Jewish family and spoke perfect Yiddish. He took direction wonderfully and gave a wonderful performance.

How did you get the scenes that needed to be in Yiddish translated into Yiddish?

Michael Gorrin recorded the Yiddish for the actors and he did all the translations, except in those instances when the actor already knew Yiddish. The Rabbi, the guy who played the peddler, the man who played the scribe, they all spoke Yiddish and did their own translations.

What movies inspired you?

I loved so many movies. I grew up in Omaha, Nebraska and in Omaha at the time I was growing up there wasn't any television. It didn't come until I was in high school. So the amusement of the day was to get on the streetcar and go downtown and pay thirty-five cents and see a double feature. You paid thirty-five cents until you were twelve, but everybody was twelve until they were about fifteen.

I still have a wealth of movie images in my mind from that, but there are a couple of movies that I remember very distinctly from seeing them as a kid. One was *Shadow of a Doubt*. I can see why I was so attracted to it: It's about a girl whose trusted uncle turns out to be a killer. This was not a threat from outside; this is a threat from within the family circle.

I was very profoundly affected by that. I can remember in the scene where Joseph Cotten tries to push Teresa Wright out of the moving train, I can honestly remember still to this day how I felt: which theater it was, where I was sitting, where my mother was sitting, where my father was sitting. It was quite a strong childhood experience. I think I was only about seven or eight, but I really remember it to this day.

That has a certain power over you and makes you desire to re-create something like that.

What's the best advice that you've ever received about writing?

I don't think it's so much advice from another person. I think it's just the experience of looking at films.

When I first started working in film — this was pre-video — we used to go to the Museum of Modern Art and sit in the basement and see films. I would say that was the thing that taught me the most, to see the great films and then to try to study the screenplays. Oftentimes those screenplays were available and I could buy them and study them and try to figure out why they worked. I think that was the kind of advice that was the best for me.

Did you learn anything while writing *Hester Street* that you took to future projects?

You know, I think each one is so different. Certain things become a little bit easier, perhaps, but each one is so different and each one has such different requirements.

I don't know how much one really teaches you for the next. Maybe it gives you confidence to think, "I did it before, maybe I can do it again." But I think each time you're walking off a cliff.

Sweet Land
Ali Selim

MINISTER SORRENSEN

I'll wait while you pack.

OLAF

This is her place.

MINISTER SORRENSEN

How can it be?

INGE

You can let it be.

MINISTER SORRENSEN

You don't have the papers to prove it.

INGE

Prove? No. Now -- I am married in my
heart. In my heart, I am -- citizenship.
In my heart I believe.

MINISTER SORRENSEN

But, believing is different than what is
real.

Sweet Land is a remarkable achievement on a small budget for a first-time feature director. It takes place in post-World War One Minnesota among the immigrant Scandinavian farmers and concerns the relationship between Olaf and his arranged bride, the

German-born Inge. The film employs a flashback structure, start-ing in present day with Inge's death, flashing back to Olaf's death, and then further back to their meeting and courtship.

When I told director/writer Ali Selim that the purpose of this book was to help de-mystify the screenwriting process, he laughed. "First, let me tell you, I can't help you de-mystify it," he said. "To this day it's the most mysterious thing I've ever done."

What was your background before you started *Sweet Land*?

I started in the film business in 1985, began directing TV commercials in 1989. I optioned the rights to this story in 1993. So I had been directing commercials for about five years. I was ten years out of any sort of screenwriting classes that I had taken and hadn't really done much with it, besides directing commercials and learning that end of the filmmaking process.

Had you ever written a screenplay before this?

No. I dabbled. I took a screenwriting class from Tom Pope in 1984 and I churned out something to get a grade. I can't even remember what it was. Then we had this idea when I was at Departure Films in 1989 that we were going to try and make a movie and I think I cranked something out then as well. But again, I don't even remember what it was. I just didn't know any better. I thought you slap some words on a page, got the camera out and that was that.

This was really my first effort at telling a story that was structured and constructed. But had I put words on a page before? Yeah. Had I ever done anything seriously or taken myself seriously? I think this was the first time.

The story changed quite a bit, from Will Weaver's short story, "Gravestones Made of Wheat," to your screenplay. There's very little left; the central conflict, about the legality of burying someone in the wheat field instead of the

**cemetery, isn't even touched on in the film. However, the
feeling of the story is still there.**

I guess that's all that really mattered to me. It wasn't the structure
of it, but the feeling and the ideas behind it and the love story. My
initial reaction was that I loved it. It's one of the few times that
I finished reading something and I cried. I told that to Will and
he said, "That's really great, because when I finished writing it I
cried." I think we hit it off because of that.

There was the love story, and the sense of heritage and the immigration story. My father's an immigrant, my mother comes from
a Minnesota farming background, grew up on a farm in southern
Minnesota, so there was a lot about the story that I connected with.
But I think the overriding thing was, this might be a pretty simple
thing to do.

There's something very simple about the story, deceptively simple. I
think it sucked me in, in terms of production. I felt like this might
be a really simple feature film to go make. The joke is, it took fourteen years.

How did you go about securing the rights?

I called the agent and at the time when I first called, the rights were
held by the local PBS affiliate. But I had said something to the guy
who worked in the agent's office that he connected with. And so
about eighteen months later, when the rights lapsed, he personally
called me back and said, "The rights are up. Are you still interested?"

I was so excited by that and just the fact that he had remembered
and called. I called a couple of friends who had had some literary
experience and I wrote up a document myself that said I'll give you
a few hundred bucks and see where it goes. And that document
was adequate and Will signed it. And then I sent him a check every
six months for three years.

At a certain point he called me up and said something to the effect
of, "This is kind of an unused room in my house and you seem to

have moved in and moved the furniture around and made better use of it. Why don't you just live there?" And so the rights and the option agreement became very personal and liberal, and we kept it going for thirteen years, which I don't think a strict agent/lawyer relationship would have allowed.

How did that story evolve over those thirteen years? The end result bears very little resemblance to the original story.

I would argue that it all came from the page. There are words on the page that I somehow reached into and pulled out, just from a single word.

Like a single word about Olaf's feelings about God. From that I'd pull out the entire story of Inge's religious background and Olaf's response to it, and Minister Sorrensen and his side of it. As I would do that, I would also do research. I would take a word in the story that had some resonance for me, and I'm sure I would apply a lot of my own personal history, my own recollections of my grandparents' history.

But then I would also go down to the Minnesota History Center, and look through their photo databases. I tend to get more out of photographs than I do out of documents and pages of research; that's just the way I am.

I would pull out photos of church-going in 1919-1920, and in one of those photos was the banker. And that would cause me to go research what was going on at the time.

It was just at the end of a wheat boom, so I figured Olaf probably had had some good years and had some money, and he was the kind of guy who would hang on to it. But maybe his neighbor wouldn't and from that I developed the character of the neighbor, Frandsen.

So a lot of it was made up that way, with photographs from the History Center and this realization that if Olaf is going to hang onto his money, somebody else won't hang onto his money. My grandparents always had tales of the guy up the street who bought everything, like Frandsen. He bought a car and a camera and the guy was always broke. So it was personal history, stories that I heard, combined with research at the History Center.

But I think overall, I would argue — and I think that Will might join me in the argument — that movie really does come from the page. It's not just plotline stuff, it's feelings and philosophy, theology, things like that.

Do you think that your attraction to photos inspired you to make the wedding photo such a key visual element?

Probably. I'm always kind of drawn to photos. They seem to tell me more.

And it was that era, when the common man started to take photos on a regular basis. It was no longer just for the rich.

The other thing that intrigued me was something my son said when he was about three. This was fifteen years ago. I'd had a job out in California and he and my wife came out for the last weekend of it and we went to Disneyland. I shot video of him the whole day and then I cut some of it together and showed him the video two years later. He would watch it over and over and over.

Once, after watching the video, he asked me why I wasn't there. And I realized that the video I had made for him had replaced his memory. It was an intriguing idea and I thought that a lot of our memory does come from reminders like that. What did my grandparents do for memory before they had photos? Was that memory stronger?

So there had to be a photo at the center of the story, because it really is a story of memory.

At what point did you establish the flashback structure?

That's in the short story. The story starts in the 1960s and then flashes back to the 1920s. But I found that once I got into the

1920s, I thought it felt like a ride and I didn't want to get back out of it.

And then, again, there's a line at the end of the short story, something like, "From that year on, every year the wheat grew a little taller in that area." And I realized that you have to have a third time period, to relate that.

That line in the story always got me, "the wheat grew a little taller every year." I'd get all misty-eyed and choked up. I had that idea in the script for a long time, up until two months before we shot — we were going to come up with some way to make the wheat a little taller.

When I was location scouting, I would come across all these places where the wheat was a little taller. And I would ask the farmer, misty-eyed, "Is that your grandfather?" And he'd say, "No, we shut the outhouse down a couple years ago." And I realized that it just didn't have the romance that I wanted.

The flashback structure was also a result of looking at a house, a potential location. It was owned by a woman who had been an immigrant from Sweden. When we looked at it, she had just moved out of her house three weeks before, to go to the nursing home. She was 104.

I realized that this character in my movie really could still be alive in 2004. This woman was born in 1900, the same year that my character was born. And that's when I thought, maybe it's a little more romantic if we bury grandma on top of grandpa then if we say that the body fertilizes the wheat and makes it taller. That's where that change came from.

Did you think about budget at all while you were writing?

No, I guess I didn't. If I had thought about that, I think the script would look very different.

No, I just let it rip and left it up to (producer) Jim Bigham to make it happen. He was great. He's an old friend and he really connected with the script for a lot of reasons. He wasn't just a line producer, he was a guy who really wanted to see it made.

He was the one guy who would go through the script with me and say, "If we get rid of this, it will make that better." He was great about hanging on to the parts of the story that would drive it forward and yet getting rid of the things that were a little too big. He was more budget-conscious and that caused me to re-write, I guess. But while I was first writing I didn't really think about it.

I was struck at one point, after Inge's been sitting in the railway station for a bit, that although I know I saw her on a train, and I saw her get off a train, I never really saw a train.

That was an interesting one. There was a train up in Osceola and they were open to it, but our insurance company wasn't. There's a huge rider for moving trains, like $40,000 a day.

Then we did find a train about forty miles from our location in Montevideo, but our ability to use it was bound up in the Patriot Act.

A lot of the railroad up here is owned either by Burlington Pacific or Canadian National or Canadian Pacific. And the Canadian National line is considered foreign territory. And so, to move a train through that area you've got to cross all three of those tracks. And to move the train onto the Canadian National tracks, you have to get clearance from the FBI. So there was just no way we were going to be able to move a train, insurance or not.

So we moved that scene into the train depot, which I think works just fine. We built a six-by-six box, a plywood box with a hole in it for the lens, and put it on the back of a flatbed truck and drove Inge around dirt roads and made you feel like she was looking out the window of a train.

Was there anything you were sorry to lose because of budget restraints?

There was nothing I was sorry to lose.

I learned a lot from Jim about how to be efficient, not how to be cheap or just say no. When you don't have millions and millions of dollars and tons of days, I think you just naturally give up some of those shots that you would see in *King Kong*, which are great — those big, wide street scenes of New York — but I don't know that we need them in a film like this.

There were a lot of those little things along the way where, if we'd had the money, yeah, we'd get the train pulling away from the station as she was walking away, but you don't necessarily need it.

Did you re-write it at all after it was cast, to fit the actors you cast?

A little bit. I think I did a lot of re-writing for Ned Beatty, who was interested and willing to be a little more terse and mean. The character wasn't originally that way and I like what he brought to it. And so I re-wrote a lot of his dialogue to reflect that.

I re-wrote Frandsen, too. My grandparents had a friend like that character, an immigrant living hand-to-mouth on a farm in Minnesota. Yet he was more influenced by what he heard of vaudeville and what he saw at the movies than what his real life was. It took Alan (Cumming) a little while, but when he got that, we re-wrote Frandsen to make him more fun in that way.

Were you always planning on directing this script as you wrote it?

Yes.

Do you think you wrote it any differently because you knew you would be directing it?

I don't think so. I don't know what writing another kind of script is like, so I don't know if I adapted this to the fact that I was going to be directing.

I do know that my writing is vastly more sparse or suggestive than most screenwriters. My Assistant Director was always pulling his hair out, saying "It's not in the script, it's not in the script!"

And I think, actually, that's what attracted the actors to it. It doesn't have the kind of screen direction that says, "She raises her left hand and puts it on the cool granite counter." There's none of that in there. It's more just a kind of rumbling suggestion, and I think the actors really seemed to appreciate that, because they all talked about the sparseness of the dialogue, which is as sparse as the script.

I'm writing another script now and I'm finding that it really isn't just the taciturn Scandinavian farmers that caused me to write that way. It's really more my writing style.

Did you show script drafts to anyone along the way?

I put them out there to people that I thought could help, but not everybody's helpful when you hand out a script. I'd taken this script out on the road and tried to raise money, then retreated and re-written it, and then taken it out on the road and tried to raise money, and retreated and re-written.

And then I sent it to a guy who had become a friend of mine, Gil Bellows. We made a steak sauce commercial together, back in 1993. He was an actor and I was a director and I learned a lot about acting that day, because he's a real actor, not a commercial actor. We just kind of hit it off through all the misfires that we had on the set that day and stayed in touch.

He ended up having a successful career. He was in *The Shawshank Redemption*, and got one of the lead parts in *Ally McBeal*, and had quite a good string of films back in the mid-'90s. So I sent it to him and he really liked it. I think he said to me it was like the most expertly laid out campfire he'd ever seen, but it didn't have any flame. It needed a little heat.

Gil had just come off spending a summer at the Sundance Institute and he loved it. He loved what he could bring to it and loved the interaction with all the writers and directors and fledgling film-makers. But he didn't really want to leave his young family again for six weeks or whatever and go to the mountains.

So he put together his own program in Los Angeles. And he got the support of a lot people, like Jon Voight and Luke Perry, and that became the Cygnus Emerging Filmmaker's Institute. They asked for script submissions and I put mine in and it was one of two selected. That's when I really started the writing process, when I really got into hashing it out with real writers. That's when I really started to break it down.

What's the value of being part of a program like that?

It's helpful to be with people like that who have done it. It's help-ful to hear what they have to say about it. It's helpful to hear their suggestions, whether you agree with them or not. After that, it was maybe two more drafts and I felt like I was where I needed to be.

What was the reading at the Cygnus Emerging Filmmaker's Institute like?

It was really amazing. We had 350 people in the Egyptian Theater and I had Peter MacNicol and Jon Voight and Louise Fletcher — the list goes on — fabulous actors who all gave a day of rehearsal and then a Saturday morning reading. It was great. I learned so much about staged readings. I learned a lot about what works in the dialogue and what doesn't. It's a tremendously helpful process for any writer.

What did your day of rehearsal before the reading entail?

We did a read-through, had a discussion, did another read-through, another discussion, and then an actual rehearsal where they made it happen and felt it. So when the people showed up for the Saturday morning reading, it was really like a play.

The thing that I find when I go to readings now that I learned at that reading is that you need to re-write the screen direction for a staged reading. It needs to just clip along.

There was a reading I went to recently where the guys who put it on wouldn't listen to my suggestions about cutting the screen direction in their script. I think they read for two hours and fifteen minutes, and they only got to page 45. It was deadly; people were walking out and had given up.

So it was great to have the reading in Los Angeles, where the actors were brilliant and the screen direction was the right length. Nobody walked out of that reading, but when they did walk out they said, "This movie has to get made." There's a lot to be said for a really powerful, wonderful staged reading.

Did you re-write the script based on your reactions to the reading?

Oh, yeah. The first thing I did was the age-old rule of "take the first three lines and the last three lines off of every scene." I felt it, immediately, in the reading, so I went and did that.

I cut some of the dialogue. There were some good actors up on that stage, and you immediately got the sense that they don't need some of this stuff, they don't need it. And that's something that you don't get directing commercials. You don't get the feeling that the actor's really going to make this come to life.

Over the thirteen years you wrote the script, how long did you go between episodes of working on it?

I worked on it every year. It would be six weeks, then I'd get back to commercials, then I'd coach Little League, and then I'd read it and then I'd sit on it for a while, then back to commercials and more Little League.

It was hardly a full-time job for thirteen years. It was just a function of where I was in my life. If this next one takes more than a year, I'm going to go get my real estate license.

Are there any lessons from *Sweet Land* that you'll take to future projects?

I think I learned some lessons about dialogue – how much actors really bring to the show.

We did a couple rehearsal readings in Montevideo, once all the actors arrived. And immediately following those readings, I went through and cut about half of the dialogue. Just watching their faces I thought, boy, they don't even need to memorize this stuff in Norwegian or German or whatever it is. They just need to act and look and work between the lines.

And then when we started editing, I bet we lost another half of what was left. And I'm finding that it's really helpful in writing the next script. Write it for the actor, don't write it for the producer who's reading it.

What movies inspired you?

I like them all. I just like the experience.

I've always been really fond of Terrence Malick, even *The Thin Red Line*, which a lot of people don't have fond memories of. I've always been a fan of Bertolucci. I just took my teenaged son to see *The Conformist* a couple weeks ago.

I just love movies that are well-written and seem full of life. I loved *Wedding Crashers*, because it just looked like fun. In a similar vein, Ron Bass's work on *My Best Friend's Wedding*. In the hands of somebody else, it could have been like, why am I even here? But it was just right on for me. And I thought it was a well-written script.

Speed is another one. I'm sure that it was well directed too, but it was just, like, different from that kind of thing. And I don't really care for that kind of thing, but I just thought it was brilliant.

What's the best advice you've ever gotten about writing?

Oddly, it's not that profound, but I carry it with me. It's about screen direction and it's this: always write in active voice, not passive voice. I had one draft that was entirely in the passive voice and I didn't even know what that meant, even though I was an English major. I was like, "What are you talking about?"

It amounted to changing "Olaf is sitting" to "Olaf sits" and "Olaf is harvesting" to "Olaf harvests." I did that on EVERY LINE of screen direction throughout the entire script.

In doing so, the script went from this "distant, over there, who are they?" story to an immediate and present emotion. The subconscious somehow took over and suddenly actors were saying, "I have to do this film." It was weird. Prior to that they called it "soft." When I made it active they called it "lean and athletic." No scene changes. No new behaviors. No sex scenes or car crashes. Just drop the "ing" and add an "s." Go figure.

But while it was a lightning bolt for me, it is probably a "duh!" for most writers.

Screen direction should almost always be about behavior. I think a lot of poorly written scripts make it about movement — moving left, moving right, moving towards the window, moving away from the window — and sometimes that's important for blocking. But it's not as important to an actor as behavior.

I think maybe that's the thing that distinguishes *My Best Friend's Wedding* from *The Wedding Planner*. Really interesting, fresh, unique behavior that makes a character somebody we want to watch.

Keep it in the active voice and concentrate on behavior.

One last question: While you were shooting, the movie was called *The Wedding Photo*. Why and how did it change to *Sweet Land*?

The Wedding Photo was a name that one of the producers put on it the night before it went into breakdown services, because he didn't think actors would respond to the name *Quiet Breathing*, which it had been called for a while.

Here's the thing about names: we have three kids and we had these placeholder names for each of them before they were born that we never used.

We named them the moment they came into the world. It was like, "Oh, *that's* who that is!" And they were names that we had never even thought of. But we looked at them and said, "*That's* who that is!" And they stuck.

I look at the placeholder names now and I look at my kids and I think, "Oh, they were never *that*!"

And it was the same with the movie. I knew it was going to be done, we're going to watch it, and we're going to feel like, "Oh, *this* is what it is!"

CHAPTER FOUR

The Play's The Thing

Making the leap from stage to screen can be a perilous (and for some, a deadly) jump. Which is hard to comprehend, because the confined nature of a stage play would seem ideal for a low-budget movie. Yet, for every one that succeeds, two or three arrive DOA.

The two screenplays highlighted here made the leap unscathed and virtually unchanged from their stage incarnations, which may be the secret of success for those looking to duplicate their results.

Tape
Stephen Belber

                    VINCE

You think I'm a dick?

                    JOHN

Ah, no. But I do know that occasionally
you have a tendency to act in a phallic
fashion.

Three people in one room. That's always been considered the perfect construct for a low-budget movie. However, to keep that interesting for ninety minutes is a lot harder than it looks.

Stephen Belber and Richard Linklater pull it off in Tape, *primarily because they trusted the source material they were working with. Belber wrote from his gut when creating his characters and the ever-changing dynamic during their meeting in a slightly seedy motel room keeps the story constantly evolving and involving.*

(Be aware that this interview contains spoilers about key plot points.)

Where were you in your career before you wrote the stage version of *Tape*?

I was not very far along. I had just quit my day-job to work on *The Laramie Project*. It was the year that we were researching the murder of Matthew Shepard. I was going out to Laramie every couple of months and then coming home. So I was just starting to get paid. I had been writing plays for a long time, I'd come out of the Playwright Fellowship program at Julliard, but I was sort of adrift and not sure.

And then *Tape* came along. It was not one of the big plays I was planning on writing or was working on. It was something where two old friends of mine came along and they wanted to showcase themselves as actors in the New York theater world, and they said, "Can you write us something that can really show what we can do?"

So I really wrote it for them. Then one of the actors was dating this girl, so I added her because it got boring with two guys after awhile. So it wasn't like, "I'm going to write this big play." I was just doing it because I liked these guys and I liked their work and it was fun.

We produced it ourselves way off-off-Broadway for a very low budget. Eventually, a Broadway producer came down to see it, because it got a nice buzz, and he wanted to option it because he was looking for something to do with Ethan Hawke.

He was going to do Albee's *Zoo Story*, and he was looking to couple it, because *Zoo Story* had first been coupled with a Becket one-act back when Albee first wrote it. So he was looking for a young, new writer to pair up with an older writer, which happened to be Albee.

So we did a reading of it with Ethan and some other actors, and then it fell through because Edward Albee didn't want that to be the play to accompany his play. He ended up writing his own. But Ethan remembered it and when InDigEnt came to him, Ethan said, "How about this? It would be fun, quick and easy to shoot."

So he brought it to Rick Linklater. And Uma Thurman had been at that first reading that Ethan had done, so she was familiar with the play. It was all very lucky.

How did you generate the idea when your two friends said "write something for us"? You weren't thinking screenplay at that point, right?

I had written maybe one screenplay, for fun, at that point. So this was really something to get gritty — it was the antithesis of what you'd think of as a movie. It was one room, a screwed-up, fucked-up relationship.

I was thinking of something we could do low-budget, production-wise. We got together one afternoon, we tossed around a couple ideas. It could be in a motel room, they could be brothers, what is it? And then they went away and I worked on it for a couple weeks. And they came over for a reading, just in my living room. It was very subterranean and organic that way, which was nice.

It was a good lesson for me as a writer, because I tend to think epically and think I'm going to write the Great American Play and I over-plan it and I don't let spontaneity into the process. And this was good to remind me to write from the hip a little more and write closer to home. These are the types of guys I'd grown up with and I know these types of situations. These are twenty-eight-year-old guys and this was something I was familiar with at the time.

Once you determined the location, how did you generate the story? It sounds like it came pretty quickly, if the two actors came back in two weeks for a reading.

I don't know why. It was right around the time that Bill Clinton was debating whether or not to apologize for slavery and I was fascinated with the idea of apology: When is it gratuitous and self-serving versus when is it genuine and important? And that was a question that was valid at the time for Clinton. So I think that was on my mind, those types of questions.

And I wanted to write about people who were very close, so I based it on myself and another guy, the repartee that you have with your close friends. But I wanted to get to something darker beneath that and what happens when those types of competitive friendships get cross-referenced with intense issues, such as date rape.

Did you outline the story?

I don't know that I did. I certainly don't have lots of notes like I have for most of my plays. I must have realized, semi-early on in thinking about it, that there was going to be a dark secret and that the one guy was taping the other. I had no idea how it was going to end, and as I said, the girl was added on.

The play used to end when Robert Sean Leonard's character leaves the first time. And the play ended with her looking at him, like "You're an idiot." But I knew there was more there and after a public reading I went back in and said, "Well, what if he comes back and makes that effort to apologize?" But when writing it, I didn't think very far ahead in terms of what happens when a friend confronts another friend.

What was your day-to-day writing process?

I guess I'm pretty intense when I come across an idea and I don't sort of do an hour a day. My wife is French and I remember trying to describe this idea: A comedy about date rape was how I was forming it at the time. And she sort of laughed me off and said I should come up with a different idea. But I was able to keep writing. I remember starting over at one point, fairly early on and scrapping what I had when I came up with the idea that she might show up.

I was writing by hand at that time. I like to get really into it when I'm writing and get a first draft done as soon as possible, then go back in and work on it.

And you're able to do that even if you don't know exactly where you're going?

Yeah. I had, at the time, a philosophy that when you're dealing with those types of tight friendships, where you don't know yourself where the conversation is going, that it would be truer and more genuine to write within that vein and to have a general goal post that you were headed for, but to let the turns happen.

If you're writing quickly enough in your mind and keeping up with your pen, let those twists and turns come at you, almost as quickly as they're coming at the characters. At least for this type of play, where it's sort of down and dirty.

Were you hearing anyone when you wrote?

Yeah, I guess I was. I always hesitate to say this, because I'm not a date rapist, but it was myself and a very close friend of mine.

I always felt in high school that I was a step behind him. He was more popular with the girls and everything, yet at this point in life he was not sure what he wanted to do and I was really going after what I wanted. And I love the dynamic of how those friendships can shift and change over the years.

I actually wrote a whole second act to this play that takes place ten years after the event in the motel room. Things have changed, and actually Vince is married. They live a sort of antiquated, domestic life. And John has gone on to make really, quote-unquote, important documentaries.

He comes back again, there's another pretense for a reunion of sorts, where things that were obviously left unsettled that night in the motel room pop back up. I never ended up doing it, because it felt excessive and a little redundant.

But I do like the idea of thirty years of friendship and the turns that it takes. The decisions that we make at eighteen reverberate and cause different decisions at twenty-eight and those reverberate and they make up our persona at age thirty-eight.

I thought it was interesting, character-wise, that Vince is so likeable, yet isn't really that nice of a guy; John is attempting to do the right thing, yet is really not all that likeable. How do you strike that balance in creating characters?

It's so easy to make them so unlikable that the whole's thing's dismissed and people are bored. And making unlikable people likeable in context is hard; I tried it in another piece and it doesn't always work.

I think because I was basing it on a guy that I love — the Vince character — I felt that he was the most unconstrued character, in a good way. He was very organic and he came out of someone with whom I do have a complicated relationship, so it just felt easy that way, to depict him with all his flaws.

But I also just got lucky in that I happened to set it up so that we were rooting for this guy. He can snort all the coke that he wants and be as much of a jerk as he wants, but we're invariably rooting for him because he is a) trying to do the right thing, and b) his second motive is that he's doing this because he's in love and he's desperately in love, from the position of an underdog. And those are just traits that if you endow a character with them, you can get a lot of mileage out of them.

But you weren't consciously considering that while you wrote it, were you?

No, I don't think I was. I would like to say I was, but I just happened to hit upon that dynamic. I don't think I even knew how much his real motive was that he was in love with her. I sort of realized that while I was writing it. I had this notion that he was trying to compel his friend to do the right thing and apologize.

But because those two motives — the desire to have Amy love him and the desire to make his friend do the right thing — were so imbued in the same character, it made him someone we could all relate to, because we all have mixed desires.

I think so often when you go to playwriting school they teach you about single intention, and certainly as an actor you can't play two intentions at once, and from moment to moment that's probably true. But I love trying to create characters who have these both genuinely deeply rooted intentions. It's great. Plus, he's a fun character to play.

Ethan Hawke, when he did the reading of the play, he played John. He was more of the good guy and that was more of his reputation up to then, playing that sort of higher than thou characters. I think he realized that he could stretch himself and show another side of himself, so when the movie came around, he very much wanted to play Vince, which I totally understand.

It's not just playwriting school that teaches that; screenwriting schools do the same thing, telling you to create characters who have one goal that they're going after. But in *Tape*, their goals shift constantly.

Yeah, exactly, and the responses of their opposite guy affect their next motives as well.

And it's true, in screenwriting it's even more of a problem. They want heroes, and if not, they want anti-heroes, but less often do they want highly flawed characters who are not self-aware and who are not clear in going after their intention.

Were there other things you learned from having a reading of the play?

I went in there thinking I had a much clearer idea of what was going on. I really did want to talk about this notion of apology and the worthiness of apology. And when I came across the idea of not just bringing Amy into the room, but keeping her around and having John come back and her not allowing him to have that apology on the grounds that he wanted to have it on, I think I started to realize that the play is actually potentially more interesting than my pseudo-politically correct take on it. It's also about power and it's about gender wars in terms of power. But also the *Rashômon* element came in, in a way I had not preconceived.

I thought I was just into this relationship between these two guys, having them sock it out, have a battle, and suddenly it became about who owned the past, who owns memories, and who owns apologies.

If we're basing our personas on events that have formed us in the past and someone comes in and takes the rug out from underneath that memory, the way you've solidified that memory in your mind, you have to reevaluate not just the memory but everything henceforth. It plays a real mind game.

I don't think I was really thinking about those things until I brought John back into the room on the second go-round and realized that it's not just about right and wrong, it's about who gets to do what when, on whose grounds. And also that memories are pliable. They're not set in stone.

When you were adapting it into a film script, was there ever any talk of "opening it up"?

There was briefly talk about it. That would be the first instinct for any filmmaker.

That's the great thing about Linklater. We talked a little bit about opening it up, but his inclination was definitely not to, that it was going to be more interesting to keep it enclosed. The problem was how do you not repeat the theatrically that comes when you try to film a play, because so often it doesn't work.

Because the DV cameras allowed you to go into a motel room or a soundstage that really felt like a motel room, he was going to be able to capture a cinematic way of telling the story. So, only very briefly did we talk about doing some exterior stuff, which made me delighted, because I was worried that they were going to ask me to write stuff that didn't fit this play.

You did lose some of the timing that you get in the theatrical version, because you have two cameras that you're trying to edit together. The theater piece runs an hour ten, and this ran an hour twenty-five. They added fifteen minutes because there wasn't the overlap that you get in live theater.

The trade-off for me, which was exquisite, was the sense of intimacy and a whole other layer of my writing, which is the silences between the words. We got to look into these guys' eyes and chart their reactions.

So the reactions were not as quick as in the theater — boom, boom, boom — but we got to see them process the other person's line and then come up with a response, all within the veil of "hey, buddy-buddy," the quick cut down repartee that guys have. But we were able to even see within that and it became, for me, more interesting that way.

You can get that in theater, but film, and especially a DV camera, can get in there in a way that an audience member, who's free to choose where to look in the theater, could never get that close. So, for me, it was a great lesson.

And to watch it with a crowd in a movie theater was a great learning experience. We're taught as screenwriters that audiences don't care about dialogue, that it's all about the visuals. But I felt that it was a nice synthesis of both, of them yearning for dialogue that they don't usually get in film. They were ready to listen to these people talk and with it they were getting the unspoken subtext very intently and clearly.

In terms of losing text, there wasn't much. There's one long speech that Uma Thurman has that is not as long in the film, where she finally goes after John. That was the only thing that Rick Linklater cut, and we talked about it. It wasn't just him saying, "I'm cutting this." He explained what he thought and it made sense. It just felt very overly written. It's about twice as long in the play and it's much more intense. But it's probably not realistic that she could come up with that in the moment.

In the film you can see, if you watch closely, it's cut off. They filmed the whole speech and so she didn't really land it in the way she might have, but she does a great job. I just think she did a great job in the movie, capturing the essence of that character.

What I love about the movie is that it raises more questions than it answers. Most movies aren't willing to do that.

Well, that's the golden rule, to tie it up and provide those answers. And even in playwriting, I think, it's a very fine line. Audiences will feel ripped off if you're intentionally ambiguous for the sake of it. If ambiguity serves a purpose, at the risk of sounding pretentious, it's to turn it around and challenge them to ask themselves, "What would I do in that situation? What have I done in past situations? And what have I done about those things?" That does seem to serve a purpose, and if nothing else the movie does poke it back at you. It's so pointed at a particular generation where the words "date rape" just became a phrase.

My wife translated it into French and there is no expression for date rape in that country yet. And it's relatively new to America. So I think the people who respond to this movie are people who have grown up with those words.

So, in terms of adaptation, it sounds like you basically handed Linklater the script to the play and said "Have at it."

Yeah, he was great that way. It was the opposite of what you expect the Hollywood machine to do to your work.

Basically, they put it in screenplay form. Robert Sean Leonard's character was originally Jewish; he makes a crack about being Jewish, but we didn't think we could pass off him as that. We also changed his name. There were also one or two cultural references which we thought would potentially date the film, so we cut a couple lines. One about David Hasselhoff.

Ethan improvised a dance bit that was from his high school days that he wanted to get in there. He put the word "fag" in at one point, which I was hesitant to do because I don't like it, but it was fine because guys like that say that word in that context.

Were you involved in the rehearsal process?

Yeah, again, I was really lucky. I was out of town, working on *The Laramie Project*. When I came back into town, they had rehearsed for about two days. They spent two weeks in a friend's apartment, just going through it. I came toward the end of the first week and it was amazing. It was like a theatrical experience. Ethan has a great theatrical background and Rick studied theater in college.

They started with real, genuine table work, which is what you do the first two days of any play, sitting around and talking about intention and motive and all that stuff around a dining room table. I couldn't believe that they were doing it exactly the way I would want it to be done. It was lovely.

And when they started shooting, I showed up whenever I wanted to, it was great. They built the set on a soundstage and the set had a retractable roof, so when they wanted to get certain shots they could light it. But for the most part inside the room was a sound guy and Rick, holding one camera, and the DP holding a camera, and the actors and me. It was really nice.

So you didn't have to make any changes to fit the budget?

No. The film was shot so cheap. They rented a car, so that when you opened the motel room door you could see a parked car. That was the big luxury and that wasn't even in the script.

Rick's company completely knows how to produce at that level when they need to, and InDigEnt was scrappy and just starting out. They hadn't yet had the success that they would have. So everyone was pitching in and calling in favors. It was sort of corny but nice.

When you finished the stage version, how did you know when the script was done?

We did this first reading where it ended abruptly and I felt it was too abrupt. I knew there was more. I was so interested in the female character and I was writing out of my element so much, so I remember calling up a lot of female friends and asking what they would do in that situation. I was really clueless about the feelings that the character would be going through.

I knew it wasn't finished after that first reading, but I didn't know if I should write a whole other act or add another twenty minutes. I remember it was my first case of real theatrical soul-searching, because I knew I had something that I really liked for once. There was a nice feeling in the room and the dialogue was rolling and the characters were knowable.

So I went off for a while and I worked on that, and we did another reading, again in my living room. And that one felt like there was a nice resolution. I guess I just knew that it was finished.

Again, I don't trust myself, because subsequently we did it in a larger venue in New York. I wrote monologues and a prologue, as well as an epilogue that took place ten years later, with all the characters speaking to us from the future. We actually produced that in New York and most of the people who knew both productions said you don't need it and it ruins this nice little thing you have. I was, as a playwright, thinking I should be writing epic, three-act plays that deal with the world and time passing, but it did feel like this moment had come to a close where the play ends now.

In terms of going back and re-writing, I actually felt like I hit that one pretty smoothly. Once I got a take on the female character, that she was not necessarily going to play their games — that she was not going to cede the power to them, regardless of what happened — I don't think it's changed much since then.

Little tiny things have changed, because the initial actress really was very helpful in charting it when we were first doing it. But in terms of structure, I never went back and excessively re-wrote it or changed it structurally. Of course, there wasn't that much structure to change.

Do you ever put a script in a drawer for a while?

Oh, absolutely. I have about twenty-five things in a drawer right now.

I think if I had put *Tape* in a drawer at that point I would never have gone back, because it's not the heftiest play. But I know that it hit a chord with people, because it was compact. I always complain when I see plays that are successful that they aren't as deep and profound as they should be, but that's not what audiences necessarily want or connect to. It has a tightness that is very satisfying and a compactness — at an hour twenty, it definitely had that.

Did you learn anything from this process that you've taken to other projects?

Yes. I think letting a degree of spontaneity into my writing, which was something that I had excised at Julliard. Learning to let spontaneity back in and knowing that that makes for better writing.

I learned that there is a market and an audience out there for dialogue-heavy films and character-driven films and that this fast give-and-take actually can work. Everyone says it's so theatrical that it doesn't work, but if you put it out there, an audience will follow it. It's not particularly complex. It's not Tom Stoppard. But we're used to it and we can be conditioned, as filmgoers, to follow and like it. Dialogue that's fun and appropriate to the contemporary world is something that audiences will respond to.

And I learned that drama doesn't come from just visuals. Drama comes from classic dramatic structure and shifts in emotions.

I'm writing more and more studio stuff now and I literally do cling to that idea — and I'm sure that I'll get killed for it — but I cling to the idea that you can infuse that into even these big things that I'm trying to work on.

Do you have any advice to writers working on a low-budget script?

They'll tell you not to worry about budget when you're writing, but I think if you really are intent on doing that, you can do both at the same time. You can find low-budget ways to tell the stories you want to tell.

In theater, the best things are the plays with no set. So you have to remind yourself that "I want to tell this story. I want to tell it the way I want to tell it," but to know that if it's a period piece that takes place over forty years in five thousand locations, it's a problem. You can probably tell the same story in a different way.

What's the best advice on writing you've ever received?

Write strong. There's so much prettiness and cleverness that we all strive for, but you should write for the heart more, which is different than saying write about what you know. Write to the gut.

With *Tape*, I guess I am most proud of the fact that it feels guttural, it feels like it's coming from a very true place. I'm sure people think there are too many plot twists and stuff, but basically these are people who are talking from their gut. And especially when it gets heated, they're talking on instinct and they're talking in the moment and there's nothing "writerly" about it at its best moments.

And it's something that's so easy to forget, the better writer you become — because you do want to show that you're a good writer — is how to click back into that, write from the gut, write strong. At least in moments, to know that you can find that, access that, no matter what the situation, we can, as human beings, relate to it. Because that's why we all go to movies and theater: to see human beings.

So if we just write to the human moments, those moments of human drama, that will pay off, because people connect to it.

subUrbia
Eric Bogosian

                              TIM

          How do you get your ideas?

                             SOOZE

          Leave him alone, Tim.

                              TIM

          I want to know. I'm curious. How do you
          get your ideas?

                             SOOZE

          Tim's jealous. He wants to have ideas
          too.

Eric Bogosian's subUrbia *started its life as a play, but it came to a wider audience via Richard Linklater's film version, which starred such up-and-comers as Steve Zahn, Parker Posey and Giovanni Ribisi.*

It is, in many ways, the quintessential low-budget concept brought to life. It's essentially one location, with a small cast, and with the action taking place over one long night. However, its theatrical roots provided it with deeper characterizations and richer subtext than you'd usually find in this coming-of-age genre.

What point were you at in your career before you started the stage version of *subUrbia*?

Talk Radio (the play and the film) as well as the solo show *Sex, Drugs, Rock & Roll* had garnered much greater interest in my work. Most importantly, excellent young actors were attracted to my script.

Do you begin with story, character or theme?

I begin with character and theme. The theme dances around in my head, almost like an editing device as I put my characters in motion with a story. But before anything, I think of the people who will populate my stage.

In the case of *subUrbia*, I began with five student actors in workshop playing the characters. I had them simply hanging out and discussing a variety of topics. There was no plot to speak of in the first set of pages.

Do you outline the whole story before you start writing a script?

No. I use outlines when writing a screenplay. But when I write a play or novel, it is very important to let the interaction of the characters lead me through the story. I'll have some sort of idea of an initial conflict, a starting point, but I won't necessarily know where it's going.

How did you create the characters?

The characters are there within me. They are the archetypes I "need" to conceptualize my inner world. In the case of *subUrbia* the cast of characters derived almost directly from the cast of characters who, in my mind, represent my friends from my high school days.

In some cases, the characters are transpositions of myself. There are parts of myself in Jeff, Pony, Sooze and Nazeer.

How much backstory do you create for each character? Do you write it down?

I'm not interested in backstory beyond its importance to what's onstage. In *subUrbia*, backstory becomes part of what we're watching. It was important to the play that we hear autobiographical stories from Sooze, Tim, Nazeer and Bee-Bee explaining who they are. Their own sense of history powers their story forward.

How important is having a theme before you start to write?

I always begin with a theme. It usually morphs as I'm writing but in the long run, the theme must have importance for me in the present, as I'm writing. I need the theme to do my writing, but I don't mind if the audience doesn't see the theme or misunderstands what the theme is.

In the case of *subUrbia* I don't think many people "got" the theme as I originally conceived it. (And what is that? you might ask. My answer is: Too complicated to explain, that's why I write plays. If I wrote themes, I would be a scholar and write treatises.)

How did the play change (if at all) during the first rehearsal process or production?

I depend on the cast to help me edit. I adjust overall structure, cut speeches, edit text. Not only did I edit for the first production, I continued to edit for the second production in Washington, DC.

When it came time to adapt it into a screenplay, were you writing to a specific, pre-determined budget?

I'm sure there was a set budget, but I didn't know what it was. Rick Linklater acted as producer with his company. All I knew was that we would hew closely to the play and that I could "open" up to other locales if I so wished. And I did.

What did you do to the script that, in your mind at least, turned it from a live performance script into a movie script?

The script hewed very closely to the play. But in the movie, we see characters when they are not with the group at the convenience store. Most importantly we see them go for the ride in the limo.

Do you know why you made certain choices when opening up the play into a film script? For example, you said showing the limo ride was important. Why did you choose to start the film with Jeff in his pup tent in his garage? Why did you choose to not shoot anything at the Four Seasons?

It's all about rhythm and texture. It's not about making things more explicit. And in the one place where we did do that (when Bee-Bee steals the prescription drugs) I think it's a bit of a dead spot.

But the tent in the garage is a kind of teaser. And certainly the limo ride serves to lighten up the center of the movie. As the story progresses into deeper and darker waters, the limo ride is comic relief in a way. For those reasons, we don't need the Four Seasons scene. That scene is after the climax, which thematically and subtextually is Tim and Jeff yelling at each other in the parking lot.

In making the adaptation, were there any moments that you hated to lose?

No. I look at movies very differently than stage. If a moment is a moment that works on film, I keep it. But film demands that the story continue to unfold. That being the case, I snipped away at some of the longer, more static speeches in the play and I don't regret it.

How involved in the production were you? Did you do any re-writes while shooting?

I did not rewrite during shooting, but if memory serves me, I did some writing after shooting and discussed editing with Rick.

How did you work with Richard Linklater?

Rick gave me my head, so to speak. He wanted the screenplay to be as close to what I wanted as it could be. We created a script that we liked, that met the needs for length. I did all the cutting of the original.

We ironed out some thematic/action aspects in the last moments, especially when Tim is telling off Jeff in the parking lot, throwing food at the store. It had taken the entire run of the play and another production of the play for me to understand what was really happening there.

Beyond that, we reached a conundrum at the very end, tried different endings, actually shot them and finally decided to stick with what we had.

Can you talk about a couple of those endings and why they didn't work for you? You said you didn't do any re-writing during the shooting, but you did some writing after the shooting. What was it and how did that work?

These two questions are part of the same question. What we were trying to find was the last words of the screenplay/film. There was some question whether the focus should be brought back to Jeff's (Giovanni's) life and specifically his future. So I wrote a scene which took place outside the hospital where Bee-bee had been taken.

This scene took place between Sooze and Jeff and if memory serves, was about "Okay, so what happens now?" Although Rick filmed it, it never resonated with either of us and we stuck to the ending as it is. Which is also the ending as it is in the play, i.e. very abrupt.

What did you learn from working on that script that you still use today?

It's good to have a sense of how the director is going to shoot the film, what sort of style. In this case, Rick used a lot of two-shots and it was constructive to know that in terms of scene rhythm.

Do you think there's really such a thing as an "independent" movie?

I don't know what "independent" means to other people. Having written and acted for film and television studios, I do feel that the corporate presence overloads the writing task at hand with "too many cooks."

My two features (*subUrbia* and *Talk Radio,* directed by Oliver Stone) and one TV series (*High Incident* with Steven Spielberg) were all "independent" of the studio in that the directors acted as producers. As such they were "independent" and as such, they gave me my independence.

Given our track record, I'm for more independence, especially for seasoned directors like Stone and Linklater. Once a director has established himself or herself, I think a studio should let him do his thing. When that happens, and it does (Gus Van Sant, Robert Altman, Tim Burton), the result is "independent" cinema.

What made you want to become a writer?

I write because I need the larger canvas. Although I consider good actors to be authors in their own right, I can't be waiting for the phone call, I need to be busy. And so I write.

What's your writing process?

If I am making new pages, I write for a couple of hours a day, usually in the morning. If I am editing or polishing, I may go longer. I procrastinate, but I also write every day. And one way or another, I am working all day from about ten a.m. to six.

Do you have any self-imposed rules — like a certain number of pages per day?

When writing a novel I will force myself to write a good chunk every day. But that's only half the story. On my last novel I ended up throwing out half the finished pages. Editing and deleting is as important as writing and sometimes just as difficult because it's hard to throw stuff away.

You seem to be fearless about cutting, changing and re-writing your work. How did you learn that habit and what are the benefits of re-writing? Is there any downside?

First of all there is a downside. Sometimes something very good can be lost in the haste to "make it better." Sometimes the long way around, i.e. the long speech, the boring passage, is the better way to go.

As far as learning the habit, it's not so much that as not thinking of my writing as that precious. I see the process as one that makes use of all of our best efforts. The goal is to make the best film we can. And in the case of film as opposed to theater, the director is the ultimate author.

How do you know when a script is done?

When I don't want to change anything when I read it and when I don't skip pages as I read. I have to find every page interesting.

Do you show drafts to people during the process?

I work almost solely with the director in the case of plays or films. In the case of "work for hire," I am forced to show pages along the way. For the most part though, I write for myself.

Do you ever put a script away for a while after finishing a draft? What's the benefit of doing that?

I always "throw it in the drawer" because when it is too fresh, I am too biased toward thinking it's a great work. After a couple of months I will find it and look at it again. Sometimes it seems smaller than it was, deflated. I will then sometimes cannibalize it for other projects.

Any words of advice to a writer working on a low-budget script?

Look at plays, understand subtext as a motivating force. A low-budget drama (as opposed to a genre film like a horror movie) lives and dies on subtext. Subtext is the changing nature of the characters' relationships. Very few writers have done this successfully in our time.

And yet, if you want to stay low-budget, you must stay in a cheap location and you must rely on the dynamics of relationship. In fact, once you learn how to write this way, you can bring this knowledge to any film.

I recommend viewing *The Blue Angel*, *The Apartment* and *Who's Afraid of Virginia Woolf?*

How do you strike a balance when adapting a play into a screenplay of making it "cinematic" without going overboard?

Well, I don't know if I have struck a balance. It's good to look at past plays and see how they were "opened up." Specifically, *Who's Afraid of Virginia Woolf* (Mike Nichols, director) or *Cat on a Hot Tin Roof*, etc.

In a way, the "opening up" is an attempt to disguise the fact that the play was originally oriented in a frame, pointing at an audience, as most plays are. In the early days of film, this wasn't an issue because all films had a "frame" and a "missing fourth wall" orientation.

Many of the golden years of cinema films were based on plays. Often the movies became more famous than the plays, but no one noticed the play underneath the film.

Today, because plays are still more or less the way they were sixty years ago (*subUrbia* being somewhat of an exception because it occurs out of doors and was presented on a thrust stage), screenwriters when asked to adapt will try to trick the audience into not noticing the "old-fashioned" feel.

The most important thing about adapting a play into a screenplay is the casting. Plays tend to be more histrionic than movies and require the kind of actor who knows how to do that. The tone has to be carefully balanced by the director so that when the actors do have big speeches or anything histrionic, it isn't noticeable.

In *Talk Radio*, for instance, which is very histrionic, almost every actor in the film has a lot of stage experience and is comfortable with the non-naturalistic quality of the screenplay.

As a writer, what's the benefit of seeing a number of different actors play the roles in a variety of productions of the play?

Certainly the more actors you see play the role, the more possible directions you notice. But I write for the first company and the first productions lay in the essential vibes of the play.

Are you pleased with the way the film of *subUrbia* came out?

Absolutely. For me, to see a play of mine on film is to in a way capture something of the experience of being at the play.

Steve Zahn was with the production from the very beginning and I thought it was important to have as many people as possible see that performance. I wish I could have done the same for the rest of the original cast. But because we did go with a different cast, we got to capture Giovanni's amazing turn as well as the rest of the gang.

I love this film, I love all the actors who have been part of the *subUrbia* experience. Now I just wish it would come out on DVD!

What's the best advice about writing that you've ever received?

Keep writing.

CHAPTER FIVE

Playing with Genres

Genre: (n) *A category of artistic composition, as in movies, music or literature, marked by a distinctive style, form, or content.*

Genre movies — such as horror films, sci-fi, thrillers, action — are popular categories in the low-budget world. However, with that popularity comes responsibility: There are rules in the genre world and you break those rules at your peril.

The screenwriters in this chapter all attempted genre jumping with varying degrees of success — from the mixture of horror and comedy in *Children Shouldn't Play with Dead Things* to the retelling of the vampire legend in *Martin* to the leap from comedy to action in *Suckers* to the multiple genres represented in *Repo Man*.

Martin
George Romero

MARTIN

Things only seem to be magic. There is
no real magic. There's no real magic
ever.

There's little question that George Romero re-invented the zombie film — indeed, re-invented the horror film — when he created Night of the Living Dead. *Then he turned his attention to the vampire myth with his film* Martin, *which is like no other vampire movie you've ever seen.*

Yes, there is blood. And crucifixes. And wooden stakes through the heart. But all resemblance to traditional vampire films ends there.

What was going on in your career before *Martin*?

Night of the Living Dead was released and actually returned money. We'd made it for about $117,000, but it returned between $500,000 and $600,000. So we thought, "Wow, this is a pretty easy business."

I quickly made three other films, one that was not written by me and was a little romantic comedy written by a friend. And we had all kinds of problem with that; it was misguided. I didn't want to get trapped in horror, but you couldn't make a little romantic comedy without, in those days, Ali McGraw or somebody.

I did a film right after that called *Season of the Witch*, which was a film where the backers didn't come through and we ended up having to make the film on about half of what we expected. It's a film that I still like, and it's actually the only film of mine that I'd like to re-make — in fact, I'm working right now on an updated screenplay.

And then we did a film called *The Crazies*. None of the films did any business, certainly none of them returned any money and they barely got distributed.

How did you respond to that?

Basically I threw up my hands in frustration.

And right then I met my long-term business partner, Richard Rubenstein. He's not my partner now but he was for years. And at that time there were these tax deals, incentives for investors. They were non-recourse loans, so that an investor could invest $100,000 and write off $600,000.

So Richard came in and basically mined Pittsburgh for all of its investment potential. Our law firm also represented the Pittsburgh Steelers, and those were the years when the Steelers were really happening, that great team that they had. And so we did a series of sports documentaries. It took us a couple of years, but we did seventeen hour-long films; one of them, on O. J. Simpson, was two hours long.

We were just sort of biding our time and saying "One of these days we'll make another feature." During that time, I wrote the script for *Martin*.

I presented it to Richard and said, "I think we could do this for really low bucks." I was thinking $250,000–$300,000, and that's where it came in, around $275,000.

I tried when I was writing it to keep it within the parameters of what we'd be able to do. I had in mind, the whole time when I was writing it, that there was nothing in it — there were no big special effects — there was nothing in it that looked like it was going to cost money. It was just a story that I liked.

Where did the idea for the story come from?

Initially I was thinking of doing a comedy. I just got one of those ideas that comes to you in the shower: If there really were vampires, they'd have problems living hundreds of years. They'd have to keep changing their passport photos, they'd have all these practical problems. So I wanted to do a comedy about the practical problems of a vampire in today's age.

I had started to keep a notebook on it. One day it just occurred to me that I could do this a lot straighter and I could do a thing about somebody who's not a vampire at all.

I just thought that that would be more — not romantic — but it would be, in a way, more of a tender story and a whole new spin that was not comedic. I wanted to just spin a vampire yarn a bit differently and leave the door open as to whether he is or is not a vampire.

You left it open for the audience, but did you decide going in that he wasn't actually a vampire?

The decision that I made was that he was not. In my mind, Martin is not a vampire, he's a kid that's been fucked up by family and mythology and movies and whatever else has influenced him. You just have to make that decision in the dark room somewhere and keep both doors open.

Like your other films, *Martin* isn't really about what it appears to be about on the surface. It's not really a vampire movie, just like *Night of the Living Dead* is more than just a zombie movie. They're really more reflections on the times we're living in.

That's what I try to do. I try to use the framework and use the genre, because first of all it's the easiest way for me to get financing. Really all my films are people stories. Even at the heart of *Night of the Living Dead*, it's really about the people and how they screw themselves over and can't get it together.

I like that theme tremendously, the lack of communication, the idea that people are still working their own fiddles and have their own agendas even faced with sea changes in the world.

I also like that "monster within" thing, which is in the zombie films and in *Martin* to some extent. Even in a couple of the things I've done that Steve King has written. The ones that I'm drawn to are those, like *The Dark Half*.

What's your writing process?

I'm weird, man. I keep a notebook and I use a little tape recorder sometimes, to do dialogue. But I don't actually start writing until I know exactly where the story's going. Once that gels, I sit down and just write it, sometimes in thirty-six hours straight. That's just me. I'm weird that way.

I used to edit my own films, and I used to edit all the commercials and most of the sports shows — pretty much everything we did, I edited. So I got used to that deadline mentality. You've got to sit down and have it ready for air by next Monday. So I'll do as much thinking and stewing and trying to put all my ideas together and then I just let it flow.

It usually comes in way too long, but once it's all on paper it's a lot easier to go back. Then I usually hit the beach for a week and then come back and read it and say, "I don't need this, I don't need this," and then I just do the great big blue pencil on it.

Did you learn anything in producing *Night of the Living Dead* and *The Crazies* that helped you write *Martin* for a low-budget?

Actually, no. I mean, we had this advantage of having this commercial company and so we knew production backwards and forwards. We were able to whip it together and do an industrial film for Alcoa or do a commercial for whoever. Those little productions were actually a lot more complex than any of the first five or six features I did.

What made them more complex?

They had to be slicker. What we did, consciously, when we started to make feature films, was cut back on that kind of gloss. We made one film for Alcoa which was really slick. It was big, it looked really glossy, it looked very Hollywood.

So we were able to do that, but we knew when we were approaching feature films on very low budgets, that we just weren't going to be able to take that kind of time to light the beer glass. I can give you a whole treatise on lighting beer. I've spent hours and hours and hours on a single shot of a glass of beer.

But of course we couldn't do anything like that on the features, because we had to blow through these things and get them done very quickly. We rarely had more than thirty or forty days to do a film.

The real secret of *Martin* was that it was a very small crew. Cast and crew combined I think were fourteen or sixteen people. John Amplas, the guy who played Martin, was carrying lights. It was like that, real guerilla stuff.

Did you have him in mind when you wrote the script?

Yeah. I had the idea first — again, I had my little notebook and I'd been thinking about it for a while. And then I saw a play that he was in and I just thought, "That's Martin." It was some old Greek thing, one of those classical things, and he just had this beauty and grace and innocence about him. I just said, "That's the cat."

I spoke to him that night, right after the performance. And so when I sat down to write the script, I knew that he was going to play Martin.

And Tom Savini had just re-entered my life. Before we made *Night of the Living Dead* I had written a script, a very sort of high-minded, Bergmanesque kind of thing, set in medieval times. It was a coming-of-age story, about two teenagers during the days of the Plague, sort of like *Virgin Spring*.

I went again to local high schools to look at plays, because I needed teenagers. And the guy that I liked from seeing him in a play was Tom Savini. So we met and hung out a little bit, he was a high-school age kid at the time.

That movie never happened and we lost track of each other. He went off to Vietnam and became a combat photographer. And then one day, he walked off the elevator at our offices and slit his wrists open, right in front of us, fell down, and then said, "How did you like THAT? Do you know what I'm doing these days? I'm doing this shit!" And I said, "Wow! I'm thinking of doing this vampire flick."

But I also knew that he was a good actor. And so I said, "There's a role here as well." And so we did a little trade off — he did the effects for free, and we fed him burgers while he played the role.

The actor who played the grandfather was a guy I knew and had worked with on a couple of industrial films. And I knew him and thought he was perfect; I could hear his voice as I wrote the words.

And then I had just met Christine, who eventually became my wife. And I knew that she was going to play the daughter. So actually, before I even sat down and wrote page one, I knew who four of the actors were going to be.

At what point did you decide to play the priest, Father Howard?

I think when I started to write the priest. I thought, "I've gotta do this." I was raised Catholic and so I'm disgruntled. My Catholic experiences were not very happy ones.

The movie opens with Martin committing a very violent act, yet somehow throughout the movie he's a very sympathetic character. How did you keep him sympathetic while he was killing all these people?

Well, I think a lot of it was John. But to me, it's the classical thing about monsters: Karloff as Frankenstein's monster is tremendously sympathetic. King Kong is sympathetic. I think you connect with them, it's the "there but for the grace of God" thing.

Martin is even sympathetic in the sequence where he goes to kill a woman and is surprised that her lover is there, which is a remarkable scene.

That's my favorite sequence. I think it's the most successful sequence I've ever done.

I like its complexity. It's a very complex situation and you have to be watching the movie closely to get everything that happens in it. But what I like the most about it is the execution of it. It's very close to what I had on the page and I was able — again, because of the small, dedicated crew and all their cooperation — to do it, make all the shots. There are a hell of a lot of shots in that sequence. And the geography is clear, you don't get lost.

You can't do that sequence without a lot of shots and these guys moved fast and we got it. It was great. I still think it's maybe the best-executed thing that I've ever done.

What's the secret of making a complex scene like that work — on paper and when you're shooting it?

You have to have it in your head. Having been an editor, I knew "this will cut, that will cut." I think that's a big advantage.

I know that a lot of young filmmakers, particularly ones that have only done music videos where it's free-form, are baffled and the assistant director ends up choreographing the action.

What I love about the scene is that you're really pulling for Martin to get away with it. What he's doing is really pretty horrible, yet he remains sympathetic.

It's in the script, but a lot of it was John. It was implicit in the script, but John was just so perfect at it. The innocence with which he approached it was unaffected and absolutely honest. And he pulled it off.

Besides setting a script aside for a while and then coming back to it, are there tricks you use to ensure that a script is really finished?

Not really. I have a partner now, for the last ten years, Peter Grunwald, who's a wonderful editor. His dad was editor-in-chief of *Time* magazine for years and Peter's got that talent.

I will show early drafts to Peter, because he has a wonderful ability for saying "You don't need this and you don't need that." That's really what it comes down to, that's really what makes a script as far as I'm concerned — if you can be as terse as possible and yet get all the juice into it.

Of course, sometimes scripts, and the films that are made from them, seem to fail because they're too terse. But sometimes they just ramble, and you're taken into outbacks where you don't really need to be.

For example, I didn't like *Brokeback Mountain.* I thought it was a bit dull, I thought I could easily get twenty minutes out of it or more. I just thought that it rambled into areas that it didn't need to go into.

So I think the hardest thing is to have that eye and I don't necessarily have it. Sometimes I'll cling to a scene and say, "No, this is too important for the character."

For example, in *Land of the Dead*, I really fought for this one scene where John Leguizamo's character goes into an apartment and he finds a guy who has hung himself and who comes back to life right as John is trying to cut him down.

I fought for that scene; I fought for the money, the extra days to shoot it, because I thought it was important, because it was the only selfless act that John's character did in the film. And it was the only time that we saw someone die without being bitten or infected and still come back as a zombie. In the mythology, that's an important point to me. So I thought the scene was very, very important.

As it turns out, I wound up in the cutting room saying, "Lose it." And we did. There's an example of a scene that I thought right down until we were editing the movie, like three weeks before delivery, that I thought was super important and then came to realize that we didn't really need it.

That's the hardest thing: to pick out the stuff that you really don't need. Weed it out. Weed out the garden and just keep the essentials.

Do you think your experience as a film editor helps you as a writer?

I think it does, yes, tremendously. Because you know what sort of tricks you can do, what sort of transitions you can make, how you can keep the flow going without as much information. Not only editing features, but having edited documentaries that were totally unscripted.

So you begin to realize that you can really craft an experience out of what looks like a bunch of leftovers. You can make a meal out of it.

Was there anything you learned from writing *Martin* that you took to other projects?

Well, I'm sure there is. I can't put my finger on anything. This medium, it's elusive. And a lot of people don't bother to get fully involved in it. I think that my background made a difference. I used to light and shoot and edit and do the whole banana, and I think all of that helps you. So each time you go out of the gate, you learn a little more, or you learn from the last thing.

It's also a very parasitic medium. I think any aspiring filmmaker comes to the medium because of being influenced by other films and other filmmakers. And you don't get a chance to sketch. In a certain sense, I did, because I made more hours of films — industrial films, commercials, and all the other shit that we did — more hours of film that I've ever done over the thirteen features that I've made, probably by three times.

I did have that chance to sketch and try and experiment. But with narrative, today, nobody has a chance to sketch. I mean, John Ford, what did he make, 250 movies? I'm trying to get my fourteenth going and you don't have all those tricks in your pocket.

First you're a parasite. You say, "I'm going to steal this shot from Welles or from Ford or from Hawks," and you wind up stealing ideas. And then you start getting confident enough to try to invent your own shots and sequences and visual storytelling techniques. It gradually gets better and better.

I thought that in the film I made before *Land of the Dead*, a little film called *Bruiser* that nobody's seen, I was really able to choreograph some sequences in that film. It was the first time that I was really liberal with moving the camera around.

When I was working really low-budget and when I was first starting, my ass-saving technique was to just shoot a lot of coverage. If you have close-ups of everybody in the room doing the scene, you can structure the scene, cut it down, do whatever you want to it. And that's what I used to rely on. That was my mandate and that's what I did as a self-protection device.

In *Bruiser*, I didn't do that. First of all we didn't have the time. It was union and we were really running with the wolf at the door, so I just had to figure out how to play things in a master, somehow. And I wound up having to design shots where the camera moved and you got different perspectives even though it was a single shot.

You gradually get more and more confident and more and more able to do that. It's all learning and it all comes from things you've done before and knowing how it's going to work.

A lot of people tend to look down on genre films.

No kidding.

But aren't they actually harder than other films to do well?

Well, they are. I think what happens is that people start apologizing. And I think what you have to do is not apologize. "Here's the situation, guys."

I mean, if you go see *Shaun of the Dead*, man, that's just sort of balls out, "Here it is! This is the world." And no apologies, it's just straight ahead. Even though it's hilarious, it keeps a straight face in a certain sense. And that's what you have to do.

I think that's the secret of *The Exorcist* and *Jaws* and *Rosemary's Baby*, the classics of the genre, is that there's no apology. "Here's the situation."

In some ways you have to make it believable and try to make this scenario that the dead are coming back to life believable. You can't do it with science, you can't have law-givers trying to explain why it's happening. You just have to take it at face value. At least, that's what I've always tried to do. Don't spend ten minutes with scientists saying, "Well, here's exactly what's going on here."

Forget it! You don't need it. Just say, "Here's the situation," and if you stay true to it and don't fuck with that and don't violate it, then it becomes believable.

Children Shouldn't
Play with Dead Things
Bob Clark

                    ALAN

    Come, children. Uncle Alan is going to
    curdle your blood.

                    VAL

    Uncle Alan already does. Turns my
    stomach, too.

*Few directors have had a more successful, or eclectic, career than Bob Clark. And not many directors can claim as many classic motion pictures on their resumes: A classic holiday movie (*A Christmas Story*), a classic coming-of-age movie (*Porky's*), a classic horror film (*Black Christmas*), and a classic Sherlock Holmes film combined with a classic Jack the Ripper film (*Murder By Decree*).*

Children Shouldn't Play with Dead Things *may not be a classic contender, but it's a clever little horror film that uses its resources wisely. A troupe of actors, led by their insane director (Alan Ormsby) arrive on a secluded island to re-enact a ritual that brings the dead back to life. Before you can say "Boo," the dead begin to crawl out of their graves and carnage ensues.*

What point were you at in your career before you started
Children Shouldn't Play with Dead Things?

I went to college at the University of Miami and I was in theater. I had also worked in the Miami film industry in the late sixties.

I was doing a play in Miami, *A View from the Bridge*, and this man named Bobby MacDonald came to me and said, "You're my director." I had actually worked on a couple of his schlock films, films that were done for $40,000–$50,000.

I said, "Bob, what are you talking about? I don't know anything about films. I've been in some as an actor, but I don't know anything else." He said, "Don't worry about that, we have a great situation over in the Everglades, near Fort Myers."

So I got involved in writing and directing a movie called *She Man*, which was done by a guy named Charlie Broun. Charlie had a combination of a hydroponic tomato farm, a clothing factory and a movie studio, all in one. I went into the Everglades and wrote this thing called *She Man*.

I knew nothing about movies, but they said, "Don't worry, we've got everybody. We've got a great cameraman," who turned out to be a World War II Nazi cameraman who had never shot a movie and knew nothing about it. The editor was a guy named Hack, from the Fort Myers local. But I did have a guy named Harry Anderson, who was a legitimate production manager who had done a few Hitchcock films.

So I did *She Man* and it was dreadful beyond belief. At the same time we decided we would shoot *The Emperor's New Clothes*, back-to-back, so we shot that in Miami in a famous castle there, and actually got John Carradine to be in it and he was terrific.

So I did these two movies — I don't think they exist anymore — and I was determined after that that I would not work again until I understood what it was to make a movie. So, for the next four years I was a production manager and an AD, and I did every job, virtually, except cameraman.

Then, in 1971, Gary and Ken Goch and I decided we'd get some money and we'd make a film. In those days, to start your career, you either made a horror film or you did porno. I didn't want to do porno, so we chose a horror film and we decided to do it in Miami. And that became *Children Shouldn't Play with Dead Things*.

It was populated with my college buddies and chums and people we knew and we did it for $40,000. It was an homage to *Night of the Living Dead*, but more of a comic version, putting it on a bit. Actually, it wasn't really that much like *Night of the Living Dead*; we were just capitalizing on its success.

Where did the title come from?

I was just walking by a pay phone in New York and stepped in to call somebody in town and it just hit me. *Children Shouldn't Play with Dead Things*. I have no idea why it came into my head.

Instead of calling the friend in New York, I called Bob Kilgore immediately and said, "Bob, write this down: *Children Shouldn't Play with Dead Things*." And he said, "Oh my god, what a great title. That's hysterical. We couldn't do better." And that's how *Children* was born — by a little bolt out of the blue.

How did you make up the story?

It just came out of my consciousness somewhere. I took things that were familiar to me, like the theater group.

I was well trained by that time to take advantage of every discipline that we could to maximize the kind of film we could make. I wrote it for the two main locations, the cemetery and the house, plus the location on the island that overlooks the city. We had three locations total. I was very careful about that, because we only had ten days — actually, ten nights.

The remote cabin was actually in Coral Gables, a friend's house. It was in the middle of the city, in a neighborhood, but we pulled it off pretty well.

What were some of the things you learned during those previous four years that helped on this production?

Control your locations, control the number of characters. We actually had quite a few characters, but that wasn't very costly for us. The movie is fairly ambitious in terms of its action.

But the key was continuity, not having to make any moves to other locations. But there's nothing complex about that: Just make sure you have one major location.

Did the fact that Alan Ormsby knew how to do make-up help in the decision to do a zombie movie?

To some extent, yes. Alan was extremely gifted and I knew he could pull it off, and in a way that was superior to our very low budget. So that was a factor. The make-ups were pretty darned good.

I completed the script and we had read-throughs; I'm sure I made some adjustments at that point.

How do you know when a script is done and ready?

You use your training and your gut instinct. You go back over it to be sure that the plot points are clear without being labored and that there's clarity and also excitement.

That's basically what a screenplay is: a duel between clarity and pacing. No matter how complex it is, you need to understand what's going on, and then you need to have pace. And that can vary. Some films that aren't rapidly paced are still very engrossing. But those two factors, clarity and pacing, are the two critical factors.

I came from a classical background; I was a Shakespearean trained actor. I was a movie fan growing up, but not a movie fanatic. I liked movies but I wasn't obsessed with them. I didn't plan on going into theater. To be a novelist was my plan from the time I was nine years old. But the minute I got involved in films I knew that was where I would go.

Did your background as an actor help you in writing dialog and creating characters?

I think so. I'd done a number of classical plays, and doing Arthur Miller doesn't hurt anything at all. I'd done Tennessee Williams and Shakespeare, so you certainly gain something from that experience.

As a director, you've never shied away from doing different genres. In fact, that sort of your style — that you work well in any style.

I determined very early that I would be an eclectic director. If you want to be a darling of the critics, you're probably better off having a cohesive singularity to your vision. Some of our greatest directors do work that way, but I didn't want to do that. I wanted to try all the forms and set out to do that. It's in my nature to be adventurous, I think, so I've been able to do, fortunately, virtually every genre. It was a conscious decision, made from the beginning.

I started out in horror films, and it took me three films to get away from horror, because I didn't have any intention of staying in it.

I intended to be eclectic, and I intended that the style be determined by the needs of the work. The other thing I wanted to do was to have a visual style that was fresh and an approach that gave the audience a deep involvement in the film, like they were part of the adventure. I'm very concerned about the look and the texture of my films.

Even in my films that aren't necessarily designed to show off the beauty of the place, I'm still very conscious of my backgrounds and my textures; not so much that they overwhelm the audience, but that they feel part of the texture.

Are you surprised that *Children Shouldn't Play with Dead Things* is still popular today?

Yes. I did a film called *Now and Forever* a few years back and we were on the festival circuit. I was at the Atlantic City Film Festival, and we won the festival and I won best director. I got up to give a speech and it wasn't a young, hip-appearing audience. The audience was young to middle age.

I said to them, "I know I am identified with Hollywood films, but my first film was a little film shot in ten days, called *Children Shouldn't Play with Dead Things*." And this crowd broke out into huge applause, all the young people, the middle-aged ones, they all knew the movie. That flabbergasted me. After speaking to them afterwards, indeed the film is, among filmmakers, pretty well-known.

Is there anything you learned on that movie that you still use today?

Sure. I learned that you want to change your backgrounds. I like to move my characters and move my camera; not obtrusively, but to identify the world that we're in and to identify the dynamics and the immediacy of the shot.

That's probably the one common element in my work is the tendency to move the camera a great deal. I mean, I'll do the classical over-the-shoulder close-up stuff when it's appropriate, when you're interested in seeing into the eyes of the people. But even then, we move the camera gently during close-ups.

And now you're planning a re-make of *Children Shouldn't Play with Dead Things*?

I had decided that I would never re-do a film of mine. They're re-doing *Black Christmas*, and also *Dead of Night*, and *Porky's* is being re-done by Howard Stern. I have nothing to do with those.

But so many people said I should re-do *Children* and I started to think, "Well, maybe I could improve it."

I don't think I could improve *Black Christmas*, I really don't. And they want to re-do *Murder By Decree* and I won't let them. I wouldn't even begin to touch that. But with *Children* I figured out a way to do it and there's more fun to be had.

I've written one scene where this ghoul makes a pass at a girl, saying "I got it baby, I've still got it. You know you want me. I still got it." And she says, "Oh yeah?" And we see her put her hands down the front of him as he says, "Yeah, baby, I still got it," and she says, "Well, actually, you don't." And he looks down and screams, "Oh my god!"

So anyway, that's the tone, but we still keep the same story.

What's your best advice about writing?

Be truthful. Verisimilitude. You've got to find your reality, no matter how broad what you're doing is. If you're doing the Marx Brothers, it's wild, it's bizarre, but somewhere in there has to be some truth, no matter how outrageous or absurd or fantastical.

Suckers
Roger Nygard

REGGIE

Are we taking advantage of people? Let
us take a look. Your job is to sell
a car for as much as you can. The
customer's job is to buy the car for as
little as possible. Why should you feel
guilty about being better at your job
than somebody else is at theirs? If he
makes a good deal, he takes money out of
your pocket. If you make a good deal,
you take money out of his. What's the
difference?

Suckers *provides an inside look at just how much car salesman take
advantage of their customers. Written by director Roger Nygard
and stand-up comic (and former car salesman) Joe Yanetty, the
story takes us inside four consecutive Saturdays at a Los Angeles
car dealership, as Bobby Deluca (Louis Mandylor) learns the ropes
from sales manager Reggie (Daniel Benzali).*

*Nygard and Yanetty based their screenplay on Yanetty's actual
experiences as a car salesman, proving yet again that truth is,
indeed, stranger (and often funnier) than fiction.*

*(Be aware that this interview contains spoilers about key plot
points.)*

What was going on with you before *Suckers*?

I'd been jumping back and forth between narratives and documentaries. I had just finished my first documentary, *Trekkies*, and was looking for another narrative. I find that they both inform each other, and I've learned and brought techniques from one genre into the other. So *Suckers* has a very real feel, like you're right there — almost a pseudo-documentary style in the way it was shot.

That's true, although it doesn't look like one of those shaky-cam, fake documentaries that have become so popular lately.

I really can't stand that "shaky camera on purpose" style in shows like *ER*, because a documentary cameraman tries to hold the camera steady and he doesn't shake it on purpose. A good hand-held camera provides a little movement and a little energy to the shot without being obnoxious about it.

At that time I had made three movies. My first film was a one-man show, *High Strung*, a one-room comedy, written by and starring Steve Odenkirk. We made that film for about $350,000. Then my second film was a two-million-dollar action picture, *Back to Back*, for a company called Overseas Film Group. Their films are primarily foreign-sales driven.

I remember seeing *Back to Back*. There was, to put it mildly, a lot of action.

You've got to have five action set pieces, that's the rule for those sorts of movies. That's what's expected from the foreign buyers to make their foreign sales. We had at least five; we might have had six. But five is the minimum requirement.

The third movie was *Trekkies*, my first documentary, about *Star Trek* fans.

In doing *Suckers*, I was coming off of those three films, which were all very different and driving my agents crazy, because they didn't know what I was. Am I the documentary guy, am I the action guy, am I the comedy guy? So *Suckers* was a new thing, a sort of grisly dramatic comedy, I guess, with some action.

Where did the idea for *Suckers* come from?

My friend, Joe Yannetty, had written a one-man show about his experiences selling cars. I read portions of that and he told me some of the stories, and I said, "You've got to make a movie about this. These stories are incredible." So that's where it started.

Joe and I worked together writing the script, based on his experiences, which is a process for me as a screenwriter that works best. I almost always work with a writing partner. The reason is that I grew up in Minnesota with a pretty average background. I went to college, then moved to California to seek my fortune in the film business. I never got a job as a CIA agent, never went into the Marines, never became a fireman or a cop, didn't go on the road and get arrested or sell cars. You can't write about life experiences that you haven't personally lived, unless you research them extensively or partner up with someone who has lived those experiences.

My writing style is that I tend to write with people who have had interesting life experiences, but don't necessarily have the desire or the fortitude or the persistence to bring it to the screen.

Most screenwriters hate it when someone comes up to them and says, "My life would make a great movie," but it sounds like, depending on the person, you might sit down and talk to them.

That's how I operate. I think everybody has one good screenplay in them, based on their own life.

Your own life is often the first and best place to start for a screenwriter, because that's what you know — as long as you're willing to rip open your soul. You have to bare yourself to the world in order to write something that other people will be interested in reading and possibly make into a movie.

It's not easy. It's hard. You've got to write things that you wouldn't even tell your shrink. Those are the screenplays that really stand out.

So when I say that everybody has one good screenplay in them, it's if they're willing to bare their soul and write about those skeletons in the closet, those experiences.

How did you and Joe work together?

Joe and I sat in a room and would brainstorm. The brainstorming sessions would generally follow the format of me asking Joe questions and getting him to tell stories. I would write them down or tape them until we had all these anecdotes.

I took all the anecdotes and boiled each one down to one sentence, and put them on note cards and laid them all out on the floor. We'd look at them on the floor and start moving them around until we had an order that we liked.

You could do the same thing in a computer — just type slug lines and create what's known as a "beat sheet," which is a list of story beats. And you can move them around, up and down, until you have a sequence of plot points.

How did you come up with the idea of setting the story on four consecutive Saturdays?

That was because that's how the car business runs. Every Saturday there's a sales meeting. It's an inspirational meeting, a motivational meeting. It's a time for everybody to gauge where they are against everyone else, because there's always that competitive aspect.

So we broke it down that way because the industry we were writing about breaks itself down monthly and weekly. Every month they start over and the cycle begins again. The framework suggested itself to us because the arena we were writing about was based on a monthly structure.

How nervous were you about setting your whole first act at that first sales meeting?

You know, we broke a lot of structural rules with *Suckers*. And in hindsight, there is a lot I would do differently, having learned what I've learned since then and having seen how that experiment worked, where it worked and where it failed.

Part of the excitement of filmmaking is taking chances. Sometimes you're going to fail spectacularly. And we took a big chance structuring the first act that way. But I don't think it was the biggest chance we took.

What was the biggest chance?

The biggest chance in the script was doing a genre shift from the second to the third act, which many people found disconcerting. Audiences are not used to — and don't like it — when you shift from one genre to another in a movie.

Quentin Tarantino and Robert Rodriguez did it in *From Dusk 'Til Dawn*. It starts out as kind of a crime caper/road chase movie and then shifts into a monster movie, which threw a lot of people. I think that film was less successful than it might have been because people just don't like genre shifts. They want to know what the genre is from the beginning of the movie, what's the level of reality of the story, and then you have to stick to it.

If you don't stick to one genre, then you're either taking a chance or doing an art film.

You did put some signposts along the way that there was an undercurrent in this story, that an outside world was pushing itself into the car dealership.

That's true and that helps, it definitely helps to give signs and signals as to what's going to come and ease the audience in that direction. But it was still, I think, too big of a shift for a lot of the audience.

Personally, I like taking those chances, but in hindsight, I think if we had just stuck with car salesmen and not gotten into the crime aspect, it would have been a more successful venture. Creatively, I think it was more rewarding to take a chance and see what you can get away with.

In your defense, there have been stories of car dealerships acting as fronts for money laundering and drugs.

Yes, everything in the movie is based on a nugget of truth. I would say that 80 to 90% of that movie is almost verbatim dialogue and incidents that Joe experienced personally. The rest are things that we researched.

For instance, we knew that there was a dealership in New Jersey that had been busted for running $600,000 of coke through their dealership every month, and that's partly where we got the idea for the ending.

Did you consider other possible climaxes and endings?

I wish we had considered more, but as soon as we unearthed that story, it felt right to us. Again, looking back, yeah, I think we could have finished the movie just as engagingly and kept it in the car sales realm, without having to go into the crime and drug-trafficking realm.

But then you would have lost the opportunity to have virtually all of the film's characters shoot each other simultaneously in a very small room.

Yes, and we would have lost my favorite line of the movie: "You're so beyond fucked, you couldn't catch a bus back to fucked."

You kind of fall in love with some things, but in the editing room you spend time killing your babies. That's the term for it. Sometimes you have to cut out the things you're in love with for the good of the whole.

Were there any things you hated to lose?

Suckers was so low-budget that everything we shot is basically in the film. I don't think there's a single scene cut out, and we didn't do any re-shoots, either, which is typical for most movies. It was shot in three weeks on an empty car dealership that was then torn down about a month after we finished.

So that limited your re-shoots a bit.

Right!

What did you do at the writing stage to keep the shooting budget down?

There are a lot of things you have to consider when writing a low-budget script, because these are key considerations when the film is made. First of all, fewer locations, and secondly, fewer characters.

Every time you have a new location, it's a company move, which is very costly. And every new character is somebody who gets a residual check when the movie is released and airing in ancillary markets.

We had a pretty large cast in *Suckers*. I think we had thirty-odd characters, which is a lot. The majority of our budget went to pay their SAG minimum wages. That's why you see a lot of movies with three or four characters in contained locations.

A first-time or novice screenwriter will write scripts that take place all over the world with hundreds of characters and it's just not realistic unless it's a hundred-million-dollar blockbuster.

The more you keep budget in mind when you're writing a script, the more likely it is that that script can be made. You don't want your creativity to be restrained, but then as you're refining and re-writing you need to consider options like combining characters. Sometimes there's no reason to have this other character — give all those lines to one of your leads, because the more lines your lead character has, the more castable it will be.

Did you have any actors in mind while you wrote?

We thought of the real people that it's based on at the car dealership where Joe worked. I went and spent some time with Joe and met all those people. Once the script was done, then we started making our wish list of people to cast.

Everybody in the movie came in and read for their part. Part of the downside of casting "name" actors, which you need for distribution, is that you don't know what you're getting until they show up. You hope they're going to fit the part well. But if they come in and read for the part, then you already know what you're getting.

When you did your research at the car dealership, did they know what you were up to?

Oh, yeah, and they were excited to talk about what they do. I rarely find people unwilling to talk, whether I'm making documentaries or researching characters for a narrative screenplay. It's harder to get them to shut up, actually, then to get them started.

I went to several dealerships with my tape recorder and talked to people and asked them to tell me stories. People love to talk about themselves.

In hindsight, what other things would you have done differently?

Besides being more wary of doing a genre shift, I think I would have stuck to a more traditional structure for the beginning. It's really tempting to try to invent a new genre and to write something that's never been written and break all the rules, but the problem is that audiences don't want that. They have either become accustomed to — or it's just innate in storytelling and human enjoyment of storytelling — to like a three-act structure and what you might call the conventions of screenwriting.

That's why Syd Field's book, *Screenplay: The Foundations of Screenwriting* and Robert McKee's book, *Story: Substance, Structure, Style and the Principles of Screenwriting*, are valuable, because they explore and lay out for you the conventions of screenwriting.

And I think they're right, because if you're going to build a house, you can't invent a whole new framework and foundation. You really have to follow the fundamentals of building the foundation and framework, and then you can get creative with the cosmetic look of the house. That's where you get creative, but you have to learn the fundamentals and follow them if you want to be a successful screenwriter.

There are art films and part of the job of an art film is to teach us about the rules by violating the rules. But don't expect to make a living being an artist. There are a lot of starving artists out there.

Did you do any readings of the script while you were working on drafts?

I have done readings with some of my scripts, but we did not do a script reading on *Suckers* until we had the cast together and did a reading with them, which was so much fun that it makes me want to do that every time.

I think it's very valuable to do script readings. You see things that work and things that don't work. You see some of the surprises that will pop up later on the set, and the more you can deal with them before you get there, the more time and money you'll save.

Did you have much rehearsal?

Almost none. A half a day with the main actors, where we went over the scenes.

Daniel Benzali, who played Reggie, doesn't like to rehearse. I mean, he likes to rehearse on his own; he would be in his trailer, pounding his lines over and over and over again, driving Louis Mandylor in the trailer next door crazy.

Louis hates to rehearse. He feels he's more natural and fresh if he doesn't have the lines down, whereas Daniel is like a machine.

Which he kind of had to be, because he had so many lines in his sales meetings.

Have you bought a car since you made *Suckers*?

Yeah, and Joe came with me. It was fun. Everything was exactly as expected. They never stop negotiating until you get up to leave. You have to get up to leave and go out the door and then they'll say, "Wait, wait!" Or they'll let you leave and then they'll call on the phone. Until they are certain you're done, they will keep negotiating with you.

Speaking of done, how did you know when the script was done and ready to be shot?

Every time you feel that the script is done, put it down for a week or a month, and then come back to it and you'll see that it's not done. Because it's never done.

I would re-write everything I've done if it wasn't already shot. A screenplay is never done. Writing is re-writing. You're constantly re-writing. On the set, we were re-writing scenes and trying to come up with funnier lines and better ways to say and do something.

What was the biggest lesson you took away from *Suckers*?

The biggest one we already discussed, which is not to violate the rules so dramatically, which we did with the genre shift. That was my biggest lesson.

The corollary was to keep writing, always be writing. Like ABC from *Glengarry Glen Ross* — ABC, Always Be Closing. ABW — Always Be Writing.

The script I'm working on right now is something where I hatched the idea for it about three or four years ago, but I didn't know what to do with it. And it took three or four years of gestating within my brain before it started to form into a shape. It was an idea I told to one of my writing partners and he really sparked to it and so it moved itself to the top of the pile.

That's why you need to have a lot of ideas and a lot of projects and a lot of things going, because I think your subconscious is working on these projects at different paces. The more you've got going, the more likely one of them is going to sprout.

What are the advantages of working with a writing partner?

One of the best advantages of working with a writing partner is that you force each other to write. Deadlines are important, that's why we function well with deadlines.

There's an old saying, "If you want to get something done, give the task to a busy person." When you're busy, you get more done, and a writing partner keeps you busy, because you write some pages and you bounce it over to him or her. And then she bounces it back and it's in your court and it forces you to address it.

You brainstorm with each other, you feed off each other. We try to make each other laugh; I'll put stuff in a script that's never going to make it to the final draft, just to get a rise out of him.

Is there a downside to having a writing partner?

You gotta split the money when you sell the script. But it's well worth it. Fifty percent of nothing is nothing.

Were you still writing while editing?

Editing is the final re-write of the script. You're always re-writing and moving sentences around, sometimes words and sometimes just syllables within words. You pluck and replace. You can get actors to pronounce things differently by moving their syllables around, and it's all toward getting the most expedient way to say something. Good writing is saying something as concisely as possible.

I worked for two years writing and editing promos for TNT and that was a great exercise, because it taught me to be as concise as possible. When you have a thirty-second or fifteen-second spot and you've got to tell a whole story, you're forced to think economically.

A writer should think economically while writing a screenplay. Even though you have ninety minutes, you should treat every second of those ninety minutes just as judiciously as if you were doing a thirty-second commercial.

Show it, don't say it, whenever you can.

Start every scene as late as possible.

Cut out the walks. Nobody wants to watch somebody walk from one door to the other in a movie. You cut that stuff out, because there's no information there.

If there's no information that informs the story in a shot or a line of dialogue, it has to go. Unless it's hilariously funny. That's my exception. If something's really engaging or funny, it can stay, even if it doesn't move the story forward.

What movies have inspired you?

There are so many. *Terms of Endearment* I think is one of the greatest movies of all time, because it is a gut-wrenching drama and a hilarious comedy, all at once. It's so successful in both realms. It's a movie that amazes me. Real life is funny, real life involves drama and funny moments, and so I think those two coexist well when done well.

Evil Dead, Part II, which I think is the *Citizen Kane* of its decade because Sam Raimi invented a style of filmmaking that no one had done before. Now you see it all the time. Orson Welles invented a lot of shots and filmmaking styles that you didn't see before *Citizen Kane*, and so did Sam Raimi with *Evil Dead, Part II*.

The Hunger, similarly, introduced a new form of editing to movies. It was Tony Scott's first film and he was coming from commercials, so he was bringing that sensibility to moviemaking. He used flash forwards and flashbacks and fractured time structures, and that's where my introduction to fractured time structure in editing came from.

Dawn of the Dead was a very influential movie. George Romero is my hero; he influenced me greatly with that movie. It's so funny and such great social commentary as well as being brilliantly gory.

Any advice to screenwriters who are starting a low-budget project?

The most important thing in any movie is that you make the audience feel something. They have to laugh or cry. Or both, preferably, like in *Terms of Endearment*. If the movie doesn't do that at some point, it's not going to succeed to nearly the same degree that a movie can succeed with an audience when it's done well.

That's the most important thing: your work has to touch people in some way. And how do you know it does that? Because it has to touch you, first, when you're creating it and writing it.

That's why if you bare your soul and write about those things in your life that make you cry when you think about them, because they're so painful or so funny or both, then you know that if you feel that way, an audience will feel that way.

How did the car salesmen react to the finished movie?

Once *Suckers* was complete, we screened it for two of the car salesman that Joe worked with. It was fascinating to watch them watching this movie. They were just cringing in their seats in pain.

Afterward they said, "Yep, you got him," referring to their boss, who we named Reggie in the movie. They saw themselves and everybody else they knew and they found it all very difficult to watch.

Once the film was released — and you can see this for yourself if you go onto Amazon.com or the Internet Movie Database (imdb.com) and look up *Suckers* and look at the comments from people — most of the comments are from car salesmen who have found the movie. Many of them say that they now show that film at their car dealerships in their training meetings. It's become a motivational movie for car salesmen. They're the cult audience for this movie.

If you go to a car dealership and ask a car salesman, "Hey, have you heard of the film *Suckers*?", they'll usually freak out. I think it's like mobsters watching *The Godfather*. It doesn't make gangsters look that good, but they feel a little bit glamorized just by having had a spotlight shone on them, even if they may not look that flattering in the spotlight.

If you're buying a car, tell them you've seen *Suckers*. It could help you save a couple grand.

Repo Man
Alex Cox

                    BUD

"I shall not cause harm to any vehicle
nor the personal contents thereof, nor
through inaction let that vehicle or the
personal contents thereof come to harm."
That's what I call The Repo Code, kid.
Don't forget it. Etch it in your brain.
Not many people have got a code to live
by anymore.
                (a beat)
Hey, look at that. Look at those
assholes over there. Ordinary fucking
people. I hate 'em.

                    OTTO

Me too.

                    BUD

What do you know? See, an ordinary
person spends his life avoiding tense
situations. A Repo Man spends his life
getting into tense situations.

Repo Man *defies description, by design. It's a punk rock comedy,
a retro sci-fi flick, a buddy film, a social satire, and one of the best
films to come out of the 1980s ... or any other decade, actually.*

*Writer/director Alex Cox skillfully transcends genres as his aimless
hero, Otto (Emilio Estevez) morphs from feckless punker to career
repo man to intergalactic traveler, continually demonstrating the
mantra of the trade: The life of a repo man is always intense.*

What point were you at in your career before this project?

I had written two scripts for money, one for United Artists and one for the director Adrian Lyne, and made a short film (forty minutes) at UCLA.

Where did the idea for *Repo Man* come from?

Various sources. People I'd met in L.A., a repo man with whom I rode around, punks from that scene.

Do you begin with story, character or theme?

Urr... it depends on the project. If it's a bio-pic, it's the character.

In the case of *Repo Man,* probably theme: the imminence of nuclear war, the superficiality and stupidity of almost everything else.

The theme for the film seems to hinge on "the lattice of coincidence." How important is having a theme before you start to write?

It depends on the project. *Repo Man*'s theme probably changed when the ending was re-written near the end of the shoot and the destruction of L.A. replaced with the transcendental flying car.

How much research did you do and how did that help you write the script?

Just riding around with a repo man, going to punk gigs, and a monthly subscription to *The Bulletin of the Atomic Scientists.*

Did you outline the whole story before you started writing the script?

No, I just started writing scenes and dialogue.

What's your writing process?

Write until it's finished. Then re-write it. There were fourteen drafts of *Repo Man*. The first one probably took a month or so. Some later ones just a few days.

Was it always planned to be a low-budget film?

Yes, and much lower budget. Around $120K at one stage, of which $50K — our salaries — would have been deferred.

I understand that there was talk at one time of doing *Repo Man* as a student film. Were you a student at the time, and how would you have pulled that off?

(Producers Peter) McCarthy, (Jonathan) Wacks and I had all been UCLA students. We formed a company with the best of the UCLA critical studies profs, Bob Rosen — Edge City Productions — for the purpose of making features. The idea was that I would re-enroll to access the facilities, which I did.

How did you connect with Executive Producer Michael Nesmith, and what attracted him to the film?

We met him via another producer, Harry Gittes. Nes liked motor-themed movies, comic books (the first four pages of the script were a comic) and had had some experience with repo men in his post-Monkees days.

Do you write with specific actors in mind?

I thought about the guys in the band Fear for the four repo men. I didn't know them personally, but had formed an impression by seeing them on stage.

What's the value of going after "name" actors (like Emilio Estevez) for a low-budget movie and do you think it's worth the trouble?

It gives confidence to the financiers. Without the financiers, no film. So in that sense it's certainly worth the trouble.

At a certain point, do you feel that as a writer you give up a character and the actor takes him over?

Oh, yes. Because the writer has to think of twenty or thirty characters, and the director of many more things besides. The actor only needs to think about his/her part (we hope).

How did you come up with the idea to use all "generic" food?

We couldn't get any product placement! Apart from Ralph's Supermarket, who gave us the generic stuff, and the Car Freshener Company.

Music plays such a large role in the film. Did you determine any of the music at the scripting stage?

Only *TV Party*, which Otto sings on camera.

How do you know when a script is done?

When they give you the money to shoot it.

Did you do readings before you shot? If so, did the script change due to the readings?

I wrote a couple of audition pieces for the characters of Miller and Lite. The actors liked them, and both ended up being incorporated into the script. There was also one script reading prior to the shoot.

Do you show drafts to people during the process?

Of course — that's what they're for.

How do you process and use feedback?

Keep changing the script until it attracts the actors and the money. If it doesn't, after a certain amount of time, give up.

Do you ever put the script away for a while after finishing a draft?

Put it away if you don't like it or can't figure out a way to raise money for it. Once put away, rarely is it retrieved.

Did the story change during shooting or editing at all?

Yes, especially with the ending, and with Dennis Dolan, our wise editor, and his input.

What's the value of being open to change during production?

It depends on the project. If the script is perfect, it might be a big mistake.

What did you learn from working on that script that you still use today?

Nothing that I learned writing or directing *Repo Man* was of any particular value. It is always the same struggle, always the same problems, always the same tedious and irritating search for money.

What's the best advice about writing that you've ever received?

Set yourself a deadline and keep to it. Get to the end before you go back and start tweaking the beginning.

Any words of advice to a writer working on a low-budget script?

Don't waste your money on screenwriting software. If you can't set two tabs and remember to capitalize character names, find an easier job — actor or producer.

With Otto you created an essentially passive main character — which screenwriting books and seminars tell us not to do. How did you make it work?

Pay no attention to screenwriting books or seminars. They are as useless as screenwriting software and almost as damaging as "professional script doctors."

Write what's on your mind. Otto had to be a blank page or he couldn't have made the transition from rebel to reactionary so effortlessly.

What's your darkest memory from *Repo Man*?

It was a pretty happy experience. Miserable relations with my girlfriend, probably. Like everyone from UCLA, she too had aspirations to be a director.

What's your favorite memory of working on *Repo Man*?

Sy Richardson! The best actor I have ever worked with and one of the finest people, too.

What movies have inspired you?

Citizen Kane, Wages of Fear, The Mattei Affair, Yojimbo, Deuxieme Souffle, Killer of Sheep, Madadayo, The Wild Bunch, For a Few Dollars More, King Kong (original version).

Repo Man mixes a lot of genres and broke a lot of ground for filmmakers who came later. What's the value of mixing genres the way you did?

It's more fun. But it tends to annoy critics, who pretend to enjoy it sometimes, but are deeply conservative in their wizened little hearts.

CHAPTER SIX

Love
Stories

The love story — Boy Meets Girl — has been a movie staple
since the first silent films unspooled at Nickelodeons.

Giving that cliché a twist can set your story
apart, while also helping it connect with the
audience in a new and different way.

The small sample represented here takes the love story
in three very different directions: from an illicit affair
... to loving siblings ... to an uncle who learns to love
(or does he?) with the help of his visiting nephew.

Each of these screenwriters used their own twist
on the classic format of the love story to make
their screenplay unique and memorable.

Love Letters
Amy Holden Jones

                    ANNA

I saw that picture of you upstairs. You
had long hair.

                    OLIVER

1971. I was a lot younger. How old were
you then?

                    ANNA

Eleven.

                    OLIVER
                    (a beat)

Wow.

Love Letters *is an anomaly: It's a dramatic, heart-felt, non-exploit-ative feature produced by, of all people, Roger Corman. Written and directed by Amy Holden Jones (who would go on to write* Mystic Pizza *and* Indecent Proposal*), the film stars Jamie Lee Curtis as a young radio DJ who enters into an affair with an older — and married — man.*

Give me a snapshot of your background before you wrote and directed *Love Letters*.

I was young, for one thing. I had re-written and directed one feature for Roger Corman, *Slumber Party Massacre*. I had edited several features, and had been a documentary filmmaker.

Roger wanted me to do another exploitation film. He also distributed the Fellini pictures and the Truffaut pictures and so he had an art house distribution network. And it was just the beginning of home video and all that money. So I convinced him that if he made a film for that art house outlet and for home video, that it would make back its money.

I wrote the film on spec. I pitched the idea to him and he agreed to the idea.

His basic theory on low-budget filmmaking is one that I think is still true to this day. He felt you could make a film about just about anything, but there had to be some sort of commercial hook. I could write what he would term an art house movie, what would now be termed a festival movie, but it had to have a saleable quality to it. And by that he meant a degree of humor, sex or violence. Many of the major successful independent films have one of those qualities. Tarantino pictures, for example, have them all.

Love Letters is not a very typical Corman film.

It's the only art house film he ever made, actually.

How did Slumber Party Massacre come about?

Well, that was kind of interesting. I had come out of documentary films and couldn't make a living in them. In those days, it was not the big scene it is now. I had won the American Film Institute student film festival with a documentary. Martin Scorsese was one of the judges of that festival and he used me as his assistant on *Taxi Driver* and then introduced me to Corman.

I had no money and I had to make a living, so I became a film editor. I worked for a while as a film editor and was beginning to get successful at it. I realized that if I keep this up, I'm going to be typed as a film editor. I did several smaller movies, one for MGM and a small Hal Ashby movie, and I was going to do *E.T.* for Spielberg.

I thought, I'll be a film editor unless I make a movie, so I went back to Roger Corman, who I had edited a film for when I was twenty-two years old. I went back and said, "What would I have to do to be a director?" And Roger looked at the documentary and it didn't show him enough about what he wanted, because it was an art documentary in a way. He said, "You have to show me that you can do what I do."

I had never written anything, so I was looking for an existing script. I went into his library of scripts, scripts that he hadn't made, and I took several of them. I read one called *Don't Open the Door* by Rita Mae Brown. And it had a prologue that was about eight pages long. It had a dialog scene, a suspense scene and an action scene.

I rewrote the scenes somewhat to make it better, and then I got short ends from shooting projects — my husband was a cinematographer. My neighbor was a soundman. We borrowed some lights, used our own house. I did the special effects, and I got UCLA theater students to act in it.

We spent three days and shot those first eight pages. Then I put them together at night on Joe Dante's system — he was doing *The Howling*. I would work at night, after hours, on his Movieola and he gave me some temp music cues.

Then I dropped off this nine-minute reel for Roger that had a dialog scene, a suspense scene and an action/horror scene, to show him that I could do those three different kinds of things which make up an exploitation movie.

He called me up and had me come in and asked me how much it had cost me to do it. And I said it cost about $2,000, which is what it had cost. He said, "You have a future in the business," and asked me how much I would need to direct the rest of the script. The truth was, I had never read the rest of the script, all I had read was the first eight pages. So I just, out of the air, said "$200,000." And he said, "Let's do it. You're directing this movie."

I then finished reading the script and it was a complete mess.

I just took a leap. I called Spielberg and told him the situation and he was kind enough to release me from editing *E.T.* I rewrote *Slumber Party Massacre* in about four weeks as I cast it. And, indeed, we made it for $200,000.

What steps did you take to re-write it?

I rewrote it to be producible. Once you know how little money you have and what the situation is before re-writing it, that focuses your mind — a lot. You don't go writing scenes at a football game with thousands of extras.

You start to think very logically about what you can do and what amount of time you can do it in. And my background as a film editor and a documentary filmmaker certainly helped.

Did you end up using any of the prologue that you shot on your own?

No, we never did, because none of the actors were Screen Actors Guild (SAG) and in the end we had to have SAG actors, so we had to toss it, which was too bad. But we didn't really need it, as it turned out.

Where did the story for *Love Letters* come from?

My husband and I had written each other love letters. We had been apart after we first met; we met on *Taxi Driver*. He was the cinematographer and I was Scorsese's assistant. And then we were apart for quite a while. I moved to the west coast and he was on the east coast. So we wrote letters. That was four or five years before.

I had our daughter when I was twenty-six and did *Slumber Party Massacre* when I was twenty-seven. I was casting around for an idea for an art film and I came upon those letters. And I thought, well this is really interesting. What would happen if our daughter someday read all of our love letters? How would that affect her?

At the same time, I saw a movie called *Shoot the Moon*, which was about an extramarital affair and the traumas of the married man dealing with his wife and the girlfriend. I thought at the time, man have I seen this a zillion times. Forever I've seen the point of view of the man, torn between his wife and the girlfriend. You see it today in *Match Point*, for example. It's done over and over and over again.

But I had never seen the story of the girlfriend and what it was like for her. I put that together with the love letters and thought it would be interesting if someone came upon the love letters and realized that their parents had had an extramarital affair; if the love letters were not in fact between her mother and father, as ours were, but between the mother and a lover.

In other words, what would happen if you were confronted with an understanding of a time period in your parents' life which you never really understood — none of us have a real idea of what our parents were like in their twenties. How would that affect your life? And I thought it would be interesting if that then thrust her into an affair with a married man, trying to replicate what she saw her mother had.

Basically, it was designed to be a movie about what happens to the woman outside of the marriage, who in fiction is usually painted as a terrible villain and often is a victim who gets left in the end.

Were you writing to a specific budget?

No, but I knew I had to make it inexpensive and one of the cheap ways to do that is a limited number of locations, because every company move takes up an enormous amount of time.

You see this a lot on television today. You have something like *ER* or *The West Wing*, where they're wandering around those same halls over and over and over, and they're talking and talking and talking and talking. What they're doing is eating up page count.

That is a much faster thing to shoot than it is to shoot activities where people move from place to place.

If there's four different scenes in two pages, you have four company moves, where you have to move the entire company, re-set-up, re-light, re-do everything. And the company move itself takes half the day.

Slumber Party Massacre was all shot between a school and two houses, which were side by side. That was it for the locations, so once we had shot the ten pages that took place in the school, we were into those two houses for the rest of the twenty-eight-day shoot.

Love Letters had many more locations than that, but basically they were all in Venice. My own house is the main location, so I didn't have to pay for it. We were living in it at the time. So that kept the cost down an awful lot.

Why did you structure the film as a flashback?

I was doing an art film and unlike most people who seem today to only set out to do art films, I had been working in big commercial movies, like *Taxi Driver* and the two pictures that I had cut.

I wasn't fancying myself to be Fellini or anything like that. But I went and read all the screenplays of Harold Pinter, believe it or not, because I felt that this would be high art, and there are some great screenplays in book form by Harold Pinter. Probably there was something in there that inspired the flashbacks, would be my guess. It's certainly an overused device now.

It was originally called *My Love Letters*. One of the big decisions you make in writing a script is point of view. Multiple points of view are more complicated for a novice writer than one person's point of view. So a lot of debut films tend to follow one point of view.

For example, *Rushmore*. They're often coming-of-age stories or single person stories that have some sort of personal quality. *The*

Squid and the Whale is another good example. You have scenes with the parents without the son there, but it's basically that son's story. The way he views his parents is the sensibility of that movie.

Although you term *Love Letters* an art film, it's not a leisurely film. It gets up and running very quickly.

Well, I was a ruthless editor. I think of all the things I've done, the thing I was best at was as a film editor. That sounds like braggadocio, but what I mean is that I was better at it than I am as a writer or a director. It really suited my sensibility. I like things to move. To this day, I'm always thinking, "Why didn't I lift that out, why didn't I move it along?" I like to take an audience on a journey and go.

I think *Love Letters* is an interesting early film, compared to stuff I did later. It changed the way I work to a degree, because I came to see that it lacked humor. I don't enjoy many serious, dramatic movies that don't have, occasionally, some humor in them. I find that it can be too lugubrious.

Crash is a good example of a really wonderful, complicated arty, sophisticated movie, but it's also quite funny.

Life is funny, and I think it's a common mistake that people make doing their first features, to just be so terribly serious about themselves or their subject matter.

Well, the main character is clearly depressed and that affects the tone.

Well, there is that. Her situation was pretty bad. But when you screen it with an audience, you saw that they really enjoyed the scenes with Bud Cort and Amy Madigan a lot, and you realize that an audience really appreciates some relief from it. I mean, Hitchcock knew that: Instead of unrelentingly going in one direction, provide some emotional relief.

How much backstory did you create for the characters? In particular, I'm thinking about the relationship between Anna (Jamie Lee) and her father, where there appears to be a *lot* going on, but it's not really talked about.

I did create a lot of backstory for that. Roger Corman made everyone who directed for him take acting lessons, which I had never had even the faintest interest in. He made all the directors who worked for him take acting lessons with a wonderful old teacher, Jeff Corey, who was a blacklisted actor who taught.

I would say those acting lessons are what enabled me to write. I didn't really ever study writing or think about writing or have any interest in writing. I was interested in non-fiction stuff, like documentaries, not fiction. I wasn't interested in theater, wasn't a film buff. But when I took those acting lessons, I discovered that the process that the actor goes through was different from what I thought it was and that it's essentially the same one that a writer goes through.

It's not like you pretend to be the person. You find inside yourself some part of you that could be that person. It could be an axe murderer, but we've all wanted to kill somebody at some point.

And once you do that with every single character, you try to inhabit their skin and then you sort of free-form write from that person's point of view. You're not standing outside that person and thinking, "What would this person say?" It's much better if you are taking the place of that person, trying to feel the sort of things that they would feel, putting yourself into that person's position.

Anna's relationship with her father was pretty crucial in motivating her to do what she did. Instead of being angry when she found out her mother had an affair, she was relieved for her, because the mother had this loveless marriage. So Anna's basic feeling was that maybe she should be taking a chance, do something that is not typically considered the right thing to do, because it might be the right thing to do.

Do you start with a theme?

This is one of the few that I didn't start with a theme. I think I started with the situation and probably anger — anger's a good place to write from.

I was angry at seeing yet another movie from the husband's point of view, about how tough it was for him when he had an extra-marital affair.

That was an era that many people don't remember so much now, but *all* movies were from the male point of view. And that same anger on my part was partially behind *Mystic Pizza*, which was the next thing I wrote. At that time there were endless — and I mean endless — comedies, coming-of-age stories about a bunch of guys. Every studio did them all the time. It was the most durable genre and no one had ever done it about women.

Mystic Pizza was specifically designed to be my *Diner*. I hoped to direct it and expected to direct it and wrote if for myself to direct. And it is, in many ways, a female *Diner*. It's about similar issues.

Did Corman have precise direction on the amount of nudity in the film?

Yes. He wants sex, violence, or humor. He actually told me that lovemaking wasn't so much required as nudity. And he didn't mind if she could just be lounging around the house nude, but there had to be nudity. He had to have some way to sell the thing.

It's actually the one thing that troubles me about it. I find some of the nudity really gratuitous. But it was the price we paid to get it made.

I was really impressed with the simplicity of the Polaroid scene. It's a lock-down shot, we don't see the couple, we only see each Polaroid photo he takes of her as he drops it

into the shot. It said a lot about the relationship, but it was also very cheap to shoot.

That's one of my favorite scenes. That's a really good example of how you come up with stuff. Writing for a lower budget really focuses your mind. It doesn't necessarily mean that you're sacrificing quality.

I see so many really big budget movies, where they've had everything to spend and have covered everything sixty ways from sideways, but they never did the hard thinking about what was important in the scene. Because they had the time, they just threw spaghetti at the wall and covered everything. As a result, they never thought about what was actually going on.

Another example of writing to a budget was your staging of the funeral scene. Instead of showing the whole funeral, with extras and lighting and all, you put the scene outside the church, after the funeral, which was cheaper to shoot.

Yes. You don't have to light the interior, it's a simple exterior. And the church that we selected was within a couple miles of all the other locations. So even if the company had to move, it wasn't far. The pool-playing scene was shot less than half a mile from that church. And the house she lives in is less than a mile from there. So when we did have to move, we didn't have to go very far.

And when we were at a location, we'd shoot out the whole location. When we were in the back bedroom of the house, we shot everything that takes place there. Then we'd shoot everything that takes place in the living room of the house. You shoot everything that takes place in or around the house, then you move. Moving does eat up the most time.

So you were literally writing for locations you knew you'd be using?

Yeah, I think writing for locations is a good way to go. I really do.

I remember being conscious when I wrote *Mystic Pizza* that it would cost more money because there were more locations, that it was a certain type of town. It had one scene that I knew would be very expensive, where there's a drawbridge and a boat.

Did you write the love letters that are read in the script while you wrote the script?

Yes. They were sort of finessed and re-written. I discovered how audiences pick up narration. They don't understand it unless it's extremely clear and simple. If it's convoluted it's hard to understand when you don't see a person talking at the same time.

Do you show drafts to friends while you're writing?

It depends on the script. I don't show them partial drafts. I usually do a full draft and it's a very select group of people that I might show it to.

It's a dangerous thing, because not everybody gives good notes and everybody has a different take. There was nobody giving notes on *Love Letters*, except for Roger saying we needed more nudity. That one was one of the purest of them all.

Usually if I show a script to five people, I will pay a lot of attention to repeating comments. So if three or four of the five people say "The end doesn't work for me," then I know the end doesn't work. If one of the five says "It doesn't work for me," and four of the five say it's fine, then it's less of an issue. You do have to listen to other people's opinions. An awful lot of people fall in love with their own material when they really shouldn't.

More people should get actors together to read their scripts. That's a luxury you get when you're making a movie, you get your table read and you can re-write after that. And you learn so much when you have your first read-through.

I've done a read-through on all the films, except *Slumber Party Massacre*. It's really useful. And there are actors all over the place who will do it for nothing, who just love to come and perform.

Did you get the cast you had in mind when writing *Love Letters*?

No, I didn't get anybody that I had in mind, except for Amy Madigan. I wasn't necessarily thinking of Jamie. She fell in love with the script, and she was a star at the time, off the *Halloween* movies.

I think my first choice was Meg Tilly. I was very lucky she fell out, because she was way too soft, really, for the part. Casting is something you kind of learn as you go along with directing. And Jamie was wonderful for it. She's just marvelous in the movie.

James Keach was not at all the first choice. We went to various people and had another actor, who shall remain nameless, who backed out. He was worried about doing a low-budget movie, he was a bigger-name guy who also really responded to the script. He backed out, inexplicably, seven days before we started shooting. He was quite handsome and he and Jamie had really wonderful sexual chemistry. So it was kind of a shame when he backed out. But what can you do?

Keach was a late replacement. It was quite difficult to find a guy at that time period — and I think it's still difficult today — to find someone who will work as the second banana in a movie where the leads are women. They don't like that; they like to be the lead.

Did you do any previews of the movie before it was finished?

No, we did not preview it at all. Roger trusted his own judgment and he was wonderful about it, actually, both for *Slumber Party Massacre* and *Love Letters*. He decided I knew what I was doing and he left me alone. I don't think he made any changes at all, maybe a couple little trims here and there. He would take over whole movies from people who didn't know what they were doing. But he liked the movie and he was proud of it.

He opened it in Los Angeles and New York first, and got mixed reviews. He was kind of heartbroken at that. Then somehow, and

I don't remember how, Siskel and Ebert got it and reviewed it and gave it a rave. That encouraged him in his own opinion and he gave it a limited release. But truly its life has pretty much been on cassette or on television.

What did you learn on this script that you took to other projects?

First was not to take myself too seriously and put in more humor.

The other thing was painful at the time and this probably still happens to people. The movie is kind of sincere, and you take a big risk when you do dramas, because if it's not really good or if they're female-driven, reviewers make fun of them. The chick film, the weepie, and so on. They look down on them, whereas I think the equivalent of a chick film for guys is a Bruce Willis action film. It's equally stupid, it just has testosterone instead of estrogen.

Your heart is on your sleeve a lot with a film like *Love Letters*. You're pouring yourself into it in a way that's very personal. And when it's attacked it can be very painful in a way that doesn't really happen with a genre movie. That's a negative lesson, because it can make you afraid to take a chance and that's bad. You have to really learn to take those risks with your heart, I think.

There are several big directors working today who are in the later days of their careers who don't take risks of any kind anymore. They have big-budget movies and they are constantly covering themselves in the commerciality of those movies, more than they did in their early work, and not putting inner passion into it. Either the passion is gone or they are too afraid of failure.

You can't really be that afraid of failure. In writing the script and in going forward with it, I think I had a wonderful youthful exuberance that would be hard to duplicate today probably.

Any advice to writers who are working in the low-budget universe?

Well, it's a different market in this day and age. It's a good era, in a way, for writers starting out on a low-budget project, because you can actually make a movie for almost nothing.

I wish that I'd had the technology that young writers have now, because you can take all kinds of risks without risking all that money, if you are bold enough to write and start shooting.

I think the main thing that is still true today that was true then is that as you write you have to both tap into your heart but you also have to be aware of the very practical side of what it all costs and also what sells. It's an interesting mix.

The world is full of festival movies that never get out or go anywhere. If people are trying to break into Hollywood movies and bigger movies, not make something personal that they're going to put up on the Internet, they have to look at the commerciality of their subject matter. They have to fit what they're trying to say into a framework that is in some form entertaining for people. It has to be meaningful or moving or exciting or funny or dramatic. It can't just be what you'd tell your shrink, you know what I mean?

People perhaps don't realize that at festivals today, where all the agents go and circulate, they're looking for the movie about the couple who are left out to the sharks when they were diving. They're not looking for the next *Love Letters*, unfortunately.

If you're trying to break into Hollywood, you have to be aware of something commercial in the project. Take a look at some of the things that have sold out of festivals. For example, *Hustle & Flow*. It's about a pimp. It's about sex. And money. That's an easy sell.

How do you write for a budget without cutting off the creative process?

There are ways to shoot big stuff so that it doesn't necessarily cost as much. If a car explodes in your script and you really want a car to explode and you don't have the money, you can go right to

217

the edge with the car, swish pan around, see the person's face and make an explosion that impacts that person and throws them off their feet and then find the hulk of a car. If it's done well, you'll have the same effect as if you saw the car blow up.

There are ways to get around it and sometimes there are cleverer ways than blowing up a car. People have seen most things already, in special effects. Looking at somebody's reaction to what happened or looking at the aftermath of what happened or looking at it from a totally different point of view, there are a lot of different ways to see something. You don't have to eliminate it, you can imagine a different way to see it, too.

What's your best piece of advice to someone starting a script?

Nobody does what I tell most people to do and that's to read a lot of scripts. That's the thing that has helped me the most in my career.

I remember when I first had to write a horror movie, when I first had to write a comedy, when I first had to write an action film, I would get myself down to the Writers Guild library or the Academy library and I would sit down and read some of the best of the genre.

If I was going to do a family drama, I would go read *Terms of Endearment*, or if I was going to go do a multiple character story, I'd read *Syriana* and *Crash*. Really read them. Instead, people go and look at the movie, and they think that did it. That doesn't do it. You have to read these scripts. You can study structure and see how really good people make it work.

No one would try to write a novel who hadn't read some novels. No one would try to write a play who hadn't read plays. But all the time people try to write screenplays who don't sit down and read them. The screenplay is a completely different form.

The vast majority of young writers you tell that to, the way they look at you, you know they're never going to do it.

You can get scripts on the Internet; even if you don't have access to the Writers Guild library, you can get a hold of a whole bunch of different scripts.

Sometimes, to the young writer, it is daunting, and they realize, "Oh, gee, I don't know if I can do this." But better to feel a little bit daunted than to have too much hubris, I think, because you're going to have to work so hard and re-write so much that you might as well face the standard you're writing to. If you write a really good script, something will happen with it. I believe that, because the vast majority aren't that good and many of them aren't even commercial.

The other piece of advice to get a good title. Don't call it *Ashes & Dirt*. A good title is very, very important. *Mystic Pizza* came from the title. I had been trying to think of what could be a female *Diner* when I saw this place called *Mystic Pizza*, and I thought, "What a fantastic title."

Many people get stacks and stacks of scripts. They open the first page and they look at the title page. If the title is terrible, sometimes they don't go any further.

Then they look at the first page and they read the first page. The first page has to be grammatical, it has to be in good screenplay format, and it has to be about something right away.

Every film I ever cut and every film I directed, it was the same: the flaws that were in the script are the flaws that are in the movie. The script is the movie. You have to get it right. And then you have to cast it right.

After that, it's easy sledding.

You Can Count on Me
Kenneth Lonergan

                    TERRY

Put on your seat belt.

                    RUDY

It pushes on my neck.

                    TERRY

What?

                    RUDY

It pushes on my neck, it's
uncomfortable.

                    TERRY

Well, when someone slams into us and
you go sailing through the windshield,
that's liable to be uncomfortable, too.
Now, put on a seat belt.

*Kenneth Lonergan found success writing screenplays for Hollywood (*Analyze This, The Adventures of Rocky & Bullwinkle, *and Martin Scorsese's* Gangs of New York*), but he finds satisfaction writing for the theater, where he is able to control what happens to his script.*

He maintained that same level of control on his first film as writer/director, You Can Count on Me, *which was nominated for an Academy Award for Best Screenplay, won the Sundance 2000 Grand Jury Prize and the Waldo Salt Screenwriting Award, the New York Film Critics Circle, the Los Angeles Film Critics Circle, and Writers Guild of America and National Board of Review awards for Best Screenplay of 2001.*

What was going on in your career before *You Can Count on Me*?

I was making a living writing screenplays, doing pretty well, but my main interest was playwriting, which I was doing mostly with the Naked Angels theater company. I had just had my first big break in playwriting, with my play *This Is Our Youth*. It was very well received and it bumped me several levels up instantly, which is very unusual. So I had just become an off-Broadway playwright with some cachet and I was already basically a Hollywood screenwriter of comedies.

Why do you use the label "screenwriter of comedies" and not just "screenwriter"?

Because I started out doing comedies and they don't let you do anything that you haven't already done. You send them five dramas and they'll say, "But these are plays." They can't extrapolate. It's like the Supreme Court. There has to be a very clear precedent or you have no argument at all.

Where did the idea for *You Can Count on Me* come from?

It came from an assignment that my theater company had given. We were doing an evening of short plays based on the subject of faith and I was poking around for something to write on that topic. I had the idea of this brother and sister. I wrote a ten-minute scene with these characters, which basically was the first step in writing the screenplay. But whenever I say that, I then read that "He adapted it from his own play." But it was, honestly, twelve pages long and it was never meant to be a full-length play. As soon as I thought of it as a larger piece it was immediately a screenplay.

And that scene is still pretty much intact, right, as the first scene where Terry and Sammy meet in the restaurant?

It's that plus the scene at the end. Literally. Minus the note of hope that he expresses when he tries to tell her that he's not going back into the toilet, he actually liked being in Alaska and maybe there's something there for him. Some people have interpreted the movie as him going back into the depths, while other people have noticed that he actually is a tiny bit of a step up from where he started.

What was it about those twelve pages that made you think you had the beginnings of a feature script?

I loved the characters a lot and I thought the scene was really very good. And when it was performed it was performed really nicely. I just thought there was something very moving about the situation.

I guess I liked the idea of how crazy she was about him and the whole dynamic of her having more faith in him than he had in himself. Even though she's a little misguided about him, just liking him that much brought him up a little bit. And I liked the idea that they were at such cross-purposes, but also that they liked each other so much.

Also the idea that they had had this shared tragedy. Her reaction was a sort of blind faith and his reaction was closer to mine, which is that it has no meaning but you have to piece together your own feelings about things like that, because none of the available systems really did it for him.

I just liked that whole dynamic. I liked her taking care of him and him disappointing her — all the dynamics between them. I just liked the people a lot.

The reason I thought of it as a screenplay right away was that their relationship to the place where they lived was very important. Another two-sided element of the story was that they live in this very beautiful place that's also very stultifying. The double edge of living in a rural area is that it's much calmer and more peaceful, but if you happen to want to do anything you could just feel like killing yourself after a while because there's nothing to do. The advantages and disadvantages of being structured or unstructured, as it were.

What was the process of finding the rest of that story and getting to that ending point?

It was one of those rare, all-in-one flashes. I was watching a play which had a little kid in it. I was only partly enjoying the play, so my mind was wandering and I suddenly had the thought, "If she had a little boy who her brother got involved with and then disappointed and became a hazard to, that would be a terrible conflict for her." Immediately I saw a whole arc of a story based on that, which seemed to be very full. Shortly after that, everything else just kept kind of falling in place.

Once you had the story, how did you proceed? Did you write an outline?

I almost never do an outline. I've done outlines for assignments and even then I think I've only done them twice. I have nothing against them, I just don't usually work that way.

For *You Can Count on Me*, I split the lunch scene up, because I knew that the last part of the scene would be the last part of the movie.

I had, at one point, a whole different ending. Originally the last scene was going to be the scene with Sammy and the little boy at the kitchen table. But then, once it was all written, I realized that it should really end with the brother and the sister. So I made that adjustment.

Their affection for each other is the main thing that creates the tension, because if he's not her favorite person in the world, there's no conflict when he starts to endanger her kid, because that's a pretty clear choice. So I realized that there has to be a series of disappointments that he creates that involve the kid. I didn't really bother to think what they were at first, I just knew that there should be about three of them and that they would escalate.

I try to get a bit of a skeleton in place for the events and then I try to not think too much. I find that my whole life I've tried to get more and more toward switching off my conscious mind. The scenes that are the most alive are the ones that you think about the least, they just come out as if someone's talking to you and you're just writing it down. If you're Mozart, that's all that happens and if you're the rest of us, it happens sometimes and sometimes you have to slog through them.

I find that the best material is always from the part of you that doesn't think and doesn't really know what's going on. My technique, if I have one, has always been to try to get better at accessing whatever the part of me is that knows how to write the story. I really don't mean that in any mystical, groovy, artsy way. I think, literally, your unconscious mind has something it's trying to say. Look at how beautifully dreams are economically formed to express something. I think the same part of your brain is trying to write the script. And I've been continually astonished by how many elements that you would think a person has strung together on purpose just pop up.

For example, in this story, you have the brother and sister. Their parents died when the kids were at a young age and the siblings are basically best friends. Their names are Terry and Sammy. Now I swear to God I did not do that on purpose, but they both happen to be names that either a boy or a girl could have. Someone had to point that out to me, saying, "I loved how you did that." But I didn't mean to do it. Those were just the names that popped into my head.

Terry says to the girl that he's dating and gotten pregnant, "You better borrow some money from your brother." So she's got some kind of fucked-up relationship with her brother; Terry's got a fucked-up relationship with his sister. There are all kinds of little parallels that keep coming up and you would think that I had very cleverly laid them in because I was thematically threading them in, but they honestly just appear.

When it happens that way, people will say that the story is trying to tell them what it wants to do. It feels like there's only one right version somewhere. It feels like the story is there, and like the Michelangelo sculpture, *The Prisoners*, you're trying to hew away at the marble to let what's in there emerge. Which is very peculiar and it doesn't always work that way. All that I have to guide me are my instincts. If I'm not on the right track, I get this dead feeling and I lose interest so completely that I literally can't write the next scene. It happens every time I get stuck and it's always because I didn't figure out something that happened earlier. I hadn't believed something or proved something or something had concluded and there was no reason for the story to go on or it had taken a wrong turn.

I didn't realize that Terry's relationship with his nephew would turn out to be such a positive thing for everybody. I initially saw it as a series of incidents: he doesn't show up at this birthday; he doesn't take him fishing; he leaves him stranded somewhere. But what happened right away was this funny thing: he got along with the kid beautifully and was actually more natural with him. He also provided a male role model/father figure and that had never occurred to me, either, but it was obvious from the beginning.

The other thing that came out by mistake was this very nice thing, where Terry spoke to his nephew as if he were the same age, which was really nice for the kid and also a little bit inappropriate at times. And then, much later, an actress who was auditioning for the movie said to me, "It's just because Terry's father died when he was eight, so he's eight too." Which also never occurred to me, but I think has some validity.

Since you don't do an outline, do you have other methods of gathering your thoughts before you write?

I take a lot of notes in my little notebook. I try to write down any thought I have about the movie or I'll write a little scrap of a scene in the notebook and I'll always refer back to that. So I ended up taking a lot of notes.

Were you always planning on directing this script?

Yes. I wouldn't have written it if I wasn't planning to direct it.

Did that change the way you wrote it?

Completely. I had been aware of what professional screenwriting was like in Hollywood many years before I got into it. I got into it only to make money, because I knew there was no creative protection.

This was the first screenplay that I ever wrote the way I would have written a play, meaning putting my heart and soul into it. Every other job I'd done, including the spec script for *Analyze This*, I definitely did as good a job as I could, but I wrote knowing that the script would be destroyed. I wouldn't have written *You Can Count On Me* if I'd known it would be destroyed. I wouldn't have written it if I wasn't planning to direct it and I knew the only way to protect it was to direct it.

I knew that if it was an independent movie that I would have a fairly good chance of controlling the material. I also knew that I wouldn't do it if I couldn't control the material.

Did you think about budget concerns at all while you were writing?

No, I didn't. There's no call for anything expensive in the story anyway. I might have thought about it a little bit in the periphery of my mind, but not really. I knew it would be cheap.

Did you tweak the script after it was cast?

The only thing I changed in production was I did a little bit of cutting and re-wrote the last scene a little bit, because I felt it wasn't clear what Terry's feeling was about going away.

When you finished the script, how did you go about getting it produced?

I had an embarrassingly easy time because I had just had this successful play, *This Is Our Youth*.

I got three offers from small companies to make the play into a movie and I told all of them that I would want to direct it. They balked a little bit, but the truth is it's much easier getting something made if you're going to direct it than selling something that you're not going to direct. A first-time director sounds sort of sexy and interesting and screenwriters are a dime a dozen, so I think it makes it a little more appealing to them if you do want to direct it and you've never directed before.

I ended up going with Hart-Sharp, who made the most firm commitment to giving me complete artistic control over the material. We agreed that we would do the play as a movie and I would direct. I was almost finished with *You Can Count on Me* and I said to them, "By the way, I have this script finished. If you're interested in this, we could do this first." And then the deal for *This Is Our Youth* never really materialized because they liked *You Can Count on Me* a lot and said, "Okay."

Then they got a little nervous and brought in a partner, which unfortunately for me was Shooting Gallery, who went bankrupt owing me $200,000. But I was so happy with the response to the movie that I *almost* didn't care.

How do you know when a script is done?

It feels right. I always feel that the ending must be at least as good as the rest of the movie. If the ending isn't great, I feel like it's not a successful endeavor. And then if there's nothing else that I can work on and improve, then I basically leave it alone. You can always futz around with it, but unfortunately there's a certain point when I start rewriting it where I start making it worse. Thankfully, I think I've learned to identify that point and then I leave it alone.

How do you know when you've reached that point of diminishing returns?

When you get out of the groove of it, I really think it's dangerous to mess around with it too much. I tend to rewrite myself a lot as I'm going, but not endlessly.

I find that a lot of writers are too ready to rewrite stuff, which is dangerous because they just get lost instantly. I know I do. New writers are way too eager to take other people's comments and show it to everyone and get all the feedback they can get. The feeding frenzy in the movie culture now — which is to let everyone dive in and anyone can give notes — I just find it repellent and very bad for the scripts and ultimately for the audience.

The other thing that writers can do is not be self-critical enough. I think you have to be very much on your own side but be very unflinching about noticing when something's no good. You have to be able to step away and step back, basically trusting your own opinion and hoping that if you like it somebody else will.

I gather you're not a big fan of the Hollywood method of note-giving and using multiple writers on a script?

I think the rewrite frenzy is just appalling. It's shocking. I'm still shocked at forty-three at how cavalierly people think it's okay to just chatter away about something someone's worked on for two years and the assumptions behind it. Personally, if I'm writing a screenplay for somebody else, I would get it to where I think it's good, but I wouldn't go one step beyond that, because I know it's going to be ripped to pieces no matter what.

Basically, you get hired and they first try to get you to destroy it. Then you don't destroy it enough and then they fire you and get someone else to do it. That's never not happened to me, except when I was the last destroyer on *Gangs of New York*. But that was a little different, because even though there were script changes that I would not have done if I was making the decisions, in the end I felt there was an artist making the movie and making the decisions and getting other people to help him shape what he wanted. It's a little different when it's a rotating committee of people who don't know how to do anything, which is what it usually is.

***You Can Count on Me* is a textbook example of writing scenes where we learn things about the characters**

through their actions and not just their words. How did you achieve that?

I always have the actors in mind and when I'm writing, I act out the scene, which includes the behavior. And if the behavior's covering it, then you don't need a line of dialogue.

The reason that movies stink now is the fixation on everything being clear. Once the studio development people got the idea that they were going to get involved in the emotional lives of the characters is when things really turned to shit, because they have a terror that things won't be clear and they have a list of what every movie has to be about.

I've never been involved in a movie — except for *Gangs of New York* — in which the comment did not come up at some point that "the character has to learn to believe in himself." Every movie has to be about somebody believing in himself and if it's not that, they have to learn that "it's the heart that you want to pay attention to, not the head." That's another one, which is basically the same thing.

These are people who insist that film is a visual medium, while pounding you to death to write this terrible dialogue which basically, in words, says every single thing that the actors should be doing. People just don't say what they mean all the time.

Or they don't say anything at all. I'm thinking of the scene in *You Can Count on Me* when Sammy is riding in the car with her on-again, off-again boyfriend. She has a moment where she looks at him and you can tell she's completely reassessing the relationship, but not a word is spoken about it.

It was very clear that he showed up, he's a good guy, she's been back and forth about him, he's very stoically driving her to get her fuck-up brother out of jail and she sits there and turns and looks at him very thoughtfully. So what are you going to think, except that she's re-evaluating him? Do you need her to say, "You know, Bob, thanks." That stinks.

Plus, she's not sure she wants to do anything about it. She's just re-evaluating. It's a private moment. Do I need to have her call her best friend and say, "You know, I sat there looking at Bob and thinking, 'You know what ...'" Who needs it? Anybody would look at him and think that, but nobody would say that to him or make that call. And if they did, everyone would cringe with embarrassment.

I wish writers would hold back a little more. You want to make sure that the audience knows what you need them to know at a certain point for the scene to have the effect that you want, but writers often write what they think *should* happen. If people would write more of what *would* happen and just see if it took care of itself, I think it would.

You don't really need to know anything about the two characters in the lunch scene to have the scene be interesting, because there's so much evident tension. If this went on for a long time and I never gave you any information, that would seem like a bullshit trick eventually. It's a medium that's meant to be acted and not described and when you start saying the subtext, then there's nothing left to act.

Did you learn anything writing *You Can Count on Me* that you still use today?

Yes, but I didn't learn it enough. In editing the first cut, I thought every scene was very good but the whole thing dragged. The problem was that every scene had a beginning, a middle and an end. So I chopped the beginnings and, more particularly, the endings off every scene and suddenly the story propelled itself from one scene to the next much better. That's because it didn't have two hundred little soft resolves.

So I've been trying to think about writing in sequences instead of scenes, but the truth is I haven't really applied that, because it's very hard for me to judge that on the page. It's something I know can be dealt with in the editing, so I can't say I actually have the faith to write a really short scene.

What's the best advice about writing that you've ever received?

I think it was from Gertrude Stein. I don't remember the quote exactly, but it's someone telling a younger writer who's worried their work is no good. The quote is, "It's not your business whether it's good or bad. Your job is to keep the channel open, because there's only one of you in all of time and if you don't say it, it will never be said. So keep the channel open." I think that is really very, very good advice, because a lot of people sit around fussing whether it's good or not and I personally think that's not really any of your business. It's not helpful.

You've got to feel your way through it and trust that you're not that much smarter about it than anybody else, which is why you shouldn't listen to anybody else.

You have to be able to evaluate your evaluators. One of my best friends wasn't sure I needed the last scene in the movie *You Can Count on Me*. Now I knew very well I definitely needed it, but all he meant really was that he was saying that it wasn't working for him yet.

If you're forced to listen to what people are saying, the only part that's of any use at all is possibly identifying that there is a problem somewhere. It doesn't mean that the real problem is where it appears, because it can be like a medical symptom: the symptom may not appear where the cause is. Your whole second act is terrible and they're sure you have to change the second act; it may be because your first act is twice as long as it should be. And once you fix that, the second act suddenly is great. No one will ever know that or say that to you.

You can acknowledge that there's a symptom somewhere that someone points out — maybe — but you certainly should be very skeptical when they start talking about what the solution is or what the nature of the problem is.

Is there a real difference between writing for other people and writing for yourself?

Screenwriting for other people is completely different from screen-writing for yourself. I think writers can have more power than they think, if they're keeping it small, but they don't have any power in Hollywood no matter what and every bad thing I described will happen and does. That's all that happens. Occasionally there's an exception.

Roger Dodger
Dylan Kidd

ROGER

I could tell you that what you think
of as your personality is nothing but
a collection of *Vanity Fair* articles.
I could tell you your choice of sexual
partners this evening was decided months
ago by some account executive at Young &
Rubicam. I could tell you that given a
week to study your father and the ways
in which he ignores you I could come
up with a shtick you'd be helpless to
resist. Helpless.

Roger Dodger *is an example of how — sometimes — all the pieces just fall into place.*

Writer-Director Dylan Kidd recognized that he'd created a great character when he came up with Roger Swanson. Actor Campbell Scott obviously agreed and stepped up to the challenge, bringing an amazing cast — Isabella Rossellini, Jennifer Beals, Ben Shenkman, and Elizabeth Berkley — along with him.

Roger Dodger *proves that it's always a good idea to carry your best script with you wherever you go, because you just never know who you're going to run into.*

Where were you in your career before *Roger Dodger* happened?

Nowhere, really. I had gone to NYU film school and graduated in 1991 and then most of the '90s was spent struggling to get any kind of entry into the industry. I loaded cameras for a couple of years; I worked in real estate for a couple of years. I made a short film in 1996, which was the first directing I had done since school, and that was a nice little thing to get my confidence up a little bit. I spent a couple years doing training videos for hair salons, industrial films, you name it. So really *Roger Dodger* was a very dramatic beginning to my career.

What was the value of all those jobs when it came time to do your first feature?

At the time I was absolutely thrilled to have the work, and I still feel that any time you are — and this is more from a directing stand-point than from a screenwriting standpoint — any time I was on a set, calling "action" and "cut," it was an opportunity to learn. And it's always good to shoot and go into the editing room and slap your forehead and think, "I should have gotten *that*!" It's all part of the training.

And in terms of screenwriting, it's all just fuel for the fire. In the case of helping the script for *Roger Dodger*, I was just getting more angry and frustrated at not being able to break in, so I ended up putting all that anger into the mouth of the main character.

In my case, it was a long struggle, but absolutely worth it. I don't know how to do anything else, so for me there was no option.

How many scripts had you written before *Roger Dodger*?

I had written two other feature scripts and then one that had been sort of abandoned. So I guess, two and a half.

One screenplay was based on my experiences in real estate. Although it was nice to get it out of my system, I think I was aware when it was done that the script really wasn't good enough to show anybody.

The other one was a horror movie, an attempt to do something in a genre. It was fine, but wasn't anything that I was that excited about. *Roger Dodger* was the first time that when I finished a script, I was like, "Okay, I want to make this movie."

What was it about the script that made you feel that this was the one?

Probably the quality of the writing, but also the fact that this was the first time that I felt like I had a character that an actor would want to play. For me, a big thing about writing something that could be done for no money was trying to write a role that was so good that we could attract a name actor to work for what turned out to be peanuts.

That was a big part of my strategy: write something that somebody would walk through broken glass to play. Most of your expense in a movie is the above-the-line costs. It's difficult but possible to make a movie for a low budget. What's really hard is getting someone that anyone's ever heard of into that movie.

Every time an actor wins an award for stepping outside of their comfort zone, like Halle Berry for *Monster's Ball* or Charlize Theron for *Monster,* I think it sends a message to other actors that sometimes you need to take a chance. If you're making twelve million dollars a picture, you don't need the money. So why not take two weeks, go shoot a little indie, and maybe you'll get a statue? That was my theory, anyway.

Where did the idea for the story come from?

The real estate script I had written was big in scope and so, apart from the fact that I didn't think it was that strong, even if someone did fall in love with it, it was still a big movie. So the idea of *Roger Dodger* was to give myself the assignment of writing something that could be done for no money. That lent itself to a series of conversations and monologues.

It started with the idea of a guy who feels like he can tell everyone else what they're thinking. It was based on a friend of mine, who in college had this strange ability to go up to strangers and take their psychology apart in minute detail. It struck me as disturbing but also very compelling.

I started with Roger. It ended up being a buddy movie, but his nephew didn't come in until later drafts. You go through a certain amount of time thinking, "Well, maybe this guy is compelling enough, maybe people will sit and watch a train wreck for an hour and a half."

And then there was a point where I realized there has to be some foil, a character who we want to protect has to enter the movie. There has to be a reason for people to hang on and keep watching.

Did you have a theme in mind when you started?

I was interested in how somebody's work could bleed into their personal life. I feel that New York is very much a place where you can be so ambitious in your career that you end up translating those techniques into your personal life.

I liked the idea of a guy who works in advertising and actually ends up bringing that kind of rhetoric into the singles arena. The idea that he's literally trying to sell himself as a product, by creating insecurity in other people.

But the nephew didn't show up in early drafts?

I think I had one breakthrough draft, which was the first time when the nephew, Nick, came in, where it felt like this was the structure of the movie. After that there were endless tweakings.

Campbell Scott was very helpful, too. We were lucky enough to be able to rehearse quite a bit before we shot and Campbell helped me cut a lot of dialog. Because as wordy as the film is, the script was even more so.

Usually actors are begging for more lines, so if an actor is saying, "I think we can cut the scene here," their instincts are usually pretty right on. They're not going to tell you to cut a line unless there's a real reason for it. And Campbell is also a writer and a director, so he had a really strong sense.

Probably the most important draft of the script was created two weeks before shooting, going into rehearsal and realizing that a ten-page monologue was finished at page seven. We didn't need to keep ranting for another three pages. We probably would have figured that out in editing, but it was great to not actually have to go shoot all that.

How did you come up with the title?

I honestly can't remember. I think I remembered hearing that as a nickname for Roger Staubach and I like titles that have an alliterative quality and stick in your head a little bit.

I also thought of this character as somebody who is dodging a bit. This is a guy that the audience is sort of chasing through the movie. And so our visual approach was that this was a guy who always had a cloud of cigarette smoke or something obscuring him. You could never really get this guy to sit still.

What is your writing process?

I used to hate writing, because I didn't feel I was any good at it. It was so hard. It takes you a while to realize that it's hard for everybody. If you spend the first two weeks of a project staring at a page, you learn to forgive yourself a little bit and realize that that's part of the process.

To me, the hardest part by far is the beginning. That's the easiest time to get discouraged and give up. But I have an almost religious faith, based on the scripts I've written, where there is some point where you break through.

So for me, the first couple of months is a lot of *not* writing: thinking, obsessing, thinking this is a disaster that is never going to happen. Then something clicks and you start to write and you realize that all that worrying was really part of the process.

But I've never been somebody who can get up and put in a nine-to-five day writing. I just can't do it. At the very end, when you're racing to the finish line, then I probably could. But up until that point, if I put in three to four hours, I consider that a good day.

You're the first person I've talked to who has used the words "faith" and "forgive" to describe the process of writing.

And I'm an atheist!

I remember reading a great quote that Stephen Gaghan said about writing *Syriana*. He was describing what he goes through when he writes a script and at the end he talked about self-loathing and not being able to get out of bed.

The beginning is hard. You're trying to make order out of chaos, and chaos doesn't want to be ordered. If you can just get through that hard part, the first draft, then I think you'll be rewarded for your perseverance.

Do you follow a three-act structure in your scripts?

I guess so, but without really thinking about it. I read the Syd Field book when I was at NYU, but I think, for me, things work internally. I can't even remember thinking about the act breaks when I wrote *Roger Dodger*. I just had the sense that we were at this stage of the story and this is what should happen.

If you go to five thousand movies in your life, then without even knowing it that structure is going to be in there when you're writing. I don't think it's a front brain thing; it just ends up being in there.

I feel like the last thing you want to do in a first draft is to be thinking about what page is the act break. I'm the exact opposite of someone who knows the ending before they begin. For me, the first draft is the "spill it" draft. And after that you can look at it and think, "Well, I have a seventy-page first act. That probably can't work."

But your first time through is when your unconscious is really trying to tell you what the movie wants to be. For me it's important to follow your bliss in that first draft, even if it ends up at 180 pages or you hate everything but 10% of it. At least you've got that 10%, which is 10 more than a lot of people have.

So you don't subscribe to the "the first act needs to end on page 30" philosophy?

The first draft, because there was no Nick character, I think there was a point where I read a draft and I literally started to get fatigued around page 25.

Once I realized that we needed Nick, the original plan was to introduce him very early in the movie so you had some sense that it wasn't just going to be about Roger. Campbell's performance was so great that we decided to roll the dice and I said "I think we can hang with this guy for about twenty minutes." Then we have the kid show up in the office, and a few minutes to get to know the kid and see how they relate, and then the movie can kick in.

There's something to be said for trying to fit it into a structure that people who read scripts for a living recognize. But for me it's always been a little more organic than having file cards and saying, "By page 40 I need to be here." But everyone's different.

Although it's a buddy movie, it is all from Roger's point of view. Do you think that's a function of the character of Nick essentially being a late addition in the scripting process?

Part of what we discovered was that Roger is controlling the tempo of the movie and the subject matter of what's being talked about, but in some weird way, Nick comes in at a moment when we're really starting to figure out something about Roger.

Even if the movie isn't told through Nick's point of view, there's some way that we're linked to Nick, in that we're sitting there listening to this guy go on and on, and there's an interesting split that happens. We're aware that, as responsible people watching the movie, we feel that this kid should get away from this guy, but he doesn't.

So the more that Nick buys into everything that's being told to him and the more we realize that, "Wait, this is the last guy you want to be asking for advice," there's something interesting that happens.

It's the classic Hitchcock situation, where you've told the audience that there's a bomb under the table — you told the audience, "here's who Roger is." And then you introduce someone who doesn't know what we know. It creates suspense, because you want him to get away but you also want him to somehow redeem Roger.

That's absolutely right. And somehow we thought that would work better if you were introduced to Nick early, because we thought if you set up that collision course, people are really going to be on the edge of their seats. And then we discovered that it was actually better to have the first twenty minutes be all about Roger and then you have the kid show up.

Under the guise of a talky, chamber piece, we're actually using every trick in the book to keep people in their seats — it's a buddy movie, it's a Hitchcock movie, it's a sex movie. We were shameless in what we were doing. It's hard to have people just sitting and talking without there being serious subtext.

Were you writing to a particular budget?

No, but having a background in production was definitely a help. I had the understanding that if you could tell the movie in one night there would be only one wardrobe change.

There are basic rules that are pretty common-sensical, like don't have a car chase, don't make it a period piece, keep your locations to a minimum.

Also, a big thing for us was that we knew we were going to shoot with two cameras and that allows you to really burn through scenes more quickly. Basically, the whole second act of the movie is four people sitting at a banquette, having this extended conversation. We were able to shoot that entire thing in a day and a half because we were rolling two cameras.

There's a scene where Roger takes the kid out into the street; it's the first time where he's instructing the kid. It's a long, extended scene and even when it was written it was intended to be shot in one take. That was a twelve-page scene that we shot in half a day. If you have two sequences like that, that's 20% of your movie that's shot in three days.

Did knowing that you were writing for a small budget cramp your creativity in any way?

Not really. This was one of those movies that felt like it wanted to be tighter. There were earlier drafts that took place over a longer span of time and it just felt like it wanted to be as tight as possible.

So there's nothing in the movie that I feel we would have done differently if we'd had more money, except for the luxury of being able to shoot more. But if somebody had said, "We love it, here's two million dollars," I wouldn't have written in some dream sequence of Roger when he was young. It just felt like it is what it is, that we were dropped into the middle of this guy's meltdown, and we hang on just to make sure that the kid's going to get out of there okay.

Did you write with specific actors in mind?

I didn't and I still don't. I have a hard time doing that, because I don't want to get too attached. I didn't have anybody in mind, so when we stumbled upon Campbell in this really crazy way, it was nice not to have some presupposed notion of it has to be this guy or that guy.

How did you get Campbell Scott?

My producer partner and I got to a stage where we realized, "we're not going to get this movie made in the standard fashion." It's like that New York thing, where nobody ever finds an apartment by actually going through the real estate listings. It's always somebody you know; there's always some back door.

So, really in a fit of insanity, thinking if I don't make this movie I'm going to go crazy, I started carrying the script with me every day. I thought, "Well, I live in New York, maybe I'll run into somebody." And that's how it happened — two weeks after starting that routine of not leaving the house without the script, I walked into a café and there was Campbell.

I didn't realize that most people will not accept an unsolicited screenplay, because it opens you up to all kinds of potential litigation. But I was so clueless at that point.

Any advice to someone who wants to try the same thing when they spot the perfect actor or actress for their script?

The only advice that I have is to be really polite and make sure that you really do have a killer part to offer.

I'm not necessarily somebody who stalks people or is really aggressive or goes up to people, but I was so sure that this was a great role for somebody. I really believed. I might not have believed that the movie was going to work, but I knew this was a lot of meaty dialog for someone to perform. So I really believed that I wasn't wasting his time. If I wasn't sure, I would not have gone up to him.

If you get to the stage where you feel like you have this great gift that you can give somebody, then it allows you to feel like you're not just disturbing this guy's lunch.

Did you do any re-writing to fit the cast?

Nothing to fit the cast. We were lucky. Basically every actor in the movie was our first choice, so there wasn't a whole lot of "Oh, this person can't handle this type of thing," or "This person is really good at this — we should add more."

Fairly late in the game we added the epilogue where Roger goes back and sees Nick in Ohio. That was something that came from doing a reading. We did a reading where we found Jesse Eisenberg, who played Nick, and he was so good at the reading that we got really excited because we thought, okay, we actually have someone who can play this role.

That reading was a huge epiphany, because we realized there was an actor who exists on planet Earth who could play this role. It really lit a fire under us, because we thought Jesse would grow a beard in a year and his voice is going to drop, or whatever, so we've got to move.

It was sort of our "That's our Hitler!" moment from *The Producers*.

The other thing we learned from the reading was this huge sense of when the movie ended. The original ending had Roger putting Nick into a cab to the airport and you could just feel the air go out of the room, because the audience cared so much about Nick, because Jesse was so good. They wanted to know if he was going to be okay.

So it was combining that sense of wanting the narrative pleasure of following through and also, just for me, I really wanted to stick Roger in a cafeteria full of kids. I don't know why, it's such a guilty pleasure for me. The movie starts with Roger having lunch in this restaurant with all these adults and then by the end of the movie he's actually found his peer group.

So I think it was a combination of sensing that the audience would feel ripped off if the movie cut to black at that point and also having this visual of Campbell Scott bopping above all these other heads in the cafeteria.

Do you show drafts to friends or use readings to gauge how you're progressing?

I like readings. I'm not a fan of too much feedback. I'm stubborn that way. I like feedback, but for me the whole point of a reading is to sit in the room and you just know — you just know if something's dead or if something's working.

I do have people that I turn to and that I care about what they think. But my feeling is that, unless the comments match something I already felt in my gut anyway, or if every person has the same comment, then I know I have an issue. I generally have found that putting too much stock in feedback can get confusing, because people are going to have a hundred different opinions.

Is there anything in the movie that people tried to talk you out of that you're glad you stuck to your guns on?

I tend to be the opposite. I tend to be the guy that cuts too quickly. I loved when the Coen brothers released their Director's Cut of *Blood Simple*, and it was like eight minutes shorter or whatever. That would be me.

My experience has been that if I have a gut feeling, if I know something isn't working, I don't need to be told to take it out. And if someone says it isn't working for them, but some gut things says I want to keep it in, I guess the reward I get for writing the script and putting myself through this is that I get to say, "No, I don't want to lose that."

There has to be something in the script that gets you juiced, otherwise it's dead on arrival. I think you have to fight for that, even if you're not going to be the one directing it.

Did knowing that you were going to direct it change the way you wrote the script?

I don't think so. But I think that's probably why I say I don't enjoy writing. It's mainly because I love directing and I think of myself as a director.

So the writing is this very necessary part, but it's not the fun part. For me it's less about hating writing and more about getting impatient, because I want to get to the point where I can go and start collaborating with others.

What is the most fun part?

I really like editing, which is very much like writing. It's just more fun, because you get very tangible results very quickly.

For me, I enjoy the entire process, but I probably add the most value in the editing room. I think I'm fine as a director on the set, but I'm not some Ridley Scott genius who always knows where to put the camera, and I'm not John Cassavetes, where I would say the right thing to the actors.

But the editing room is a place where my tenacity pays off, because I just keep working the footage and refuse to stop tweaking. I just find it really enjoyable, not walking away until a scene is as absolutely good as it can be.

There's a shot right near the end of the movie where Roger is sitting alone on his couch, smoking and thinking, and the smoke disappears in front of him, like a cloud of fog lifting. Was that in the script or a happy accident?

That's the one effect that was completely scripted.

There was a deliberate structure, where the first image of Roger was of him expelling a plume of smoke. Then, we really labored over that last shot of him smoking. It's the only dolly shot in the film. Our poor cinematographer had to light it in a certain way, so that the smoke would read.

I don't know if anybody even gets it, but I still get a kick out of it when I see it. "Oh, look, he's coming out of the fog." It was even written in the script that way, something like, "Roger exhales and then the smoke lifts ..."

Although you created Roger, I'm sure there was a point where Campbell took him over and knew him better than you did. Do you remember when that point was?

Probably by lunch on the first day.

I had a really interesting thing happen with Campbell. I think good film actors work really small. There's a great interview with John Travolta where he says he always has to remind directors that they might not see what he's doing on the set, but they'll see it on the screen. These guys are working at a level where the camera can almost read their minds.

My initial concept for Roger had been much more manic. But Campbell brought this total James Bond sophistication to it, where he's saying these horrible things but it's going down so smoothly. That was a total surprise to me and I had a panicked reaction. We talked and he said it's going to be fine. And I thought, I've cast this guy and he's great. Maybe this is not what I had in mind, but maybe that's the whole point.

Since then I've learned that that moment of surprise is the very best feeling you can experience on the set. If you don't feel surprised, you're in trouble. The whole point is that you write a script and then the actors turn it into something so much better and richer and different than you ever thought.

It wasn't until the end of the shoot that I realized how right Campbell's choice had been. The only way people would stand this guy was if he was kind of suave about it. If he had done what I had pictured in my head, the movie would have been a disaster. So that was a great lesson.

I think I imagined the character as constantly pushing people away and what Campbell was doing was more of a push/pull thing, where he reels you in and *then* pushes you away. That's so much more interesting than what I had in mind.

I don't think I'll ever make a movie that turned out so much better than I imagined. I thought the script was good, but the actors added so much.

**You were quoted once as saying you wanted every charac-
ter in this movie, even if they only had one line, to be so
well drawn that they were worthy of their own movie. How
do you go about doing that?**

I think that's something that's easy to say, but in the end it comes down to the actors. It's very easy to say that you want people to feel that you could go off with any character, but unless it's Jennifer Beals who's riding off in that cab, maybe you're not really going to give a shit and you'll say, "I'll let her ride away."

I think it was more about just wanting to instill in the actors some sense that everyone is important, that there are no supporting characters. But I do believe that it's the responsibility of the writer to love every character equally. Once you start writing a character who is only there in order to fulfill some piece of plot machinery, then nobody is going to care about that person.

I have this clear memory of being about twelve years old and going to a James Bond movie. There was a scene in the movie where the main henchman gets in a fight with an extra character in the movie — some Secret Service guy we'd never seen. And it ends up being a really long fight. I remembered being so thrilled that this guy, who you'd think would be dispatched immediately, gets a nice scene.

I always enjoy it when characters come in and you make a snap judgment about them and then they surprise you, either by claiming more of your attention than you thought or just being richer than you thought.

It's our job to remind audiences that every character has something going on and everyone has a story to tell. It sound pretentious, but that's where our heads were at when we made the movie.

What did you learn writing _Roger Dodger_ that you still use today on higher-budget projects?

The main thing that I learned from that script was that it was the first time ever when I was writing something that I thought, "This is good, this is working."

My other scripts had been okay, competent, but the hair on the back of my neck didn't stand up. For me, the most important thing now is trying to make sure that I get as close as I can to that feeling.

I never want to settle for, "Oh, this is okay." You want people to read it and get genuinely excited about it and want to shoot it.

You've got to get to a place where you are genuinely pumped with what you're doing. As hard as it is, you can't give up on a script until you've gotten to that place.

What's the best advice you've ever gotten about writing?

I have to say it was that Stephen Gaghan quote I mentioned earlier. That was the first time that it really hit home for me that it's hard for everybody and that 90% of writing might just be staring into space or reading a book and feeling like you're procrastinating.

Writing is so hard that I only want to do it if I'm absolutely dying to tell that story. My advice would be, particularly in the beginning, the only thing that is going to make your script jump off the page for a reader who's read a hundred scripts that day — the only thing that's going to make a difference — is that there's something about it that's getting you up each morning. Even if it's the least commercial idea in the world, I have to believe that somehow that passion translates to the page.

My experience with *Roger Dodger* was that I had written two other scripts that I thought were good, and then it wasn't until I wrote *Roger Dodger* that I realized that there's a difference between just "good" and "holy shit this is good." The industry is tough enough and competitive enough that if you're going to go out to somebody, whether it's an agent or an actor or you're going to submit it to a studio, it has to have that holy shit feeling.

CHAPTER SEVEN

Original Visions

Now, that's not to say that the other screenplays profiled in this book are in any way unoriginal. But the three screenplays highlighted in this chapter vehemently resist categorization.

Instead they present original stories in original ways, which in a nutshell is really the goal of all independent films.

Paris, Texas
L.M. Kit Carson

WALT

You've been gone a long time, Travis.

TRAVIS

How long have I been gone, do you know?

WALT

Four years.

TRAVIS

Is four years a long time?

L.M. Kit Carson has the rare gift of often being in the right place at the right time. When his friend Jim McBride needed to re-shoot his fake documentary, David Holzman's Diary, *after the original footage was lost, Kit just happened to be there — and his life just happened to mirror what was going on in the movie.*

Years later, when his young son, Hunter, was cast in Wim Wenders' Paris, Texas, *Kit was there when the production of the movie — about Harry Dean Stanton's search for his son (Hunter) and his lost wife (Nastassja Kinski) — came to a halt.*

Again, Kit's life mirrored the story on screen, and he was put in the unique situation of coming onto a movie that was already in progress (the screenplay that Wenders had shot up to that point had been written by Sam Shepard) and working with the director as they attempted to collaboratively create an emotionally satisfying conclusion to the story.

What was going on in your life before *Paris, Texas* happened?

I did *Breathless* with Jim McBride, so I'd done my first Hollywood film. After *Breathless* I was not exactly hot, but I was lunch. So I went to lunch a lot and was offered projects, and none of them was anything that I really wanted to do.

At the same time, my son, Hunter, had been cast in *Paris, Texas*, so I got to know Wim Wenders very informally because of that. So while I was doing lunch with all of the studios and executives from all the different agencies and all that, I was watching the progress on *Paris, Texas*. I knew that they had gotten started and that there was a stop date on Harry Dean and there was a stop date on Nastassja, so they had to start shooting.

They went off and started the beginning of the movie down in Texas in an area called The Devil's Playground in the desert. Wim was out there for two weeks and then came back. I wandered into the office one evening to see how it was going, and he was at his desk, with his head in his hands.

I said, "What's the matter?" And he said, "We have shot the beginning of the movie. It sets up this great mystery, and then the script explains it all away. And I don't want to do that."

He went on to say, "I want this movie to be about love, a movie in which love triumphs at the end, but it's not sentimental."

That was the thrust of the movie. He'd shot the opening mystery, the first twenty minutes of the film. And then he didn't like the rest of the script. I asked him what the script was like, and he said, "There are two versions."

One version was that Nastassja's father was a big Texas oil man and his goons had gone and beat up Harry Dean and grabbed Nastassja and stuck her in a penthouse. The other version was Nastassja's mother was under the thrall of a televangelist and, of course, he ran heroin dens and whorehouses, just like all televangelists do. His goons came and beat up Harry Dean and grabbed Nastassja and stuck her in a heroin den/whorehouse.

And I said to Wim, "Those are kind of corny." And he said, "Yeah."

And I said, "What if they did it to themselves?"

And he looked up and he said, "Exactly."

Wim explained to me that Sam Shepard had gone on to *In Country*, the film where he met Jessica Lange, because he and Wim couldn't get satisfied with the scripts. And so Sam just sorta said, "You figure it out. I'm outta here. I gotta go do this movie."

So Wim said to me, "Give me the weekend. I'll call Sam and tell him that I want you to do this." And I said, "Okay, but I'm going back to New York this weekend. I'm stopping in Texas first to see my folks. You call me by Sunday and tell me in which direction I'm going — either back to L.A. or on to New York."

So I didn't hear from him and I didn't hear from him, and on Sunday night at the last possible minute when I was about to go get my ticket and get on the plane, Wim called and said, "Come back."

So I came back and they resumed the shoot, and I stayed two weeks ahead of the shoot with new pages.

When we were finishing shooting in L.A., the production designer was getting ready to head for Texas to set up the place in Houston where Harry Dean finds Nastassja.

We had decided that it was a "talk house." Wim had talked about when he was doing *Hammett*, he would go to a bar right near the studio at the end of every day — it was a topless bar, with all the girls on poles and stuff like that. He said that the sexiest thing and the real action of the bar was the girls coming to the bar and talking to customers.

So he decided that was a business, to build a bar around talking. And we had to figure out what that was — on the last night, right before the production designer was heading for Texas the next morning.

We knew it was a bar, and we knew it was people talking, and we knew that there were certain rules — Harry Dean could not touch her. And so we decided it was a booth, some kind of talk booth.

Okay, so we had to decide, is it like a voting booth? Is it like a phone booth? And in that evening, until 3:00 in the morning, we came up with talk booths that were dioramas.

That's how the movie was made, with the collaboration of everybody. And that's why it has, I think, a certain energy. It feels like it's figuring itself out as you watch the film.

And then at the end of it, when we got to Houston and we were going to shoot the talk rooms, Wim called Sam and said, "Here's what happened." And overnight Sam dictated the monologues that Harry Dean and Nastassja do in the talk room. And Wim continued the rest of the movie until the end.

Did you have a sense while you were making the movie of the impact it would have and the status it would achieve?

No. What I want to keep emphasizing about *Paris, Texas* is that it was not important. There was nothing fancy about what was going on. It was really just a bunch of guys driving around Texas in pickup trucks making the movie. There was nothing that seemed important going on. We were not shooting a film that was going to win at Cannes. It was just a bunch of guys trying to do something.

We had brilliant collaborators: Production designer Kate Altman — brilliant. Cinematographer Robby Müller— brilliant. And the actors are all brilliant. But it was wide open in the sense that all we were doing was serving the movie. There was nothing else going on except trying to figure this out.

And this was all happening with very little money, right?

I remember that the movie had a budget of about $750,000. That's probably not the official budget, but that's what I knew we had. I was paid, partly, with a '57 Chevy Bel Air, with the fins. That was part of my pay. Nobody was paid anything, really, on this movie.

You look back at it now and you say, "How could you guys do something this good without any luxury at all?" But the intention was so high; there was nothing in the way of trying to do something honest and out of your heart.

What was your working process with Wim?

He's challenging, in the sense that he's in the middle of the movie and he keeps changing things. For him, change is an ongoing process.

He said to me at one point, "I don't think Harry Dean should get the kid. You're going to have to prove it to me." And he knew he was playing with me, because this movie has a lot of my own life in it — myself and my son's relationship was embedded in this movie, because I had gone away. I had gotten divorced and I had gone away and I came back. So I had to beat that game.

And then when we were heading toward the end of the movie, and we didn't know how to pull that off, at dinner one night Wim said, "Well, the audience doesn't know the end of the movie when they go into the theater. So it's not fair" — and he pounded the table — "for us to know the end of the movie when we do it."

So that's his dynamic, always questioning what you're doing. That keeps your mind really going.

Another example of how Wim keeps everything open was when we were in the hotel room at the end of the movie and Nastassja and Hunter are seeing each other for the first time in years. And I'm trying to figure out what they say. So I'm in the next room, working on what the dialogue is, how it can't be sentimental and all of that, and Wim comes running around the corner and he says, "Stop! Stop! Hunter just wrote the last lines of the film!"

In the improv that they were shooting, she lifts him up and spins him around, and pulls back after the spin around and he says to her, "Your hair. It's wet." And he improvises clipping it with his fingers. And that's it, it's the last line of the film. And it's great, because it somehow brings tears because "Your hair. It's wet" is so indirect. It's a release moment, because they're touching again.

It's like when we shot the talk-house sequence. I'd written it so that Harry comes in the front door and finds a bar and all these people. The day before we shot it was Alfred Hitchcock's birthday. And Wim said, "Okay, you were born the day before Alfred Hitchcock and I was born the day after Alfred Hitchcock. So, we're going to honor Alfred Hitchcock. We're going to do a Hitchcock version, in which Harry Dean comes in the back of the building, doesn't know what's going on, and has to piece it together, just like a Hitchcock hero does — they always come into things and don't know what's going on."

Then as we were shooting, Harry Dean spots Nastassja's back — she's leaning against the bar and John Lurie's standing beside her, looking toward Harry Dean and Harry starts toward them.

Wim waved at me and said, "Come up with a Hitchcock line." In the middle of shooting the scene.

And I go, "Ummmm. John Lurie says, 'Sorry, sir, you're too early. It's not time yet.'" Which is a Hitchcock line, because it's metaphorically correct — it's too early for him to find the Nastassja Kinski character — and it's physically correct, because the bar's not open quite yet.

That's what Wim does to your head when you're working with him.

How much fun is that?

I loved it. I loved it. But I love the rub, I love spark that's made out of not knowing what's next and two creative forces rubbing heads.

You've had the experience of working on two classic movies — *David Holzman's Diary* and *Paris, Texas*. How do you react when people always want to talk about those two movies?

It makes me want to do that again. At this point in my life, it's really fucking bizarre. I just went to Santa Fe and got honored, then went to Sundance and got honored. They're doing a new DVD of

Paris, Texas. Jim McBride has now got a new DVD coming out of *David Holzman's Diary*. And then I was called three days ago to be on the new DVD of *Texas Chainsaw Massacre, Part Two* that's coming out.

What's fulfilling is that these things don't go away. That makes you feel like you did something that's going to last.

Is there anything that you learned working on *Paris, Texas* that you still use today?

Silence. I learned that.

The first part of the script was Sam's and it was full of silence. I found out about the power of silence from thinking about that over and over and over again. Thinking about how the characters relate to each other. There's a lot of silence in this movie and it's very powerful.

I've learned and applied that to everything else.

What's the best advice you've ever gotten about screen-writing?

Paul Schrader once, when we were talking about writing, said off-handedly, "Well, you know, a scene is like a party. The best way to go to a party is that you come in late and leave early." And I think that's a great way to talk about writing a scene.

What is your favorite memory from working on *Paris, Texas*?

My favorite memory was when we were at Cannes. I was doing a film in Berlin for Wim's company at the time, and I got permission to go to Cannes, because the film was showing. I slept on the floor in somebody's hotel room.

So I'm sleeping on the floor and I had rented a tuxedo in Berlin, which was a classic double-breasted tuxedo from the thirties. And then the movie showed.

And the audience went nuts, they stood up at the end, the applause was roaring, and people started throwing money. This is what they do in France — they throw coins at you. And we were ducking these coins — Nastassja and Harry Dean and Wim and myself. That was kind of astounding and hard to repeat that moment.

The other memory I love was when we shooting in this little town, Nordheim, where Harry Dean stops in a bar after he runs away from Nastassja and gets drunk and Hunter brings him back and basically makes him drive back to Houston.

So we were shooting at night on the main street of Nordheim, and the whole town was out watching us — "the whole town" meaning about fifty or sixty people. And there's a scene where Hunter walks Harry Dean, who's drunk, down a street and Hunter's holding him up, and they cross the street, and Wim yells, "Cut!"

And the whole town burst into applause. Wim turned to me and said, "These are the best reviews I've gotten in years!"

How do you jump into a movie that's already shooting and keep it going, while making the work your own?

Don't think that. Think about what the movie means. That's all I was doing. I wasn't thinking about making it my own. I was thinking about what I thought the movie meant and Wim agreed with me.

I said the movie is about the son resurrecting his father and Wim agreed. But that's what I could bring to it. I could bring that part of the story to it.

Isn't it interesting that you were there, at that time, with that unique perspective?

I have no way of explaining that, but it happens like that a lot in my life. Somebody else is writing the plot and they turn around and there I am, in the story.

Eve's Bayou
Kasi Lemmons

MOZELLE

Life is filled with good-byes, Eve. A
million good-byes. And it hurts every
time. Sometimes I feel like I've lost so
much I have to find new things to lose.
All I know is there must be a divine
point to it all and it's just over my
head. That when we die, it will all
come clear and we'll say, "So that was
the damn point." And sometimes I think
there's no point at all and that's the
point. All I know is most people's lives
are a great disappointment to them and
no one leaves this earth without feeling
terrible pain, and if there is no divine
explanation at the end of it all, oh,
that's sad.

As you watch this beautiful movie, it's occasionally hard to believe that Eve's Bayou *is a film from a first-time feature director working from her first solo screenplay. It's an assured and ambitious and emotionally satisfying story of life in the South in the early sixties, following young Eve (Jurnee Smollett) during a life-defining summer.*

Writer/Director Kasi Lemmons (best known to filmgoers as Ardelia in The Silence of the Lambs*) deftly mixes Southern gentility, voodoo and magic, and a touch of* Rashômon-*style storytelling to present the sometimes comic, sometimes tragic events of that summer from a child's unique perspective.*

What was going on in your life and your career before you came to write *Eve's Bayou*?

I had been an actor for a long time. I'd done a couple of plays with really good companies, Naked Angels and Steppenwolf, and then I went to film school. When I got out of film school I had a short film that was festivaling around, called *Fall from Grace*. And then I did *Silence of the Lambs* and moved to Los Angeles.

I'd written with other people, but *Eve's Bayou* was the first thing I wrote by myself. At that point in my life I was starting to think about the future. I'd been to film school, so it wasn't a completely foreign concept that I would start to marry all of these elements, the things that I'd been doing for years.

What I really wanted to do was to write the perfect role for myself. To write the perfect part. If you could write a perfect part for yourself, what would it be? So I wrote the character of Mozelle for me to play when I got a little bit older.

Also it was very much an experiment in a certain type of language and a certain writing style. It was very ambitious. I knew what I wanted to do, but it was more of an experiment. And then when I was finished with it, I showed it to Vondie Curtis-Hall, who was my boyfriend at the time, and he said, "You've got to show this to somebody else." He was the person who said, "You can't put it in a drawer. You have to show it to somebody."

Where did the idea for the story come from?

I remember the first time I told any story from *Eve's Bayou* was at an audition. The casting director didn't want to see a scene from the show. He wanted us to talk. So I started spinning *Eve's Bayou* stories. I talked about my aunt who had gotten married five times and all of her husbands had died. That was true. The more fantastical parts of the story are true.

I wrote that story down as a short story and I wrote some other short stories. One was about two little kids, a brother and sister, who go and look in their grandmother's room. It talks about all of her medicines and the way in which her room was very evocative. And then another was about Eve and Jean Paul Batiste and how a bayou came to be named after this slave who saved her master's life with voodoo and witch-doctoring. So I had all these stories, but they weren't really connected. There was some connection in my mind, but I hadn't found it yet.

Then I invented the character of Louis Batiste for the stories to revolve around. Way before I wrote anything down I could tell you the entire story of *Eve's Bayou*, the entire thing complete with flashes of lightning. I could tell you the whole movie. I had it all in my head.

How long did it take you to get it out of your head and onto paper?

From the time I could tell it all the way through, maybe a year.

I was in therapy at the time and I was very conflicted about what to do with my life, how to approach the next step, the next phase of my life. My therapist said, "You really need to take this pilot season off, don't audition for anything and write that story that you keep telling me about." So basically my therapist told me to stay home for a few months and write it down and that's what I did.

Were you thinking about budget at all while you wrote?

I wrote it as a literary experiment. So I wasn't thinking about anything other than wanting to get this story down on paper. As a matter of fact, when I first started writing it I thought it might be a book. And then I ended up writing it as a screenplay and I had the idea of playing the role of Mozelle. But I wasn't really sure if it was going to turn into a book or a screenplay or what was going to happen with it. I just let it come out. I wasn't thinking about budget and I wasn't thinking about directing it at all.

Do you know what it was that tipped the balance for you between it being a book or being a screenplay?

It came out that way. It came out as a very literary screenplay. The first draft was very literary, it was a bookish screenplay. But it was definitely a movie. If I really look back I always knew that. When I would describe it, it was very visual, but then the best literature is very visual.

How often did you tell the story of *Eve's Bayou* and how did that help you when you sat down to write it?

I think I told it fairly often. I remember at least three times that I told someone the whole movie. It helped shape it in my mind. Not so much that I did it for feedback, but it helped to shape the story in my mind.

Once you had a draft done, how did you get feedback?

I have a select group of people who read every script. There are about five of them. They are the most critical people I know. I process their comments carefully. They usually don't agree on many things, so I look for the things they all agree on. If five people tell you something is bothering them, then maybe you need to look at that. I take what somebody says and try to see what resonates with me or if they say something that I've been thinking already.

As you wrote the screenplay, were you still thinking of yourself for the role of Mozelle?

I guess I was, in some vague way. Not in a specific way, but in a vague way. Like, "I'll write this thing, I'll put it in a drawer and one day maybe it might serve me in some way."

What was it that made you decide to direct it?

I took a bunch of meetings that were a little bit frightening to me. I started to realize that I'd written a very delicate piece of material that could be misinterpreted very easily. In fact, it was just as easy to misinterpret it as it was to interpret it the way I intended. I took some scary meetings where I thought, "Oh God, I'd rather keep it in the drawer than let people interpret it this way."

My producer kept saying, "What's a sexy idea of a director? Who's sexy?" And I was thinking, "Who's sexy? Who's sexy?" Literally I woke up on my birthday and it was an epiphany. I was like, "You know what? I'm going to direct it."

After that moment I never vacillated. I went to the producer and said, "I went to film school. My short film did really well and I've decided I'm going to direct this." He almost fell off his chair. But he was very supportive. The first thing he said when he recovered from shock was that he wanted to produce a short film for me to see what I could do. Something with a 35mm camera, real crew, the whole thing. And that's what he did. My agent put up half the money and he put up the other half. It was really amazing.

Did you change the script at all once you locked in on a budget?

At first the Batiste house was reminiscent of my grandmother's house. It had an elevator that went up to the third floor. And the little marketplace/fair where they meet Elzora, the voodoo priestess, was a huge, traveling fair that had a Ferris wheel. I took that out. I took a lot out of it and made it much, much simpler.

Was there anything that you hated to lose?

There was nothing that I hated to lose until the edit and then I lost something I *hated* to lose. It was extremely painful. It was a character named Tomy.

A whole character got excised?

A whole character. He was a member of the family. It was actually a lot of work to cut him out.

He was a great-uncle who lived in the house. I never explain exactly what's wrong with him, but he's mute. He was modeled after my great-uncle who had cerebral palsy. In the director's cut, he's in a wheelchair and he's actually sitting in the room when what happens between Louis and Cisely happens. So he knows the truth but he can't speak. He was the mute witness and to me it was very beautiful that there was a mute witness in *Eve's Bayou*. Even though Louis and Cisely remembered it differently, there was actually somebody who knew the truth.

At the end of the movie, when you see the little girls and they do their scene and they're standing on the bayou, I cut to him on the porch in his wheelchair and he knows what happened. But he can't say.

You did a masterful job of cutting him out.

He's in the movie, but I would have to freeze frame and point him out to you. There are places where we didn't remove him but you just don't see it, your eye doesn't go there.

What drove the decision to cut this fairly major character out of the movie?

What drove it was notes from the producer, Mark Amin, who was running Trimark. He *hated* that character. He hated it from the beginning. It was one of those elephants in the room that doesn't go away. In *Eve's Bayou* the people are very conspicuously pretty and then there was this older, disfigured person. To me it was beautiful that there was this older, disfigured person who lived in the house, it wasn't just the beautiful people. It was a relative in the house and I thought it was very black and very Southern that there would be some relative that you had to take care of.

He really didn't like the character and we went back and forth over it. Finally I lost him and it was very painful. My crew made t-shirts with an empty wheelchair that read, "Where's Tomy?" Tomy was my real great-uncle's name so it was a real big deal that we lost that character. But it was something that I had to do and honestly, I'm pretty sure I like the version without Tomy better. It took me a while to come to that point of view. I like my "director's cut" an awful lot, too. But probably the version without Tomy is my favorite.

Once you decided to direct it, did you ever consider also acting in it?

No. I find directing to be a very, very voyeuristic art form. Almost a perversion. You're really watching other people's intimate moments and trying to get those moments out of them. But I don't think there was ever a question of me wanting to be in it once I decided to direct it.

What was the benefit of your acting background when it came to writing the movie?

I think the characters are always talking to me. But I think writers are like that whether they're actors or not. Being an actor definitely helped me to hear the characters.

What was the benefit of your acting background when it came to directing the movie?

I didn't really think that much about it until I saw in the electronic press kit that almost all of the actors said I was a good director because I was an actor. But I hadn't really thought about it until then.

I don't scream direction across the set. I'll go up and talk to an actor intimately. I would treat them the way I would like to be treated, in that it's always, always, always a private conversation so nobody can listen to me direct actors.

How do you process notes from producers? In the case of Tomy, you had that note before you started shooting but you didn't make the change until you were in editing.

You make the perfect movie when you write the script, where the world is your oyster and you're making the perfect movie. And then as preproduction goes along you start getting reality checks. So you try to incrementally excise things and see how much pain you feel. At the time I was shooting I would have felt way too much pain if I had gotten rid of that character. I never would have forgiven myself.

I remember one day my agent said to me, "It's not a painting, Kasi." This was after I had made the film and people were starting to comment on it and I was resisting notes. It's not a painting. It's really a collaborative medium and it requires an audience. It's not just for me alone. It's not even my money, right? It requires cooperation.

The trick is to cooperate and hear your fellow collaborators without losing your vision. Because they're trusting you not to lose your vision, so they're going to push you as hard as they can and they're trusting that you will keep the vision. That at a certain point you'll say "No" to them, you'll take it as far as you can and then you'll say "No." It's one of the things that they're trusting you to do as much as they're trusting you to collaborate.

That's the tricky thing and that's something that's a little tricky to learn. Some people don't have to be told. They learn it right away and they always know their boundaries and where their line in the sand is drawn.

Did you have much rehearsal time?

I did. I had about two weeks. I used it mostly with the little girls, not exclusively but almost exclusively. I thought that these two little girls have to carry a movie and it's a very complicated movie. Some of it I wondered, was it over their heads? Jurnee Smollett was a very contemporary little girl, so I had to take her back into the 1960s. How you stood and what I thought her body language would be and who I thought Eve was, where the boundaries between Eve and Jurnee were. She's so facile, within three days she was Eve.

Did you do any tweaking of the script in rehearsal?

No. I think I had gone through about eleven drafts by then, so I was pretty locked on the one that I liked.

What movies have inspired you?

I was inspired a lot by Hitchcock. By Euzhan Palcy's film *Sugar Cane Alley*, which had a little bit of magical realism. Spike Lee, *She's Gotta Have It*. But Hitchcock, definitely. His way with suspense and a certain way of unfolding a story.

After I had written the script, I would see films that reminded me this is what I'm trying to do. One was *The Piano*. One was *Like Water For Chocolate*. Julie Dash's film, *Daughters of the Dust*.

Was it much of a struggle for you to get that tone you felt in the script up onto the screen?

Not really, once the actors nailed the language. The language to me, and I really haven't felt this way with other things that I've written, but the language in *Eve's Bayou* was like Shakespeare. That's because it started out as a language experiment, so I made them say it word for word. And the words were really important to me. So they had to say it as it was written. Once they nailed the language, that really helped them fall into the tone.

When you were writing, how did you create that language?

It was definitely as if you were trying to make poetry out of the language you heard as a child.

How tough was it for the actors to get that and make those speeches work? I'm thinking in particular of Mozelle's "Life is filled with good-byes, Eve" speech.

That's my favorite speech. Debbi Morgan's such a wonderful actress. She came in and her audition was wonderful. Wonderful.

She really got it. And once she got the words exactly, like, "Well, you musta been thinking something right before you was thinking that, what led you to that particular thought?" Once you could nail the words and you're not improvising on the words, you're saying those exact words, the words help with the character. But she was so wonderful, she was wonderful from the beginning and she understood Mozelle. There was a part of her that was Mozelle.

Did you learn anything writing *Eve's Bayou* that you're still using today?

You know, there's an innocence when you write your first script. You don't know what the rules are. It's almost something that's really hard to reclaim. So that's what I'm always trying to get back to, that innocence, to try and be that pure. I don't know that I can ever do it again, but to try and remember to be that unleashed in a way.

Have you found any tricks to get back to that state?

Yes. When I'm writing the first couple of drafts I really try to write in a box. I might tell people the story, but I don't listen, I don't shape the story with other people. I tell the story to myself the way I want to tell the story, in a pure storytelling way. I don't think about budget, I don't think about anything. I think about purely the story.

It's very easy for me, it happens pretty much automatically in the time between sleeping and being fully awake, it happens in a dream space. I have a million stories. Some of them are short, they're not always long and complicated and full-blown. They usually develop in a dream space and all of a sudden I'll have this story and I won't know where it came from. I might recognize certain events that were around the conception of it, but I don't recall the conception. It's as if it tells itself to me. So that's my trick: I try to listen to the story telling itself to me. Where does this story want to go? What wants to happen? What's trying to come out? It's hard. You get used to yourself and you get used to the world and it's a hard thing.

There's something about everybody's first script that I love. All my friends' first scripts, young filmmakers that I meet. When it's their first script, there's something magical about it.

What's the best advice you've ever received about writing?

I'm not sure who gave me this advice, but it's understanding that people usually don't say exactly what's on their mind. There's nothing more tiresome than a script where people say exactly what's on their mind all the time. It's just not the way people talk.

As an actor, you need subtext and intention. You know what the character wants from each scene and you think of them as if they were real people talking in your ear.

What was the best part of your experience on *Eve's Bayou*?

The collaborating. I love collaborating. I like writing, too, but writing's really lonely. You're in a room and you're by yourself and your friends are all going out to lunch and you are stuck with your computer. Directing is a collaborative art.

One of my favorite things is hiring brilliant people to work around you. And hopefully what you've written has inspired them to want to come work with you. It's like you are plugged into their genius. You're not just relying on yourself. It's not lonely; as a matter of fact, there's a feeling of security in that you've put together a team and they each know how to do their job and you can't live without them. I love collaborating. It's my favorite thing.

Me and You and Everyone We Know
Miranda July

                    RICHARD

Those are comfortable?

                    CHRISTINE

I guess so. I mean, they kind of rub my
ankles, but all shoes do that. I have
low ankles.

                    RICHARD

You think you deserve that pain but you
don't.

                    CHRISTINE

I don't think I deserve it.

                    RICHARD

Well, not consciously, maybe.

                    CHRISTINE

My ankles are just low.

                    RICHARD

People think foot pain is a fact of life.
But life is actually better than that.

Miranda July's Me and You and Everyone We Know *is an intri-
cate tapestry of interlocking stories about the different ways in*

which people create connections in the contemporary world. But don't let that description scare you away. This is a funny and completely engaging movie that is far more sophisticated than it may first seem.

Although July stars in the film (in addition to writing and directing), the movie is a true ensemble, where the whole is greater than the sum of its parts. With her script — her first attempt at a feature — she does an artful job of juggling multiple story lines and bringing them together in ways that seem, ultimately, inevitable but still always surprising.

What was going on in your career before you started *Me and You and Everyone We Know*?

The main thing I was doing was performing live, multimedia one-woman shows. I had a lot that were scripted and kind of dialogue heavy — I performed all the dialogue. And I had also made about six short movies, some with kids in them, and with me in almost all of them. The movies had gotten progressively longer and the live performances were feature length.

Where did the idea for the script come from?

I had the idea for a while that I would eventually write a feature film and that I'd make it. I didn't really know anything about the industry, but I figured that if I'd made a half-hour movie I could make one that was an hour and a half.

The way that I write anything is pretty free-associative and magical. Usually I just start with a structure. The idea was to have these multiple story lines that converged in surprising ways. That structure gave me the freedom to write from where I was each day and add characters as I needed to.

Did you know where you were headed with the story and the characters when you started?

No, but I had a strong feeling, an emotional touchstone in me. That feeling was in me from the beginning and I knew when I would write a scene that would be filled with that feeling or when I would write a scene that was irrelevant to that feeling.

For example, one day I wrote the scene that was eventually the ending — the tapping the quarter thing — but I wrote that probably a year before I actually finished writing the script, so it wasn't like I wrote chronologically or anything.

The feeling that you worked from to create the script — would you consider that feeling the *theme* of the movie?

Well, a theme implies a kind of intellectual participation and for me it's important to not have my mind working in that way. When I write badly, it's because I'm thinking, "Oh, people are coming together and it's about connection." It has to come from a more unconscious or subconscious place than that for me. The themes come later, once you start talking to the press.

What is your writing process?

At the very beginning, I just sit down and write dialogue. Writing dialogue was very familiar to me, because I'd been doing that for performances for a long time. Then I act out the characters as I'm writing that dialogue.

But I usually start with some really irrelevant detail, seemingly out of left field. Like, "I know she has a powder compact in this scene." So I'm starting with that, rather than starting with, "She needs to connect with this man." There's something about the irrelevance and the physicality of something like that. And often it's humor that gets me into a scene, because I'm enjoying myself when I'm writing something funny. And in enjoying myself, just as hopefully the audience will, you kind of open up and then other stuff can come out, maybe deeper stuff.

So it's never starting with the big idea; it's always something physical or quite often something visual. For example, a little door peephole that a girl can open in the door. Sometimes I'll write a scene and I won't know until later why that little door will be opened. It seems very magical to me, like, "Oh, Richard knocks on the door because he's looking for his son," but I actually already wrote a version with a girl opening a peephole, without any clear objective.

At what point do you start to connect these disparate scenes?

Pretty quickly there are characters. And characters have intentions, whether you're conscious of it or not and pretty quickly there's a set of problems. So then much of the scenes come out of trying to solve problems. Like, how can the audience be reminded that she's thinking about him? And that becomes the scene with the "Me" and "You" shoes. There's a certain point where there's just enough stuff where you establish problems and at that point you start solving problems.

Did you include incidents from your own life as you were creating the script?

Not in the way people think. Nothing in the movie happened to me. Some things happened to friends of mine. And if I did take things out of my life, they're not usually very emotional things. For example, I did have a job where I had big magnets that I had to put on the sides of my car. Again, they're often physical things that end up holding a lot of power, because the door magnets leads to the job which leads to the relationship with the older man.

Did knowing that you would eventually play the lead in the film have any impact on how you wrote it?

I honestly didn't think about it that much as I was writing it — it was kind of second nature that I would be in it. But I pushed to make that character a little more embarrassing than other characters. I often cringed at the things I was writing. You're already so vulnerable, so I sort of felt that this must be important if I'm cringing. So I guess she ended up being a receptacle for a lot of fear and embarrassment in the movie.

I feel that I am pretty hard on myself, except when I'm writing and creating work, so in that sense it's kind of a healing process. If I can put my most unlovable sides into it, then potentially I can heal those parts of myself.

Did you write with any specific actors in mind?

No. I knew that I would cast all new faces. Although the only one I wrote for specifically was the art curator, played by Tracy Wright. I had seen her in *Last Night*. I wrote that part with her in mind, even though pretty early on she said she had no interest in playing it. I persisted and made the part better and better, eventually.

Why didn't she originally want to do it?

In a certain sense I was type-casting her, based on her role in *Last Night*. I totally admitted that. She actually isn't really all that interested in screen acting; she's a stage actress. So for her it was like, "Is it worth it to play a role that I've essentially already played?" And that pushed me to make it more complex and she saw that.

Did you do any other re-writing once you'd cast the film?

I had a reading early on, before I was really casting it, but I did find one actress, Natasha Slayton, who played Heather, the more dominant teenage girl. I knew when I saw her audition for the reading that I would cast her in the movie. And seeing those lines actually said, I realized that the teenage girls were going to be pretty compelling and that my character was going to suffer for that — or that was my fear, that I wouldn't be able to keep up with them or be as interesting.

All the story lines are competing and they all have to be as interesting as each other. There were actually at that point two female characters about the same age: there was my character and then there was a woman who had the romance with Richard, who worked at the make-up counter. I combined the two characters. I suddenly realized, "Oh, wait, if my character has the romance, then it's going to be a lot more interesting." That decision was made pretty late in the game. But that change stuck and it was really the last big change.

And that change all came about because you had a reading and heard the script out loud?

Yes, it came out of the pure fear of not being able to compete with a teenager. Which I think was a good instinct.

Did you lose any other subplots or characters in the writing and re-writing process?

Yes. The parents of the little girl were bigger characters at one point. And then I started to realize, "This is great, but at this point anything that's not adding to these main characters is actively taking away from them." So I slimmed that down.

Did you re-shape the story at all in the editing?

Not dramatically. We lost one small character in the editing and there were some big chunks moved around. It all had to do with flow, so we just changed the order of a few things.

Do you think your background in live performance helped you as you refined and shaped the movie?

Yes. I have to say that my sense of timing is a lot of what I've got going for me. A live performance is deathly if you don't have timing, whether it's humor or something really sad. To feel like you have an audience with you and that you're moving out of things not too early, not too late — that kind of thing turns out to be so crucial. You're imaging it when you're writing and then you're perfecting the reality of it when you're editing it.

It also helps to act it out. I acted the whole script out, every character, for my director of photography before we shot. I knew we weren't going to do storyboards and we had very little time. So I thought at least if we both know what emotionally is the core of each scene — what we have to get — I thought the best way to show that was to make him feel it. Of course, who knows? He may have just been humoring me during that three-day performance I subjected him to.

It took three days?

Yes, because we'd stop and talk about it and make sketches and then I'd move on. So, yeah. Three days.

The movie has a lot of great and original scenes, and I'm wondering where some of the ideas came from. For example, the scene where you're following the car that has the goldfish in a plastic bag on its roof. How did that scene come about?

That's a good screenwriting story, because originally — the first time I wrote that scene — it was just about the dialogue between my character and the older man. I was just writing some B-roll things that the man might see out the car window as they were talking. It was like, "A woman walking by with groceries, a kid with a goldfish in a bag," and some other things. Then later I was running some errands and I thought, "Wait, a kid with a goldfish? That is so dumb. That's so Disney. I can't believe that I wrote that. I'll have to take that out and put in something less cartoony." And I sat down to change it and I wrote that scene.

It just started taking over and instead of deleting it, the fish in the bag ended up on the car and I wrote exactly the scene that you see in the movie. And all this emotion that couldn't come out through the other characters came out through this ridiculous goldfish that I was going to delete.

It is just amazing how there is a lot of information in your "mistakes." Your mistakes are often your unconscious, trying to say, "Me, me! Look at this feeling!"

Another scene that I loved was the macaroni scene, where your character puts a request at the end of the videotape she submits to the art curator to call her and say "maca-

roni" and hang up if the curator actually got to the end of the tape. Did you ever do that in real life?

No, I didn't. When I wrote that scene I had been nominated for, applied for, and been rejected for the Rockefeller Film/Video grant four years in a row. (I actually finally got it after making this movie!) I even applied with the script for *Me and You and Everyone We Know*. So that was the feeling.

Sometimes I do audio dialogues, like radio plays, and I had done one about a boy calling a girl and she was supposed to call back and if she loved him she was just supposed to say "peanut" and then hang up. So there's not a great leap from "peanut" to "macaroni."

I find myself saying things like that to people. Like, "Can you read this version of the script and if you think it sucks, just shake your head and I'll know and we won't have to talk about it." And they'll say, "Hey, that's in your movie." So you have to kind of be careful after you expose yourself like that.

What did you do when you were done with the script?

I was lucky enough to get into the Sundance Screenwriting Lab and Filmmaking Lab. And then through one of my advisors, I was introduced to my producer, Gina Kwon, and we spent about nine months looking for money. At the end of that time we had a deal with IFC and Film Four. It felt excruciating long, but we were obviously pretty lucky.

Did you have to alter the script based on the budget you raised?

We were given less than a million dollars and we had a lot of locations. I now see that it was really well produced, it worked, but it was very ambitious. I remember an early draft actually had a blimp in it that fell. Luckily I cut that scene for dramatic reasons, not for budget.

Really the goldfish/car chase scene was the only expensive scene, and it probably took a big portion of the whole budget.

How did attending the Sundance Labs help you and the script?

I think the biggest way it helped was with confidence. I had all these professional writers and directors telling me that I had what it took. I'm a self-starting person, but it's easy to feel like you wouldn't belong in that industry. And it was certainly a real blessing to have the nicest people invite me in and that's what it was.

You don't get financing or anything like that through the Lab, but I felt ready by the time I was done and had kind of a chip on my shoulder. Like, "Who's going to get the honor of financing my movie?" Not really, you're begging, but I had some pride and that was worth a lot.

In the Filmmaking Lab, they try to simulate what a shoot might be like. They actually have someone come in and cut you off at a certain time, because that happens on a real set. And so you have to make those decisions, like, "Shit, I can't get both scenes, which one can I lose?" and things like that. And it's grueling enough that it actually does sort of pre-brutalize you in a way that takes the edge off the real experience, so you're not in as much shock as you would be.

How much did the script change as a result of your time at the Lab?

I don't think I made any changes based on notes that I got at the Lab. But I left the Lab with a crystal-clear sense of what wasn't working. That is to say, everyone's solutions were their solutions and I came up with other ones.

That's the main thing, to really know what you have to fix. I had never heard of the three-act structure or all that film-writing stuff, but people were pretty respectful. They liked the script and a lot of the advisors had the attitude of, "I don't want to fuck too much with your process, because it seems to be working, but maybe you could think about this..."

Everyone's different. Some were like, "Here's what you've got to do. In the second act, she's going to run away." They'd give you these really specific notes and you're like, "Oh my god, this is a nightmare." But you learn a really great process for getting notes from producers: You learn how to distill what the problem is from the solution they're providing.

Did you learn anything working on this script that you'll take to future projects?

The thing that I most admire now about what I had then, writing my first screenplay, which is now something I'm trying to defend with my life, is the interior freedom. Not thinking about logistics or other movies or critics, all that stuff you think about once you've been through the mill. There are a lot of monsters you have to keep at bay. And so my job every day when I write is basically to find my way back to feeling totally free, like I could write anything at any moment. And realizing that it doesn't have to make sense, it doesn't have to be perfect, no one's looking at it, no one's judging it, no one can see into my computer right now. To me, that's the beginning and that's what you need. Once something takes root you have other issues.

If you feel like you're forcing yourself to write, then maybe it's a good time to take a walk around the neighborhood. And then the second you give up — really give up — that's when your insides allow you to change and have some new thoughts.

Thirty (Highly Subjective) Lessons

There are a myriad of lessons to be found in the preceding pages. It's safe to say that just about any approach to screenwriting (and its polar opposite) could be successfully debated from these interviews.

Therefore, the lessons that follow are, by their very nature, selective and subjective. You may agree with all or none of them. I harbor few doubts that other screenwriters could assemble a wholly different and equally valid set of conclusions from these same interviews. And when they have their own book, they're welcome to do so.

With those caveats in mind, here are the thirty most important lessons I took away from these interviews.

The Final Chapter: Thirty (Highly Subjective) Lessons

Beginning Is Hard

Is it just me, or does knowing more about screenwriting make it harder to sit down and actually write a script? When I first started out, I knocked off spec script after spec script without breaking a sweat. Now, lo these many years later, my brain brimming with the rules and theories about the precise nature of screenwriting, I find it harder and harder to even get started. Perhaps a little knowledge *is* a dangerous thing.

Dylan Kidd defined this problem (and its solution) best when he said, *"The hardest part by far is the beginning. That's the easiest time to get discouraged and give up. The beginning is hard. You're trying to make order out of chaos, and chaos doesn't want to be ordered. If you can just get through that hard part then I think you'll be rewarded for your perseverance."*

Listen to Dylan. Don't give up before you've even started. Trust me, you'll have plenty of opportunities to give up later on.

Screenwriting Software and Seminars

The most frequent questions I'm asked about screenwriting usually involve things that have very little to do with the actual writing process. "Should I buy screenwriting software?" and "What are the best screenwriting books and seminars?" are two of the most common.

When it comes to screenwriting software, I used to agree with Alex Cox, who said, *"Don't waste your money on screenwriting software. If you can't set two tabs and remember to capitalize character names, find an easier job — actor or producer."*

I still agree with that idea in principle. However, (and I paid full retail for this product so this is not a paid plug), "Final Draft" from Final Draft, Inc. is a terrific piece of software that really does let you just focus on the writing and ignore the formatting. Plus it has some wonderful organizational tools. So I've come around on the topic of screenwriting software. It won't make you a better screenwriter, but it will make it easier to be whatever kind of screenwriter you are.

Alex also went on to say, *"Pay no attention to screenwriting books or seminars. They are as useless as screenwriting software."* Well, I'd look pretty silly saying that you shouldn't read books on screenwriting, particularly at this late point in the book. But I will say that it's surprisingly easy to become addicted to studying screenwriting (i.e., buying books and going to seminars) at the expense of actually sitting down and writing.

There is certainly value in reading books on screenwriting (start with the masters: Syd Field, Robert McKee, Linda Seger) and it can't hurt to attend a seminar or two. But after that, stop spending money on learning resources and get down to the real learning. You'll do that by writing draft after draft and script after script. With screenwriting, as with many things, one learns best by doing.

Read Scripts

While I think you reach a point of diminishing returns when all you're doing is reading books on the screenwriting process, I do think you should never stop reading screenplays themselves.

As Amy Holden Jones recounted, *"That's the thing that has helped me the most in my career. I remember when I first had to write a horror movie, when I first had to write a comedy, when I first had to write an action film, I would get myself down to the Writers Guild library or the Academy library, and I would sit down and read some of the best of the genre."*

She's right. You can learn so much about how to build a script by examining in detail how someone else successfully did it. I think it's arrogant to attempt the process without having gone through the experience of reading multiple scripts. As Amy put it, *"No one would try to write a play who hadn't read plays. But all the time people try to write screenplays who don't sit down and read them. The screenplay is a completely different form. The vast majority of young writers you tell that to, the way they look at you, you know they're never going to do it."* So, make Amy proud and just do it.

There are tons of places on-line to find screenplays, but before you dive in and start reading the collected works of the Farrelly Brothers, one word of caution: Be sure that you're reading the screenplay and not simply a transcript of the movie. There is a world of difference between the two.

The actual screenplay is more educational, because it shows you where the writer *intended* to go — which you can then compare with the finished movie to see where they actually ended up.

When I teach screenwriting, one of the sessions is spent watching *Body Heat* while we read along with the screenplay. This lesson provides a couple of key learnings. First, it demonstrates to the student that there is nothing magical about screenwriting: Lawrence Kasdan wrote the words on paper and then the actors and crew brought it to life. The student can see what he wrote and how that was made manifest on screen.

The other lesson they learn is that screenplays change when they become movies. Scenes are cut, lengthened and moved around. In order to follow along with the screenplay of *Body Heat* while watching the movie, the reader really has to jump around, because Kasdan moved things around in the editing. That's a good lesson to learn: nothing is set in stone.

Write What You Know

"Write what you know" could easily win the award as the Biggest Writing Cliché That Is Actually True. There is tremendous power in your own experiences and perspectives.

Roger Nygard said it best when he told me, *"I never got a job as a CIA agent, never went into the Marines, never became a fireman or a cop, didn't go on the road and get arrested or sell cars. Your own life is often the first and best place to start for a screenwriter."*

In that case, the best perspective you can offer is your own unique perspective, based on your life experiences. As Tom DiCillo explained, *"Whatever you write, you have to tap into something personal for yourself. I used to have an acting teacher who said to me, 'If it ain't personal, it ain't no good.' I absolutely believe that if you can find a way to tap into something that's very personal, and then make a creative leap from there, that's the best way to do it."*

However, in order for this to work, you have to be willing to be honest and dig deep. Roger Nygard feels that *"You have to bare yourself to the world in order to write something that other people will be interested in reading and possibly make into a movie. It's not easy. It's hard. You've got to write things that you wouldn't even tell your shrink. Those are the screenplays that really stand out."*

Now this is not to say that every script you write should be a literal autobiography, because no one wants to see that. But you should draw on your own emotions and experiences to create real, truthful scenes.

It's all about telling the truth, whether you're writing about your life growing up in a small town in the Midwest — or saving the world from an alien attack. As Bob Clark put it, *"Be truthful. You've got to find your reality, no matter how broad what you're doing is. If you're doing the Marx Brothers, it's wild, it's bizarre, but somewhere in there has to be some truth, no matter how outrageous or absurd or fantastical."*

Readers will respond to that truth. Actors will want to play it. And audiences will get caught up in it.

Make the Public Domain Your Domain

If you're searching for a great story, don't overlook the thousands of stories that are sitting out there in the public domain, just waiting to be re-told.

That's where Stuart Gordon turned for his first feature, *Re-Animator*, and he took a good lesson away from the experience. He learned that you should make sure that the people who say they own the copyright to a work really do own that copyright. In the case of the H. P. Lovecraft stories he wanted to use, a quick copyright check proved that the work was in the public domain after all, saving the production the cost of paying for rights that were free to begin with.

As Stuart recalled, *"That made things a lot easier for us. If they had asked for a lot of money, that would have been difficult, because our budget was small. Finding out that it was public domain was great, it was one less thing to worry about."*

So hire a good lawyer and make sure that the work you're using is really available for your use. A good rule of thumb is that if the author is alive, or was alive less than seventy-five years ago, then the story is off limits. But don't take that as a blanket rule: Heirs have been known to keep some authors' work out of the public domain long past those limits. Get a lawyer and get it right.

Tell the Story

It's amazing to me that screenwriters — who are, at the very heart, storytellers — are often unwilling to tell anyone the story they're working on, for fear that it will somehow kill their inspiration or frighten their delicate muse away.

On the contrary, I think the more you tell your story out loud, the better the story will become. You'll begin to notice gaps and repetitions, find slow spots and areas of confusion.

In the case of *Eve's Bayou*, Kasi Lemmons was not shy about telling her story. *"Way before I wrote anything down I could tell you the entire story of* Eve's Bayou, *the entire thing complete with flashes of lightning. I could tell you the whole movie. I had it all in my head. It helped shape it in my mind. Not so much that I did it for feedback, but it helped to shape the story in my mind."*

I think that's a good practice to get into. It forces you to admit to holes in logic and weaknesses in your storytelling long before they appear in print. And it could also inspire you to head in new, fun directions, based on the verbal (laughing) and non-verbal (napping) cues you receive from your listener. So don't be afraid of telling your story aloud. You are, after all, a storyteller.

Find Your Genre and Stay There

Audiences are a fussy lot. While they may suspend their disbelief while watching a movie, that disbelief runs down a surprisingly narrow highway. Stray too far from that road and you'll lose the audience, perhaps for good.

If you've given them a romantic comedy, keep it romantic and keep it funny. Turning it into a slasher film halfway through will only annoy the audience. If it's a drama, don't turn it into a farce in Act Three. If it's a thriller at the beginning, it better still be a thriller at the end.

That's a lesson that Roger Nygard learned the hard way, *"Audiences are not used to — and don't like it — when you shift from one genre to another in a movie. People just don't like genre shifts. They want to know what the genre is from the beginning of the movie, what's the level of reality of the story, and then you have to stick to it. If you don't stick to one genre, then you're either taking a chance or doing an art film."*

That's not to say there's anything wrong with art films, if that's what you're setting out to write. But a movie is like a contract with the audience, with certain built-in promises. One of those promises is to play fair (i.e., if you set up rules that govern your cinematic universe, then you better stick to those rules). The other is to take the audience where you promised and then (with any luck) beyond that. That doesn't mean you can't surprise them along the way — in fact, if you're not surprising them, you may want to start that re-write right now. But if you change horses in mid-movie, don't get pissed if the audience doesn't follow you.

Don't Apologize/Don't Explain

And speaking of genres, the best way to succeed with a genre film — such as a horror film — is to treat the subject matter directly, without unnecessary explanations or excuses.

George Romero knows how to do that, in spades. *Night of the Living Dead* and *Martin* are still iconic examples of genre films that don't apologize for being genre films. As he explained, *"I think the secret of* The Exorcist *and* Jaws *and* Rosemary's Baby, *the classics of the genre, is that there's no apology. 'Here's the situation.' You just have to take it at face value. Don't spend ten minutes with scientists saying, 'Well here's exactly what's going on here.' Forget it! You don't need it. Just say, 'Here's the situation,' and if you stay true to it and don't fuck with that and don't violate it, then it becomes believable."*

Stuart Gordon agrees with that sentiment: *"One of the great things that Lovecraft said was 'Never explain anything.' I always thought that was a really good note. There's this tendency to want to explain everything — to the point where you kind of take away all the magic."*

For me, the classic example of that is the final "explanation" scene in *Psycho*, where Simon Oakland takes us through a laborious and completely unnecessary dissertation on what Norman's problem is and why Norman did what he did. Not only is it a waste of time, it also sucks the energy out of the end of the movie. (A bit of that energy comes back in the final shot, thanks to the brilliance of Anthony Perkins.)

Granted, in a mystery you want the audience to finally understand what happened, but you don't have to hit them over the head with it. *The Usual Suspects* does a brilliant job of putting all the pieces together in the last two minutes, without making the audience feel stupid. *The Last of Sheila* is another wonderful example of how to tie things up while keeping the screws tightened.

When it comes to explaining things in movies, less is always more.

Listen to the Voices in Your Head

Screenwriting is not a science, it's an art. As such, you can really only apply so much theory to the process. After that, it's often better to let your gut take over and see where it leads you. That won't work on every draft and rewrite, but it's a good way to approach the first draft that pours out of you.

As Dylan Kidd observed, *"Your first time through is when your unconscious is really trying to tell you what the movie wants to be. For me it's important to follow your bliss in that first draft, even if it ends up at 180 pages or you hate everything but ten percent of it. At least you've got that ten percent, which is ten more than a lot of people have."*

Later drafts is when the craft kicks in and you start to edit and hone and tighten and improve. But don't saddle your muse with too many restrictions right out of the gate. Rigidity kills creativity.

Ignore the Voices in Your Head

Of course, all those voices in your head aren't necessarily trying to help you. As you write, you may start trying to second-guess critics or producers or directors or the audience or (worst of all) yourself. You've got to learn to ignore those voices, because they won't help you write a good script; they'll just help you destroy your inspiration.

Dan Futterman looked at the voices this way: *"You cannot have that in your head while you're writing. You simply have to be thinking, 'Do I like this? Do I believe it? Is it interesting to me?' You already have enough voices in your head — and the superego perched on your shoulder, saying, 'That's terrible, that's not good enough' — so the fewer voices you can add to that chorus, the better."*

For Stuart Gordon, that meant not worrying about how people — especially critics — would react to the film: *"I just wrote off the critics. In a way, that was a very healthy thing, because if you're worrying about the critics it can paralyze you or you'll get too self-*

conscious about what you're doing. To just be able to ignore them completely was actually a very healthy thing."

Screen Direction: Active Voice

Ali Selim provided me with one of the most interesting bits of screenwriting advice: *"Always write in active voice, not passive voice."*

To be honest, I didn't really understand what he meant and so I had him explain further: *"It amounted to changing 'Olaf is sitting' to 'Olaf sits' and 'Olaf is harvesting' to 'Olaf harvests.' I did that on EVERY LINE of screen direction throughout the entire script. In doing so, the script went from this 'distant, over there, who are they?' story to an immediate and present emotion. The sub-conscious somehow took over and suddenly actors were saying, 'I have to do this film.' It was weird. Prior to that they called it 'soft.' When I made it active they called it 'lean and athletic.' No scene changes. No new behaviors. No sex scenes or car crashes. Just drop the 'ing' and add an 's.' Go figure."*

Write Characters Actors Will Want To Play

This seems like it should be obvious, but how often do we really set out to do this? Most of the time we create characters that will move the plot forward or spout our funny lines or die at the right time. Instead, we should be writing characters that leap off the page and scream to actors, "Play me!'

This wasn't news to Dylan Kidd. *"That was a big part of my strategy: Write something that somebody would walk through broken glass to play. Most of your expense in a movie is the above-the-line costs. It's difficult but it's possible to make a movie for a low budget, but what's really hard is getting someone that anyone's ever heard of into that movie."*

Creating a strong (interesting, unique, challenging, fill in the blank) character will attract talented people to your script. And that's always a good thing. So, how do you do that? Go back to

Write What You Know. If you are writing honest characters in the throes of truthful scenes, you're on your way.

Few Characters, Fewer Locations

When you're first starting out, it's easy to forget that each new location and each new character will make your movie more expensive to shoot. When I did my low-budget digital feature, *Grown Men*, which consisted of five interlocking stories, I repeatedly ran into this issue with the writers on the project. One of the short segments, which had to be shot in four days, had over fourteen distinct locations. That's three and a half separate locations each day. On a low budget — heck, on any budget — that's tough to pull off.

So keep in mind the mantra intoned by Stuart Gordon: *"With low budget, it really has to be minimalist. You have to have as few sets and locations as possible and as few characters as possible."*

So why do you want to control the locations? Amy Holden Jones explained it this way, *"I knew I had to make it inexpensive and one of the cheap ways to do that is a limited number of locations, because every company move takes up an enormous amount of time."* And time is money.

Why worry about cast size? Simple: more characters means more people to shoot, more people to move, more people to feed and more people to pay — both during production and later as well. As Roger Nygard explained: *"Every new character is somebody who gets a residual check when the movie is released and airing in ancillary markets."*

The economy of limiting locations and actors can actually work to your advantage, both financially and artistically. Richard Glatzer learned that on *Grief*, which essentially takes place in one suite of offices: *"To conceive of a film from the outset as ultra-low-budget is the way to do it. You don't start with a bigger idea and then whittle it down. To me the movie gained its identity and meaning from being limited to the office. That was a budgetary limitation that ended up working in the movie's favor."*

There's also a unity that limited characters and few locations bring to a movie. It focuses your energies among a few characters in just a few places, which can create its own tension. *Tape* is an extreme example of that philosophy in action. For another take on how to make that set-up work, rent the movie *Cube* — six people in one room and it never gets boring.

Know Your Mid-Point

Writing a script is a long, lonely journey and it's easy to get lost along the way. One way to stay on track is to cut the journey in half and establish a mid-point.

John McNaughton compared it to the long road trips he often takes from Los Angeles to his home in Chicago. *"Most movies get in trouble in the middle. But establishing a mid-point for me was like knowing that I was going to drive from Los Angeles to Chicago but I'm going to stop in Omaha. That was really an incredibly helpful idea."*

Most people, if they break the script up at all, break it into three sections: Act One, Act Two and Act Three.

But Act Two, which is usually the longest, is the one where most of us have trouble. By dividing the script in half, you're essentially dividing Act Two in half, which makes it easier to figure out if you're going astray long before you reach the end of that act. Breaking up the journey into smaller, more manageable steps is a good way to ensure that you — and your story — will make it successfully to the end.

Keep Lester Awake

Stuart Gordon learned this lesson while directing theater, but it applies to film as well. While he's directing, he's always thinking of Lester, his audience member who was prone to nodding off during shows.

"Lester was notorious for falling asleep in the middle of the plays, and sometimes snoring. So I was always, in the back of my mind,

*thinking 'We've got to keep Lester awake. We have to have some-
thing going on every moment to keep Lester from falling asleep.'
And I think I'm still trying to keep Lester awake."*

So while you're making your journey to the mid-point and beyond,
stay focused on keeping Lester awake. And how do you do that?
By making sure that every scene in the script is necessary to getting
to your destination. You can't get distracted and meander around
the countryside — you're got to get to where you're going in the
most direct fashion possible.

Dan Futterman learned this from his wife, who is also a writer.
*"She was clear and strict with me, saying 'If there are any scenes
where people are just talking, cut it, because if it's not moving the
plot forward it doesn't belong in the script.' And that was important to learn. It has got to move."*

Not only should every scene move the story forward; each scene
should also contain its own intrinsic tension. As Stuart Gordon
explained: *"Every single scene should have some tension in it. You
really can't have any scenes with people just sort of sitting around
and relaxed. You have to find the tension in each scene. What you
really want to do is to keep people on the edge of their seats all the
way through."*

The lesson here is to look at every scene with a cold, clear eye and
ask yourself: "Is this moving the story along or is it just going to
put Lester to sleep?" If it's the latter, then it's got to go.

Watch Out for Repetitions

And while you're moving that plot forward, make sure that you're
not repeating yourself. Audiences are smart. They get it. Tell them
something once and they'll remember.

Not only is this good storytelling, it's also cost-effective storytelling according to Rebecca Miller: *"Comb through [the script] for
internal repetitions which you might not be aware of, but will only
cost you money that you don't need to spend shooting scenes that
you're going to cut later in the editing room. If you say the same*

thing two different ways, usually you don't need to do that. It's a very powerful medium."

Watch Out for Repetitions

Just kidding. Wanted to make sure you're paying attention.

Look for Connections

While you're looking for repetitions, also be on the lookout for connections — those little moments that make a character richer, focus the story or add to the depth of the narrative. A prop in the beginning of your story may turn up in a surprising way later on — like the comically-large suitcase in Act One of *Henry: Portrait of a Serial Killer* which turns up for a much darker purpose in Act Three.

You don't necessarily need to add anything — just look at what's already there. As John McNaughton described it, *"Once you lay out your story and your script, then you start to see these connections that can be made to really strengthen that through-line, so everything connects in some way or another. If you have time, you can work on those details. If you don't, you just shoot the script and hope for the best."*

Make the Part Work for the Whole

You'll be amazed what you can't afford when you're making a low-budget movie. The simplest staples of big-budget moviemaking are outside your grasp. Therefore, you need to be abundantly clever and tell your story with the fewest elements required to get the point across.

Joan Micklin Silver referred to this as *"Making the part work for the whole. In writing low-budget films you often have to do a part of something; a part has to stand for something larger."* For her, that meant that she couldn't recreate Ellis Island. Instead, she had to come up with a way to express the idea of Ellis Island and do it within her meager budget. Her solution? A simple chain-link fence.

This solution cost only $800 and it got the visual point across as effectively as an $80,000 set. So look for those parts of the whole that you can afford that will help to tell your story effectively, as well as cost-effectively.

When we were shooting a short sequence for my digital feature, *Grown Men,* we needed a jail cell for a very short shot of the door closing on our hero. Oddly enough, jail cells are hard to come by, and the only one we could find was sixty miles away. Plus they wanted a few hundred bucks to let us come in for this one shot.

Poverty forced us to realize that we didn't really need a jail cell — we needed the feeling of a jail cell. So we put the actor in front of a cinder block wall in a parking garage and pulled some evenly-spaced black PVC pipes in front of the camera. In post we added the sound of a cell door slamming shut and we had our shot. As they say, necessity (and no cash) are the mothers of invention.

Not Talking Is Just as Powerful as Talking, Sometimes More So

Film is a visual medium. (I'm probably not the first person to point that out, but who knows.) Many writers — including myself — have a tendency to fall back on dialogue to drive their story forward.

I learned from L.M. Kit Carson (who learned it from Sam Shepard) that *not* talking can be just as powerful — or more so — than talking. As Carson explained, it's all about silence. *"The first part of the script was Sam's and it was full of silence. There's a lot of silence in [Paris, Texas] and it's very powerful. I've learned and applied that to everything else."*

So much can be said with a look, a gesture, or no action at all. Look at the scene in *The Remains of the Day* where Emma Thompson takes Anthony Hopkins' book out of his hand to see what he's reading. His silent reaction says volumes. Or the look on Dustin Hoffman's and Katharine Ross's faces in the last shot of *The Graduate.* Or the truly classic moment in *Harold and Maude* when Harold's mother gives him the once over after he's frightened off yet another computer date.

So the next time you have a character open his or her mouth, think about whether it might not be stronger to skip the clever retort and instead have them say nothing at all.

Act It Out

And speaking of not speaking, one of the best ways to minimize the amount of dialogue you're writing is to act out each scene, playing all the parts, in order to determine what actually needs to be said out loud and what can be expressed via action and behavior.

As Kenneth Lonergan said, *"I always have the actors in mind and when I'm writing I act out the scene, which includes the behavior. And if the behavior's covering it, then you don't need a line of dialogue."*

Acting out the scenes is also a good way to get your vision across to your artistic team, as Miranda July did to an extreme on her first feature: *"I acted the whole script out, every character, for my director of photography before we shot. I knew we weren't going to do storyboards, and we had very little time, and so I thought at least if we both know what emotionally is the core of each scene — what we have to get — I thought the best way to show that was to make him feel it. Of course, who knows? He may have just been humoring me during that three-day performance I subjected him to."*

Write the Text, Act the Sub-Text

And while we're on the subject of dialogue, remember that in real life people don't always say exactly what they mean. Instead, they talk around their real meaning or intention. Kasi Lemmons feels *"There's nothing more tiresome than a script where people say exactly what's on their mind all the time. It's just not the way people talk. You need subtext and intention."*

Kenneth Lonergan agrees. *"People just don't say what they mean all the time. I wish writers would hold back a little more. You want to make sure that the audience knows what you need them to know at a certain point for the scene to have the effect that you want, but writers often write what they think* should *happen. If people would write more of what* would *happen and just see if it took care of itself, I think it would."*

One of the best examples of sub-text writing can be found in the 1946 Howard Hawks' version of *The Big Sleep*. Watch the scene where Humphrey Bogart and Lauren Bacall discuss horse racing. Trust me, they're not talking about horse racing.

Readings

One thing I heard over and over while conducting the interviews for this book has been the value of doing readings of your script as you rewrite and refine it.

Surprisingly, no one expressed the view of my late screenwriting teacher, Frantisek (Frank) Daniel, who disliked readings because he felt they placed too much emphasis on the script's dialogue to drive the story. I think Frank was correct on that point, but there's no denying that hearing your script read aloud by actors is still a great way to quickly learn what's working, what's not, and what needs to go.

Stuart Gordon's experience was similar to most: *"It was good to hear the script read aloud. It amazes me that that is almost never done. We could see which lines sounded kind of clunky or other lines that weren't needed. In a couple of places we found dialogue that we really did need that was not in the script and we had to fill in some things."*

A good piece of advice on how to stage a successful reading came from Ali Selim, who said, *"I learned that you need to re-write the screen direction for a staged reading. It needs to just clip along."* So do some serious surgery on stage directions before subjecting an audience to your script. You may find that most of it was superfluous anyway.

Getting Notes #1: Too Many Voices

Just as there's an art to screenwriting, so too is there an art to receiving and reacting to notes. Most screenwriters agree that having a handful of close associates look over your script is a good thing. They also agreed that you don't need to react to every single note you get. As Amy Holden Jones put it, *"Usually if I show a script to five people, I will pay a lot of attention to repeating comments. So if three or four of the five people say 'The end doesn't work for me,' then I know the end doesn't work. If one of the five says 'It doesn't work for me,' and four of the five say it's fine, then it's less of an issue."*

Dylan Kidd agreed with her, adding, *"I do have people that I turn to and that I care about what they think. But my feeling is that unless the comments match something I already felt in my gut anyway or if every person has the same comment, then I know I have an issue. I generally have found that putting too much stock in feedback can get confusing, because people are going to have a hundred different opinions."*

Whit Stillman takes a different tack, suggesting that the screenwriter is better off, ultimately, by going it alone. *"I'm not sure it's very helpful having a lot of voices in on the creation of a script. I think they try to smooth things and homogenize things and explain things. It's better making it a kind of goofy voyage and ride, when you have to just be honest with yourself about what you're doing and where your mistakes are and what isn't working."*

Getting Notes #2: Listen to the Problem, Ignore the Solution

Identifying the problem is not to be confused with finding the solution. And, of course, everyone has an opinion. Miranda July realized that after her screenplay went through the Sundance Labs, where some advisors provided extremely specific thoughts on what needed to be changed in her script. Miranda recalled, *"Some were like, 'Here's what you've got to do. In the second act, she's going to run away.' They'd give you these really specific notes, and you're like, 'Oh my god, this is a nightmare.' But you learn a really great process for getting notes from producers: You learn how to distill what the problem is from the solution they're providing."*

Also, people will often find fault with one area of the script, and not realize that the blame for that problem lies elsewhere in the script. As Kenneth Lonergan explained, *"It doesn't mean that the real problem is where it appears, because it can be like a medical symptom: the symptom may not appear where the cause is. You can acknowledge that there's a symptom somewhere that someone points out — maybe — but you certainly should be very skeptical when they start talking about what the solution is or what the nature of the problem is."*

So, if possible, try to balance two points of view while getting notes and re-writing: First, from Miranda July: *"Everyone's solutions were their solutions and I came up with other ones. That's the main thing, to really know what you have to fix."*

And then, Eric Bogosian: *"There is a downside (to re-writing). Sometimes something very good can be lost in the haste to 'make it better.' Sometimes the long way around, i.e. the long speech, the boring passage, is the better way to go."*

If you can balance those two approaches, I think you'll find your way to a better script.

Listen to the Actors

One group of artists that you'll encounter on your journey who can often provide terrific notes and insights are your actors. My experience has been that when an actor wants to change a line or (God forbid) cut a line, it's well worth your time to sit down and listen to their reasoning. They often know the characters better than you do and their insights can be compelling.

Richard Glatzer had a similar experience. *"My actors were a really smart group of people, so I could trust them if they said 'Wait a minute' about their character. Most of the time they were right and that was really good, because it was a great sounding board. Actors are always like that, but I think some actors are better able to see what's missing or know when something's not sounding right than other actors are. I credit them with a lot of that."*

A Moral Debt

When you're writing about real people — especially people who have passed on and can't defend themselves — you have an obligation to tell their story truthfully. Legally, if they're public figures, you may have plenty of leeway. But just because it's legal doesn't mean that it's necessarily right.

Dan Futterman learned that on *Capote*, when he combined several actual people into the real-life character of William Shawn. It was a hard-learned lesson. As he explained, *"Even if the people have died, there is a moral debt owed to them in terms of trying to adhere as strictly as possible to the truth. It's something I tried to be very conscious of, but in this particular case, I think I came up short. It didn't occur to me at the time that any of the things I had him doing could possibly be upsetting to anybody, but that was my own take and I see now why his sons are upset. Looking back now, I would try to find a way to fix it."*

Write, Wait, Re-Write, Repeat

As I pointed out in the Introduction, a continuing theme throughout this book has been the idea that scripts need to be rewritten and refined over a number of drafts. You don't just write it and shoot it. Not if you want it to be good, anyway. As Eric Bogosian said, *"Editing and deleting is as important as writing and sometimes just as difficult because it's hard to throw stuff away."*

While there's very little disagreement on the need to rewrite (Kenneth Lonergan did warn, *"I really think it's dangerous to mess around with it too much"*), there is some disagreement on how long to let it sit before you tackle it again.

Roger Nygard advises, *"Every time you feel that the script is done, put it down for a week or a month, and then come back to it and you'll see that it's not done. Because it's never done. Writing is re-writing. You're constantly re-writing."*

Of course, if you keep doing that, your drawer may get pretty full. Stephen Belber admitted, *"I have about twenty-five things in a drawer right now."*

The contrary view is espoused by Alex Cox, who said, *"Put it away if you don't like it or can't figure out a way to raise money for it. Once put away, rarely is it retrieved."*

You need to decide for yourself how long you want a script to sit before tackling the next draft. However, I think a short vacation always does the writer — and the script — a world of good.

Just Try It

Screenwriting has a lot of rules or implied rules. Now, I'm not promoting ignorance of those rules. But I also don't believe in slavish devotion to a rule just because it's a rule.

If you've got a different idea, a new approach or a radical vision, give it a shot. Or, as Tom DiCillo learned, don't be afraid, just try it. *"Whatever you're doing, if you're trying something, just try it. Just try it. Things don't have to be instantaneously perfect or whatever, but if you really are trying something, then trust it and just try it."*

Make Your Own Kind of Movie

Henry Jaglom scolded me slightly when I asked him how someone would go about making a movie like his. And he made a good point: *"It's really simple: Don't do my kind of movie, do your kind of movie. Figure out what your kind of movie is. And once you've figured out what your kind of movie is, don't let anybody diminish your enthusiasm or excitement about it. Try as much as you can to tell your own particular truth on film. Insist on not letting anybody change your mind about what your truth is, what your goal is, how you should convey it. You can learn all kinds of technical things and become very proficient, but most people lose the impetus that made them want to be filmmakers to begin with because they learn all kinds of things that people tell them you shouldn't do or you can't do."*

The Best Advice

And, finally, the best advice of all. I'm quoting Eric Bogosian here, but this could have been said by any writer in this book: *"Keep writing."*

Afterword

We've reached the end of the road, at least for now.

If you've gathered nothing else from these conversations, I hope it's the understanding that there really is no right or wrong in screenwriting — there's only what works and what doesn't.

Or, to paraphrase W. Somerset Maugham,
"There are three rules for writing the screenplay. Unfortunately, no one knows what they are."

For every "rule" that someone throws at you — never use narration, never use a flashback or a flash-forward, never set your story in only one room, never use non-actors, never write a period piece, never get involved in a land war in Asia — you'll find a successful movie that shatters that rule into a million little pieces.

So worry less about rules and more about the passion that you need to bring to your script. If you're passionate about your story, and have the talent and drive to tell it well, then I say Godspeed to you.

Keep reading. Keep writing. Keep watching movies.

And keep in touch.

John Gaspard
www.graniteproductions.org

The Movies

The majority of the movies in the book are available on DVD; the rest can be found on VHS, either new or for sale used somewhere on-line. All are worth a look.

Bubble — © 2006, HDNet Films, 2929 Productions, Magnolia Pictures, Section Eight Ltd.
Capote — © 2006, Sony Pictures
Children Shouldn't Play with Dead Things — © 1972, Geneni Film Distributors
Eve's Bayou — © 1998, Lions Gate
Grief — © 1993, Strand Releasing
Henry: Portrait of a Serial Killer — © 1986, Greycat Films
Hester Street — © 1975, Midwest Films
Living in Oblivion — © 1995, Sony Pictures Classics
Love Letters — © 1984, New World Pictures
Martin — © 1977, Libra Films International
Me and You and Everyone We Know — © 2005, IFC Films
Metropolitan — © 1990, New Line Cinema
Paris, Texas — © 1984, Twentieth Century Fox Film Corporation
Personal Velocity: Three Portraits — © 2002, Metro-Goldwyn-Mayer
Re-Animator — © 1985, Elite Entertainment Inc.
Repo Man — © 1984, Anchor Bay Entertainment
Roger Dodger — © 2002, Artisan Entertainment
subUrbia — © 1996, Sony Pictures Classics
Suckers — © 1999, Creative Light Worldwide
Sweet Land — © 2006, Carbon Neutral Films
Tape — © 2001, Lions Gate Films
Venice/Venice — © 1992, Rainbow Releasing
You Can Count On Me — © 2000, Paramount Classics

About the Author

 John Gaspard has directed and/or produced six low-budget features, including the digital feature, *Grown Men*, which premiered at the Ashland International Film Festival and won the "Best of Fest/Best Screenplay" award at the Black Point Film Festival.

He directed and co-wrote the award-winning feature film, *Beyond Bob*, and directed the science-fiction comedy feature film, *Resident Alien*. He was also a writer and story editor for the international television comedy/western series, *Lucky Luke*, starring Terence Hill.

His screenplay, *The Sword and Mr. Stone* (co-written with Michael Levin) was the first winner of the Barry Morrow Screenwriting Fellowship, as well as a finalist at the Austin Heart of the Film Screenwriting Competition.

John wrote the companion book to this one, *Fast, Cheap and Under Control: Lessons Learned from the Greatest Low-Budget Movies of All Time*. He also co-authored, with Dale Newton, the books *Digital Filmmaking 101: An Essential Guide to Producing Low-Budget Movies* (first and second editions) and *Persistence of Vision: An Impractical Guide to Producing a Feature Film for Under $30,000*, all of which are published by Michael Wiese Productions.

He can be contacted via his website, *www.graniteproductions.org*.